Sustainable Concrete Solutions

Professor Costas Georgopoulos
Chair in Structural Engineering Practice
Kingston University London

Dr Andrew Minson
Executive Director
MPA - The Concrete Centre

WILEY Blackwell

This edition first published 2014
© 2014 John Wiley & Sons, Ltd

Registered Office
John Wiley & Sons, Ltd, The Atrium, Southern Gate, Chichester, West Sussex, PO19 8SQ,
United Kingdom.

Editorial Offices
9600 Garsington Road, Oxford, OX4 2DQ, United Kingdom.
The Atrium, Southern Gate, Chichester, West Sussex, PO19 8SQ, United Kingdom.

For details of our global editorial offices, for customer services and for information about how
to apply for permission to reuse the copyright material in this book please see our website at
www.wiley.com/wiley-blackwell.

Library of Congress Cataloging-in-Publication Data

Georgopoulos, Costas.
    Sustainable concrete solutions / Costas Georgopoulos.
        pages   cm
    Summary: "The book will provide students with a thorough evaluation of the advantages and
disadvantages of concrete a sustainable building material"– Provided by publisher.
    Includes bibliographical references and index.
    ISBN 978-1-119-96864-1 (pbk.)
    1. Concrete construction–Environmental aspects.   2. Sustainable buildings.   I. Title.
    TA681.G46 2014
    624.1'8340286–dc23

                                                    2013031272

A catalogue record for this book is available from the British Library.

Wiley also publishes its books in a variety of electronic formats. Some content that appears in
print may not be available in electronic books.

Cover illustration courtesy of the authors
Cover design by Andrew Magee Design Ltd

Set in 10/12.5pt Minion by SPi Publisher Services, Pondicherry, India
Printed and bound in Malaysia by Vivar Printing Sdn Bhd

1   2014

Contents

Foreword

Professor Jacqueline Glass
Chair in Architecture and Sustainable Construction
Loughborough University, UK

This book on sustainable concrete solutions sets out a practical and up to date manifesto for the design engineer to create low carbon, sustainable buildings and civil infrastructure using concrete. The materials that make concrete are global and plentiful, but we have a duty to deploy them in an environmentally sensitive and socially responsible manner. This publication by Georgopoulos and Minson brings together the current thinking on engineering design practices and materials science – an unusual and helpful combination for the engineer keen on delivering more sustainable buildings and civil engineering projects.

Beyond the introduction of sustainable development principles, there is a healthy balance of theory here, which is appropriately and neatly articulated with practical considerations. This is reflected in the logical structure which acknowledges implicitly the significance of the role of decision-making in the design process which is, ultimately, a key determinant of the success of sustainable buildings. Written through the eyes of a design engineer, the publication essentially shows how we can avoid the specification gap which often prevents projects achieving their full sustainability potential. Examples and case studies are featured extensively.

Indeed, the book is very much written with the designer in mind and while it covers the fundamentals, it also brings to light emergent challenges around life-cycle assessment and responsible sourcing of construction materials. What makes Georgopoulos and Minson particularly interesting therefore, is that it worthily and legitimately goes well beyond the more traditional interpretations of sustainability in the context of cement and concrete (i.e. replacing Portland cement).

This book is a valuable addition to the sustainable design and specification area and I would commend it to construction and engineering practitioners, academics and students alike.

Preface

The challenges facing twenty-first-century humanity include climate change, natural disasters, population growth, overconsumption of resources, over-production of waste and increasing energy demands. The sustainability opportunity for construction practitioners is to create a built environment that provides sustainable solutions with better whole-life performance by using less primary materials, less non-renewable energy, wasting less and causing fewer disturbances to the natural environment. Solutions are needed that will mitigate climate change, but also that help mankind address the consequences of climate change.

There is a growing pressure from governments and clients to create a built environment that meets the needs of today's communities without compromising the needs of future generations, in other words, a more sustainable form of development. Concrete is ubiquitous in the built environment being used in schools, hospitals, homes, offices, transport infrastructure, energy supply, water distribution and so on, for centuries and second only to water as the most consumed substance on earth. It is therefore essential that concrete is used in the most sustainable way and, this book contributes to constructing a sustainable built environment with concrete by offering a range of sustainable concrete solutions to practitioners.

Teaching and learning sustainability at universities is a challenge as it is a relatively new and fast evolving subject. In the UK it was initiated by the Royal Academy of Engineering in 1998 and incorporated into the competences of engineering graduates by the Engineering Council in 2004. Since then, sustainable development has been embedded into engineering curricula but very often, students and academics are not exposed to innovations in sustainable construction that are mainly developed by the industry. This book contributes to closing this gap of knowledge by offering a range of sustainable concrete solutions to students at all levels and academics of engineering and other construction related degree courses.

Specifying modern concrete mixes, designing to new state-of-the-art techniques and standards and, constructing using latest innovations are more challenging with demands to implement sustainability. The aim of the book is to serve as an introduction to and an overview of the latest developments in sustainable concrete construction. It provides useful guidance with further references to students, researchers, academics and practitioners of all construction disciplines who are faced with the challenge to design, specify and construct a more sustainable built environment.

1 Introduction

To set the scene, definitions of sustainability and sustainable development and the role of the design team in sustainable development are presented and followed by the sustainability credentials of concrete and, the book layout and context.

1.1 Sustainability and sustainable development

A distinction must be drawn first between sustainable development (the process, or journey) and sustainability (the aim, or destination). Sustainable development involves maintaining our current rate of development whilst leaving suitable resources behind for later generations to continue to develop. Therefore, environmental problems such as emissions must be tackled by considering their relationship with both the state of the economy and the well-being of society. We must take a holistic approach to each facet of sustainability: the environment, the economy and society. Taken together, this triple bottom line includes everything that we need to consider for a healthy, prosperous and stable life (Figure 1.1).

In the 1980s, increasing concern about the effects of economic development on health, natural resources and the environment led the United Nations to release the Bruntlandt Report 'Our Common Future', 1987. This report defines sustainable development as 'development which meets the needs of the present without compromising the ability of future generations to meet their own needs' (Bruntlandt, 1987).

The three strands of sustainability, that is, environmental, social and economic, being always diverse and sometimes conflicting can be used both as

Sustainable Concrete Solutions, First Edition. Costas Georgopoulos and Andrew Minson.
© 2014 John Wiley & Sons, Ltd. Published 2014 by John Wiley & Sons, Ltd.

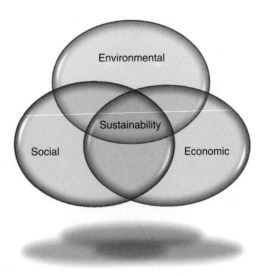

Figure 1.1 The triple bottom line of sustainability.

justification and as a barrier. For example, the London 2012 Olympic Park's environmental credentials – grey water recycling, combined heat and power plant, demountable structures, robust long lasting legacy structures – helped fulfil London 2012's pledge of hosting the most sustainable Olympic Games ever held and to establish sustainability benchmarks for the development of future Games facilities. Surely, one might argue, the most sustainable decision for London would have been to not hold the Games at all – not to use water and power, not to have hundreds of thousands of people flying to London, not to build structures for a few weeks. This would have been true if the emphasis had been placed on the environmental pillar of sustainability. Nevertheless priority was given to the economic and social pillars of sustainability as the Olympic Park helped regenerate the economy and society in a deprived area in London. Decisions are always based on one or more pillars on which emphasis is placed so projects always satisfy one or more pillars of sustainability. As a result, very few, if any, projects end up looking entirely unsustainable.

Although there are environmental impacts associated with cement and concrete production, we must not lose sight of the role that concrete and cementitious materials play in our built environment and the value of this built environment in our quality of life. The British Cement Association (BCA), in association with Forum for the Future, developed a business case for sustainable development with the purpose of assessing the costs and benefits of the UK cement industry in terms of its economic, environmental and social impacts (BCA and Forum for the Future, 2005). The overall findings of the business case are positive (Figure 1.2).

This work highlights the importance of approaching sustainability holistically; all facets, social, environmental and economic should be considered equally. To consider only one element skews the perception of the overall

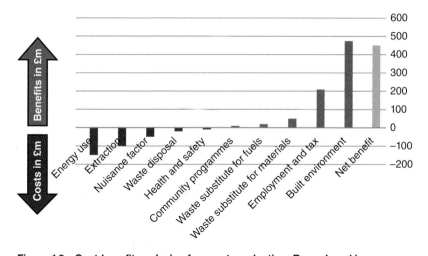

Figure 1.2   Cost-benefit analysis of cement production. Reproduced by permission of The Concrete Centre.

performance; embodied and in-use or upstream and downstream facets must be considered if we are to achieve real sustainability.

Detailed aspects of environmental, social and economic sustainability in construction are examined in Chapter 2.

1.2   The role of the design team in sustainable development

To enable the most sustainable construction and operation of a building the right decisions need to have been made at the design stage. A range of professionals have input into the design of a building and can contribute positively or negatively to sustainable development. A summary of the role of key contributors to the building design team is presented in Table 1.1. There is an overlap between roles, but for the purpose of considering sustainability, the different responsibilities have been allocated where possible. Some sustainability design decisions are truly integrated across several disciplines and this is indicated at the foot of the table.

1.3   Sustainability credentials of concrete

To demystify doubts about how sustainable concrete is, its sustainability credentials are presented in Table 1.2 and are further examined through the book. This draws on data obtained from the Sixth Concrete Industry Sustainability Performance Report (TCC, 2013) or is previously unpublished information from The Concrete Centre.

Table 1.1   Opportunities to impact sustainable development (Minson, 2008).

Client	Architect	Structural Engineer	Services Engineer
To develop, reuse or maintain status quo Scale of development Functional requirements Location	Concept design Orientation Massing Cladding Internal finishes Fire* Acoustics* Lighting* Thermal comfort$^\lozenge$ Air quality$^\lozenge$ Minimum water use Landscaping Flooding New sustainable architecture	Structural materials specification Efficiency of design New structural concepts	Energy/CO_2 Thermal comfort Air quality Equipment specification Operation manual New servicing strategies
	$\longleftarrow$ New integrated design solutions $\longrightarrow$		
$\longleftarrow$ Long life/loose fit or Deconstruct/reconstruct $\longrightarrow$			

*Specialist consultancy (not tabled) may be used on larger/complex projects
$^\lozenge$Responsibility is another discipline listed in this table

Table 1.2   Summary of Sustainability Credentials of Concrete (drawing on data from published data (TCC, 2013) unless otherwise referenced).

The sustainability performance benefits of concrete
Fire
Environmental Concrete does not burn and therefore it reduces noxious emissions from a fire, and wastage of materials.
Social The resilience of concrete reduces damage and limits the potential loss of livelihood or homes through a fire. During construction there is no risk to neighbours of the concrete frame being a fire hazard.
Economic Regulations require safe evacuation of occupants but not property safety. Concrete structures comply with life safety regulation but can also resist fire to enable cost-effective repair and re-use.
Thermal Mass
Environmental Concrete's thermal mass allows it to be used to reduce heating and cooling energy of buildings.
Social The thermal mass of concrete can be used to reduce overheating in a building. Occupants affected by public funding and CO_2 targets, in social housing and schools, are at risk of overheating if energy use cannot be reduced by no cost options.
Economic Using the thermal mass of concrete will lower running costs of a building. It will also reduce the plant needed on site, leading to reduced maintenance costs.

Acoustic Performance

Environmental
Concrete has good acoustic performance and there is less reliance on finishes and materials which have a short lifespan. Hence less material is used and potential waste is avoided.

Social
Concrete's mass absorbs sound, ensuring quality of life, particularly in high density living, where dwellings are prone to acoustic break-in.

Economic
Concrete walls and floors provide required acoustic separation with minimum finishes, hence minimum cost and maintenance.

Durability

Environmental
Due to the long life of all concrete structures, material impacts on the environment are kept to an absolute minimum.

Social
The durability of concrete structures means that, once built, they are rarely out of use for maintenance and hence have minimum social disruption.

Economic
Concrete is a very stable and durable material with an extremely long life. As a result, maintenance costs are minimal for concrete structures.

Robustness/Security

Environmental
Concrete structures are robust, reducing risk of damage to finishes, hence less use of materials through the whole life cycle of structures.

Social
Solid concrete party walls provide safe, secure buildings. Prevention of intruders helps to build safer communities. Concrete infrastructure is robust against vandalism/terrorism minimising social disruption.

Economic
Concrete structures, particularly if finishes are minimised, will suffer less damage and cost less to repair and maintain.

Flood Resilience

Environmental
The flood resilience of concrete means it retains structural integrity, resulting in minimum wastage of materials following a flood event.

Social
A concrete structure will resist water penetration, keeping inconvenience and disruption to business, homeowners and the community to a minimum following a flood event.

Economic
Downtime of businesses, homes and essential community services, is minimised if flooded buildings are constructed in concrete.

The Sustainability Credentials of Specified Products: Precast, Ready-mixed and Reinforcement

Precast Concrete Products
CO_2: A commitment to use additional cementitious materials where performance requirements permit exists throughout the industry. Transport distance for the average delivery of precast concrete products is 106 kilometres.

(Continued)

Recycling: Recycling systems capture virtually all process water, slurry, aggregates or cement and these are re-used in the production process. Around 96% of the waste produced by the precast sector is recycled or re-used.

Resource depletion: Over 21% of aggregates used in the precast sector are recycled or from secondary sources. The sector has set a target to increase the use of additional cementitious materials to 25%. Precast products can often be re-used in their entirety.

Waste: The precast concrete sector uses more waste than it produces. A tonne of precast product uses 210kg of secondary materials and by-products and produces only 1.76kg of waste that goes to landfill. Concrete buildings can be designed with less finishes reducing the associated material waste.

Water: Dependency on mains water supplies is being drastically reduced across the industry as companies adopt recycling systems and alternative water sources such as rainwater harvesting. Approximately 132 litres of water are used per tonne of precast concrete product; 36% of which is from licensed non-mains sources. Water-reducing admixtures also minimise water use.

Emissions: The precast concrete sector is closely regulated by the Environment Agency. In 2012 the sector achieved an increase in the percentage of tonnage covered Environmental Management Schemes (EMS) to over 88%. A target has been set to increase this to 95% by 2020.

Biodiversity: Companies with factories in more rural areas are increasingly committed to protecting and enhancing the natural environment. A site in Yorkshire was the first manufacturing site to attain The Wildlife Trust's 'Biodiversity Benchmark'.

Health and Safety: The comprehensive British Precast health and safety scheme has helped members reduce their overall incidence rates by two thirds compared to 2000. Admixtures are used to produce self-compacting concrete which does not require vibration leading to quieter working environments.

Ready-mixed Concrete

CO_2: Additional cementitious materials and admixtures are used by most concrete manufacturers to optimise cement content and can reduce the embodied CO_2 of the concrete. Transportation CO_2 is minimal with the average delivery distance of ready-mixed concrete being 12 kilometres and 50% of ready-mixed plants are located at the aggregate extraction site.

Recycling: At the end of the life of a structure, all cured concrete waste can be recycled to create new construction materials.

Resource depletion: Every tonne of ground granulated blast-furnace slag (GGBS) or fly ash used in concrete mixes saves about 1.4 tonnes of raw materials and fossil fuels. Aggregates are abundant the world over and the UK has enough aggregate reserves to last for hundreds of thousands of years at current rates of usage (McLaren et al., 1999).

Waste: Modern formwork systems and efficient site management minimise ready-mixed wastage which is estimated at less than 2% of production output. Systems are available to re-use 'returned ready-mixed concrete' and this does not go to landfill. Concrete buildings can be designed with less finishes reducing the associated material waste.

Water: A cubic metre of fresh concrete contains 140 to 190 litres of water. The use of admixtures can reduce the water content by up to 30 litres per cubic metre. Ninety per cent of ready-mixed concrete already includes water reducing admixtures.

Emissions: All ready-mixed plants have dust suppression systems in place.

Health and safety: The ready-mixed sector is an increasingly safe place for people to work. Lost time injuries and reportable injuries to direct employees have been both reduced by a factor of 4 in the period 2009 to 2012 inclusive.

Sustainable formwork: Formwork suppliers and contractors have responded to the sustainability agenda by, for example, increasing the number of re-uses of formwork on site, refurbishing forms with surface treatment rather than replacing, and using vegetable-based release agents.

Reinforcement

CO_2: Manufacture of steel reinforcement bars for reinforced concrete could be a source of significant energy consumption and a large contributor to embodied CO_2. However, the UK industry uses the Electric Arc Furnace process, which generates up to six times less CO_2 than those emanating from the Basic Oxygen Steel making system that is used for making other UK steel.

Recycling: UK produced reinforcement for concrete is manufactured from around 94% recycled UK scrap steel. Scrap steel reinforcement from demolished buildings is recycled to manufacture new steel reinforcement. Two thirds of reinforcement used in the UK is produced in the UK. The majority of imported reinforcement is also produced from scrap steel by Electric Arc Furnace.

Resource depletion: The use of Electric Arc Furnaces allows reinforcement steel to be made from 100% scrap metal, reducing the specific energy (energy per unit weight) required to produce the steel, but also relieving pressure on the Earth's natural ore resources. The UK is a net exporter of scrap steel.

The Sustainability Credentials of Constituents: Cement, Cementitious Additions and Aggregates

Cement (MPA Cement, 2012)

CO_2: Direct annual CO_2 emissions were reduced by 44.8% since 1990 in absolute terms, thereby surpassing the UK's 2010 Cement Industry Climate Change Agreement target. The target was actually met four years in advance. This compares favourably with the UK construction industry, which overall recorded an increase in CO_2 of more than 30% over the same period (BCA, 2006).

Recycling: In 2011, the sector replaced 39.7% of its fuel from waste-derived material including scrap tyres, pelletised sewage sludge and meat and bone meal.

Biodiversity: All cement plants and quarries have, or are linked to, biodiversity action plans.

Resource depletion: The consumption of natural raw materials needed to make cement has reduced significantly over recent years. Between 1998 and 2011 the sector has increased the use of waste-derived raw materials by over 80%.

Waste: The cement sector is a net user of waste. Waste-derived materials are actively sought as replacements for natural raw materials and fossil fuels. In 2010 the sector used over 1.3 million tonnes of waste in this way and produced only 14,000 tonnes.

Emissions: The cement industry has worked hard to reduce its emissions to air by investing in new technologies. From 1998 to 2011 significant reductions have been achieved; SO_2 emissions have reduced by 84%, dust emissions by 82% and NO_x by 60%.

Health and Safety: Zero Harm is the overriding health and safety priority. Lost Time Injuries were reduced by 85% in the 8 years to 2011, and a target of 50% reduction has been set for the 5 year period to 2014.

Cementitious Additions

CO_2: The use of 50% GGBS can reduce embodied CO_2 by over 40% compared with a traditional 100% Portland cement concrete mix. Thirty per cent fly ash can reduce embodied CO_2 by over 20%. Limestone fines can reduce embodied CO_2 by 15%.

Recycling: The concrete industry recycles by-products from other industrial processes. GGBS, a by-product of iron production, and fly ash from electric generating plants can both be used as additional cementitious material in concrete mixes.

Resource depletion: Every tonne of Cementitious Additions used in concrete mixes saves about 1.4 tonnes of raw materials.

Waste: GGBS and fly ash are by-products of other industries. These products can be diverted from landfill by being used as Cementitious Additions in concrete mixes. As a proportion of total cementitious materials used in ready-mixed and precast concrete 30.2% is Cementitious Additions based on 2012 data.

(Continued)

Aggregates

CO_2: On site CO_2 emissions from aggregates supply are 4–6kg per tonne. Fifteen per cent of UK aggregates are transported by rail and ship/barge. The average road delivery distance is 43 kilometres.

Recycling: With a growing commitment to recycling construction waste materials, there is now little evidence that any hard demolition and construction waste is sent to landfill (DCLG, 2007). Recycled and secondary aggregates account for 29 per cent of the total market: this is the highest for all countries in Europe.

Biodiversity: Over 700 Sites of Special Scientific Interest (SSSI) in the UK are current and previous sites of mineral extraction. The aggregates sector is actively involved in site stewardship and biodiversity initiatives, including encouraging exemplar restoration projects.

Resource depletion: Aggregates are abundant the world over. The UK has enough aggregate reserves to last for hundreds of thousands of years at current rates of usage (McLaren, 1999).

Health and safety: With improving working practices, year on year aggregate extraction is becoming an increasingly safe industry. The Mineral Products Association (MPA) achieved in 2012 their 2014 target of a 50% reduction in Lost Time Incidents (LTI) for direct employees and contractors, with an overarching aim of 'Zero Harm'.

Other Issues

Responsible Sourcing

The concrete industry is the first industry to link its sustainable construction strategy to the responsible sourcing standard developed by the Building Research Establishment (BRE), BES 6001 – 'Framework Standard for the Responsible Sourcing of Construction Products'. Ninety-two per cent of UK concrete is accredited as responsibly sourced. The reinforcement sector has both Eco-reinforcement which is accredited to BES 6001 and CARES Sustainable Reinforcing Steel Certification (Greenbooklive, 2012).

Local Sourcing and production

Local production using local materials is an important principle and covers social, environmental and economic aspects. For the UK, concrete and reinforcement are local products compared with alternatives that are imported, often from beyond Europe.

1.4   Book layout and context

After this introduction, Chapter 2 sets the scene by outlining the challenges of implementing sustainability in construction each followed by example responses drawn from the concrete industry. Chapters 3, 4 and 5 follow the logical sequence of a construction project, from inception to end of life, namely Chapter 3 on conceptual design, Chapter 4 on material specification and, Chapter 5 on construction, Operation and End of Life. Each chapter includes a summary and references at the end. The Appendix consists of specialised subjects and further information referenced in the main chapters. Appendices A, B, C and D cover thermal mass, biomass product substitution, options for concrete floors and worked example on embodied CO_2 for a building slab respectively. Concept definitions and where feasible case studies are included in the text.

In Chapter 2 the main challenges of implementing sustainability are presented, each followed by example responses drawn from the cement and concrete industries. The chapter starts with climate change, being sustainability's biggest challenge and causing temperature rise, flooding and wind damage. environmental protection is covered by looking at resource depletion, emissions reduction, transport of construction materials, preserving biodiversity and site restoration. Social progress follows under the headings of functionality, safety, durability, robustness and security, aesthetics, archaeology and community involvement. Economic growth is examined at national, local and household levels. Finally a section on regulatory responses outlines current global, European and UK regulations influencing progress in sustainability implementation.

Chapter 3 is the largest subject in the book covering the conceptual design of buildings and infrastructure. After a comprehensive introduction emphasising the importance of conceptual design, the buildings part starts with the client's brief followed by whole building design that includes design life and future flexibility, life time energy, design for deconstruction, orientation and integrated design. In keeping with the philosophy of moving from the whole to the parts, the following sections on buildings cover substructures, lateral stability, frames and flooring, cladding and roofs. Finally the buildings part is completed by looking at innovations, environmental assessment schemes and life cycle CO_2e studies. Conceptual design of infrastructure covers a selection of sustainable solutions using modern concretes or cements including ground remediation with stabilisation / solidification, hydraulically bound mixtures for pavements, road construction and pipes, new modular precast concrete bridges, sustainable urban drainage systems, wind towers and environmental assessment schemes.

Chapter 4 covers material specification being an integral part of the design process. The chapter starts with the introduction of new terms under the title Assessing Environmental Impacts of Materials that includes project context and functional equivalence, range of environmental impacts, life cycle of materials, life cycle impact assessment and, international standards and concrete product category rules. Responsible sourcing, being an increasingly important factor, is outlined next and is followed by the sustainability impacts and benefits of all constituents of concrete under the headings of cements and combinations, aggregates, water, admixtures, novel constituents and reinforcement. The chapter is completed with special concretes, specification examples and key guidance to specify sustainable concrete.

In conclusion Chapter 5 looks at construction, operation and end of life.

References

BCA and Forum for the Future (2005) *The UK Cement Industry: Benefit and cost analysis*, British Cement Association (BCA) and Forum for the Future, UK.

BCA (1999) *Concrete Through the Ages – from 7000 BC to AD 2000*, British Cement Association (BCA), UK.

BCA (2006) *Performance: a corporate responsibility report from the UK cement industry*, British Cement Association (BCA), UK.

Bruntlandt, G.H. (1987) *Report for the UN World Commission on Environment & Development, Our Common Future*, Oxford University Press, UK.

DCLG (2007) *Survey of Arisings and Use of Alternatives to Primary Aggregates in England 2005*, Department of Community and Local Government (DCLG), UK.

Greenbooklive (2012) www.greenbooklive.com

McLaren, D., Bullock, S. and Yousef, N. (1999) *Tomorrow's World: Britain's share in a sustainable future*, Friends of the Earth, Earthscan, UK.

Minson, A.J. (2008) *Sustainable Design & What Concrete Can Offer*, 7th International Congress, Dundee, UK.

MPA Cement (2012) *Sustainable Development Report* 2011, Mineral Products Association (MPA) Cement, UK.

TCC (2013) *Concrete Industry Sustainability Performance Report, 6th report: 2012 performance data*, MPA-The Concrete Centre (TCC) on behalf of the Sustainable Concrete Forum, UK.

2 Challenges and Responses

2.1 Introduction

It is important that we manage the natural and built environment and our resources to ensure a better quality of life for everyone, now and for future generations, moving towards what is called 'one planet living' (UN, 1998).

Measuring sustainability has proved to be quite a challenge for engineers who are increasingly asked to think holistically and produce sustainable solutions based on modern qualitative non-measurable values rather than traditional quantitative measurable criteria. The challenge is to translate a problem defined by complexity science to a solution delivered by Newtonian science (Fenner et al., 2006). One hopes that the continuing interaction of engineers with other disciplines and the fast evolving changes in engineering education and practice that are driven by the need for holistic design will improve the way sustainability is measured in the future.

In this chapter the main challenges of implementing sustainability in construction are presented and each is followed by example responses drawn from the concrete industry. The chapter starts with the challenge of Climate Change, continues with challenges under the three usual headings of Environmental Protection, Social Progress and Economic Growth and finishes with a short outline of Global, European and UK Regulatory Responses.

2.2 Climate change

The greenhouse effect has been known since 1858, when John Tyndall, an evolutionary atmospheric scientist, concluded after experiments that 'The solar heat possesses the power of crossing an atmosphere; but, when the heat

Sustainable Concrete Solutions, First Edition. Costas Georgopoulos and Andrew Minson.
© 2014 John Wiley & Sons, Ltd. Published 2014 by John Wiley & Sons, Ltd.

is absorbed by the planet, it is so changed in quality that the rays emanating from the planet cannot get with the same freedom back into space. Thus the atmosphere admits of the entrance of the solar heat, but checks its exit; and the result is a tendency to accumulate heat at the surface of the planet' (Fleming, 1998). We now can explain that the earth's surface radiates back some of the energy of the sun's rays, at a different frequency. Some gases in the atmosphere absorb some of this reflected radiation, and re-radiate it in all directions, including back towards the earth causing the earth to warm up. These gases, known as greenhouse gases, include most gases with two different atoms and all with three or more, of which the most important is carbon dioxide (CO_2). Burning fossil fuels – coal, gas and oil – releases CO_2 into the atmosphere, so increases the strength of the greenhouse effect, and hence causes global warming (Allwood & Cullen, 2011). But how much of global warming is anthropogenic?

Sources of anthropogenic CO_2 include fossil fuel combustion, changes in land use (e.g. forest clearing resulting in less CO_2 being absorbed by trees) and cement manufacturing. Concentrations of CO_2 in the atmosphere are expressed in parts per million by volume (ppmv). The Industrial Revolution circa 1700s increased the CO_2 concentration from 280ppmv to 380ppmv (GWA, 2007). The first increase of 50ppmv took 200 years from 1770 to 1970 but the next 50ppmv increase took place over 30 years, from 1970 to 2000. This dramatic and accelerating anthropogenic increase of CO_2 in the atmosphere has been implicated as the primary cause of global warming.

It is very likely that anthropogenic influences have led to warming of extreme daily minimum and maximum temperatures at the global scale. It has been estimated that the 500,000Mt of CO_2 released since the start of industrialisation – an amount not experienced for at least the last 800,000 years – has caused just under 1°C of global warming. There is medium confidence that anthropogenic influences have contributed to intensification of extreme precipitation at the global scale. It is likely that there has been an anthropogenic influence on increasing extreme coastal high water due to an increase in mean sea level (IPCC, 2012).

Climate change is one of sustainability's biggest challenges and a significant threat to global security and prosperity. Despite doubts on the pessimistic predictions of the future climate as expressed by sceptics there is a duty of care that requires construction professionals to be fully aware and try to both reduce the contribution their projects may make to future climate change and reduce potential impacts of climate change on buildings and infrastructure. There is also an economic driver that prompts immediate action. According to the *Stern Review*, the cost of reducing CO_2 emissions to the planned target in the UK would be about 1% of GDP, although the cost of climate change if nothing is done would be at least 5% of GDP (HM Treasury, 2006).

A changing climate leads to changes in the frequency, intensity, spatial extent, duration and timing of extreme weather and climate events. Since

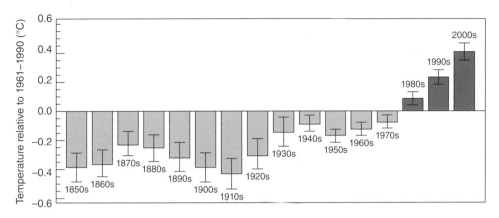

Figure 2.1   Observed global average temperature for each decade from 1850 to 2009 relative to 1961–90 (Met Office, 2010). Crown Copyright. Contains public sector information licensed under the Open Government Licence v1.0.

August 2003 when Europe experienced the most intense summer heat wave on record and the end of the last decade which was the warmest since the 1850s (Figure 2.1), global warming and climate change scenarios have come to dominate the sustainability agenda worldwide.

Extreme events are rare, which means there are few data available to make assessments regarding changes in their frequency or intensity. The more rare the event the more difficult it is to predict long-term changes. Global-scale trends in a specific extreme event may be either more reliable (e.g., for temperature extremes) or less reliable (e.g., for droughts) than some regional-scale trends.

In the Special Report 'Managing the risks of extreme events and disasters to advance climate change adaptation' (IPCC, 2012), that is based on evidence from observations gathered since 1950, the extreme events identified are temperature rise, increased flooding and higher wind speeds. These are based on probable climate projections and scenarios with inherent modelling uncertainties and are considered below together with examples of damages resulting from climate change such as toxic mould and insect damage.

Actions that range from incremental steps to transformational changes are essential for reducing risk from climate extremes. Responses to climate change are twofold:

- Mitigation: reducing impacts to climate change from buildings and infrastructure by minimising greenhouse gas emissions.
- Adaptation: changing new and existing buildings and infrastructure to deal with the impacts of climate change as it happens.

In the UK, these two central actions are covered in its regulations outlined in section 2.6.3.

2.2.1 *Temperature rise*

CHALLENGE

Based on available meteorological records, there has been an overall decrease in the number of cold days and nights, and an overall increase in the number of warm days and nights, on the global scale. In many (but not all) regions over the globe the length or number of warm spells or heat waves has increased. Climate models predict substantial warming in temperature extremes by the end of the twenty-first century. It is virtually certain (99–100% probability) that increases in the frequency and magnitude of warm daily temperature extremes and decreases in cold extremes will occur in the twenty-first century on the global scale. It is very likely that the length, frequency and/or intensity of warm spells or heat waves will increase over most land areas. The 1-in-20 year extreme daily maximum temperature (i.e., a value that was exceeded on average only once during the period 1981–2000) will likely (66–100% probability) increase by about 1 °C to 3 °C by the mid-twenty-first century and by about 2 °C to 5 °C by the late twenty-first century, depending on the region and emissions scenario (UKCIP09, 2010).

In the UK, even under a medium to low emissions scenario, the average summer temperatures are anticipated to increase by between 3 °C and 4 °C in the south of England and 1.5 °C to 2 °C in Scotland by 2080. In London, due to the Urban Heat Island (UHI) effect – that is, the rise in temperature of any urban area, resulting in a well-defined, distinct 'warm island' among the 'cool sea' represented by the lower temperature of the area's nearby natural land-scape – the increase could be as high as 8°C, taking the peak summertime temperature to well over 30°C. This will have a considerable impact on the temperature of the internal environment of buildings, especially buildings of lightweight construction which are likely to be overheated by 2020. This over-heating may increase the need for energy-intensive air conditioning to make them bearable and this would compromise the UK government's target for reduction of CO_2 emissions.

These predictions now need to be taken into account in designing the per-formance of buildings – particularly hospitals and care homes where high temperatures can be a risk to life and safety – even though they have yet to be adopted in approved design guidance.

RESPONSE

An inherent benefit of concrete is its high thermal mass (see Appendix A). In the summer, exposed concrete absorbs heat and that together with the provision of solar shading, can keep internal temperatures 6–8 °C below the peak external temperatures. Night-time ventilation is then used to cool the building priming it for the next day (TCC, 2005). In the winter, concrete's thermal mass stores the energy from the heating system, passive solar energy and heat gains from the occupants and internal sources such as electrical equipment, cooking, lighting, people or other internal sources. This stored energy is then released at night thereby sustaining warmer overnight temperatures and reducing the use of heating energy.

Independent research, carried out by Arup Research and Development, highlighted the energy savings that can be achieved by utilising thermal mass. Comparing lightweight timber homes (see Appendix B) with medium weight and heavyweight masonry and concrete homes, the research found that the latter has the lowest total energy consumption and therefore CO_2 emissions over the lifetime of the house, due to the reduced need for air conditioning and reduced winter heating requirements (Hacker et al., 2008). The results for housing are of relevance to other buildings such as offices where a major design challenge is to keep cool. Here, adequate ventilation, solar shading and utilisation of thermal mass can avoid overheating through passive cooling. The moderate to high cooling loads associated with office environments enables significant energy savings to be realised if thermal mass and night ventilation are utilised to avoid or minimise the need for air conditioning. This will in turn result in a reduction in the operational CO_2 emissions thereby enabling the embodied CO_2 of the building's structure to be offset.

2.2.2 *Flooding*

CHALLENGE

The impacts of a changing climate include an increase in the frequency, intensity and duration of heavy precipitation and storms as well as a rise in sea levels. It is likely that the frequency of heavy precipitation or the proportion of total rainfall from heavy falls will increase in the twenty-first century over many areas of the globe. It is very likely that mean sea level rise will contribute to upward trends in extreme coastal high water levels in the future. There is limited to medium evidence available to assess climate-driven observed changes in the magnitude and frequency of floods at regional scales because the available instrumental records of floods at gauge stations are limited in space and time, and because of confounding effects of changes in land use and engineering (IPCC, 2012).

Flooding is identified as the most significant risk from climate change, currently and in the short term, across the UK (DEFRA, 2012). Wetter winters with extreme rainfall events happening twice as often are predicted by the 2080s. Sea levels are expected to rise in most areas of the UK between 250 and 860mm by the end of the century. When these rises are coupled with increased storm surges and high tides they will produce more extreme high water levels with consequential flooding. With increased development and associated hard surfaces not adequately designed as part of SUDS (see Chapter 3) local flooding and runoff may also be an issue. Flash and river flooding already causes damage to energy, road and railway infrastructure such as scouring of bridge foundations as well as buildings in vulnerable locations.

RESPONSE

Concrete submerged in water absorbs very small amounts of water over long periods of time, and the concrete is not damaged. In flood-damaged areas, concrete buildings are often salvageable. In the rebuilding of New Orleans after Hurricane Katrina in 2005 and Japan coastal towns after the tsunami in 2011, architects and engineers have realised that lightweight construction is unable to sustain the force of water and they are looking at structures that will keep water out and not shift or float away when subjected to floodwaters. The best solution is using reinforced concrete for both external walls and internal floor slabs.

Concrete normally provides a good dry environment in buildings and will only contribute to moisture problems if it is enclosed in a system that traps moisture between the concrete and other building materials. For example, a vinyl wall covering in hot and humid climates will act as a vapour retarder and moisture can get trapped between the concrete and the wall covering.

Concrete is the preferred construction material for many coastal and river flood defence systems such as breakwaters, barriers, slope stabilisation, erosion control and water dispersion. In urban areas where a greater proportion of the land surface is covered by hard impenetrable materials, Sustainable Urban Drainage Systems (SUDS), comprising elements of concrete permeable paving, are used to prevent flash flooding and better manage the run-off water by facilitating rainwater storage. (see Chapter 3)

2.2.3 Wind damage

CHALLENGE

The maximum wind speed of average tropical storms is likely to increase, although increases may not occur in all ocean basins. It is likely that the global frequency of tropical storms will either decrease or remain essentially unchanged. For example, the frequency and intensity of hurricanes – that is, tropical storms with wind speeds over 74 miles per hour – in St Lucia, Caribbean is likely to increase by 2025 with the result that the basic wind speeds for buildings should be increased by 10–15% (which results in a 20–30% increase in pressures) (The Structural Engineer, 2011). Beyond areas subjected to tropical storms, serious consideration should be given to modifying wind speeds where national codes may be based on out-of-date wind speed data.

In the UK, increased temperatures would lead to increased energy and moisture in the atmosphere and this could lead to increased wind speeds in the future.

Residential buildings may be more vulnerable to wind damage than commercial buildings as they may not have the same degree of construction reliability as major projects. Damage from storm events is often caused by flying debris and so elements attached to buildings such as cladding must be fixed properly and be robust enough to sustain potential damage from flying projectiles.

RESPONSE

Research conducted by the Texas Tech University's Wind Engineering Research Centre concluded that an exterior concrete wall is one of the premier systems for ensuring safety for homeowners from debris carried by tornado- and hurricane-force winds. University researchers conducted a series of analytical and physical tests of numerous exterior wall systems for residential housing, subjecting them to projectiles driven by the severest of winds. Only concrete wall systems were proven to withstand 100% of all known hurricane-force winds, and over 99% of tornado-force winds. Concrete safe rooms help provide protection from earthquakes, tornadoes, hurricanes, fires, and other disasters.

Concrete is not affected by wind-driven rain and moist outdoor air in hot and humid climates because it is impermeable to air infiltration and wind-driven rain. Moisture that enters a building must come through joints between concrete elements. Inspection and repair of joints will minimise this potential. More importantly, if moisture does enter through joints, it will not damage the concrete.

2.3   Environmental protection

With the world population doubling every 40 years – although it is currently stabilising steadily – and resource consumption doubling every 20 years there is a pressing need for environmental protection – whilst a small population may not suffer the consequences of causing environmental damage, at some point an increasing population will.

Concrete has embodied environmental impacts as a result of the quarrying of raw materials, the energy used in its production and the carbon dioxide emissions. As with all products it will eventually reach the end of its useful life. The cement and concrete industries are sometimes mistakenly perceived as arch-polluters in the industrial landscape. In fact, they are far from complacent in the face of the need for further improvement in environmental performance. Both industries are positively involved in activities to reduce the environmental impacts of the production of concrete, including:

- Reduction in the amount of polluting and 'greenhouse' gases emitted during the creation of concrete.

- More efficient use of resources in concrete production, including re-used materials and by-products from other industrial processes.
- Better re-use of waste and other secondary materials such as water, aggregate, fuel or other cementitious material.
- Lower reliance on quarrying material or sending construction and demolition waste to landfill by maximising the use of recycled material where practical.
- Development of low-energy, long-lasting yet flexible buildings and structures.
- Exploiting the thermal mass of concrete in a structure to reduce energy demand over the lifetime of a building.
- Environmental restoration after industrial activity has ceased.

Concrete's environmental impacts mainly consist of embodied impacts attributed to cement production. In putting these impacts into perspective, embodied impacts are very small in comparison with in-use impacts. For example, the US cement industry accounts for approximately 1.5% of US CO_2 emissions. That is a very small amount in comparison with heating and cooling homes and offices (40%), driving cars (33%) or industrial operations (27%) (NRMCA, 2012).

Furthermore, concrete uses only about 7–15% cement by weight depending on performance requirements. As a result, the embodied CO_2 in one cubic metre of concrete is only approximately 100–300kg depending on the concrete mix. Therefore notwithstanding the benefits of thermal mass and related operational CO_2 savings, the embodied CO_2 impact of concrete compares favourably to other building materials.

In this section the environmental challenges of resource depletion, emissions reduction, transport of construction materials, preserving biodiversity and site restoration are presented each followed by responses from the cement and concrete industries.

2.3.1 Resource depletion

2.3.1.1 Fossil fuel

CHALLENGE

With increasing fossil fuel prices, the peaking of North Sea oil and gas production, and the peaking of oil production in 15 of the leading oil producing nations (it is still rising in eight), more and more attention is being focused on the need to use alternative sources of energy. Even in the US the Federal Government is beginning to promote the manufacture of alternative fuels, such as ethanol which is produced from wheat, to plug the energy gap. Analysts are far from a consensus on this issue, but several prominent ones now believe that the peak in global oil production is imminent, after which there will be less oil available for consumption. 'Peak oil' is described as the point where oil production stops rising and begins a long-term decline. In the face of fast-growing demand, this means rising oil prices. Even if oil production growth simply slows or plateaus, the resulting tightening in supplies will still drive the price of oil upward, albeit less rapidly. Even if oil was not becoming scarcer and harder to find the fact that the combustion of fossil fuels contributes to the acceleration of climate change is enough reason to reduce our reliance upon them.

RESPONSE

Throughout the concrete supply chain there are concerted efforts underway to reduce reliance on fossil fuels. For instance the performance indicators below demonstrate how the cement industry in the UK is making strides in reducing both natural materials and the amount of fossil fuels that it uses per tonne of Portland cement manufactured.

Table 2.1   Performance indicators (MPA, 2011).
(Natural materials - in kg/t - and fossil fuels for primary energy - in % thermal - per tonne of cement manufactured)

	1998 (base)	2010 (target)	2010 (actual)	2015 (target)
Natural materials (kg/t)	1498	1420	1377.6	1400
Fossil fuels (% thermal)	94.3	75	61.9	70

In terms of fossil fuels, a 2010 target of 25.0 per cent replacement against a 1998 baseline of 5.7 per cent has also been surpassed with the actual 2010 industry figure being 38.1 per cent. This level is higher than the replacement target for 2015 of 30.0 per cent. To reach this high level of replacement, a wide variety of wastes have been used including solvents, waste tyres, paper and plastics, waste oils and wood, sewage sludge, meat and bone meal. The industry supplies positive answers to UK waste problems: lifting materials up the waste hierarchy from disposal to energy recovery. The industry only selects wastes that are safe and compatible with the cement manufacturing process and hence have no adverse effect on product quality or public health (BCA, 2008). Similarly, energy efficiency activities are underway throughout the sector. Quarries are installing new highly efficient rock crushers and concrete companies have applied energy management systems to reduce their energy use and costs.

2.3.1.2   Material resources

CHALLENGE

The construction industry is the largest consumer of material resources of all UK industries, both directly and from its supply chain of materials producers, fabricators and stockists. About six tonnes of materials are consumed per person per year. Most of these resources are massively abundant minerals or wood. For example, there are reserves of aggregates in the UK for hundreds of thousands of years (McLaren et al., 1998). Nevertheless sustainable use of materials is an integral part of environmental protection.

RESPONSE

A study (Wayne, 1993), sponsored by National Resources Canada, compared logging for wood products, iron ore mining for steel products, limestone quarrying for cement making and aggregate quarrying for concrete. The study measured the overall environmental impact in four areas:

1. Extent – the physical range of the affected area.
2. Intensity – the degree of damage to a site.
3. Duration – the length of time on the affected site.
4. Significance – the biological and ecological impact to the site.

As shown in the tables below concrete measures as good or best in all four of the categories. In addition, concrete has the lowest rating of the three materials on the Impact Index, the measure that was produced by the survey.

Table 2.2　Weighing the environmental impact of resource extraction.

	Extent	Intensity	Duration	Significance
Concrete	Low to moderate	Moderate to high	Moderate	Low
Iron Ore	Very low to low	High	High	Very low
Wood	High to very high	Moderate	Variable, complex	High

Table 2.3　Impact Index.

Concrete	Steel	Wood
1.50	2.25	2.5

Unlike limestone and aggregate quarries, iron ore extraction often involves very deep pits which are rarely restored. This is likely to be the case because these quarries are all overseas, many in countries with a much lower level of regulation compared to the UK.

The use of recycled aggregates (i.e. materials from previous construction projects) and recycled secondary aggregates (i.e. by-products from other industrial processes) in concrete support waste minimisation and reduce resource (i.e. virgin aggregates) depletion. The government sees this as such an important issue that the construction and demolition waste recovery rate is one of the national sustainable development indicators (DEFRA, 2013).

In the UK (2011 data), 148 million tonnes (Mt) of materials are quarried every year for use as aggregates, cement and other building materials, and 60 Mt arise from recycled or secondary sources. The Waste and Resources Action Programme (WRAP, 2012) was created to support the government's aim of increasing the use of recycled aggregates in England to 60Mt per annum by 2011. The Environment Agency has also set a target to procure 20% of the aggregates used for flood defence works from secondary sources. Road construction (sub-base layers) and fill materials for car parks, foundations, roads and runways are the main applications for 10 Mt of recycled aggregates, but this has changed with the introduction of *BS EN 12620: 2003 Aggregates for concrete*, which allows the use of suitable recycled aggregates in concrete (see Chapter 4).

Alternative materials are also used in the production of cement, making good use of wastes and enabling the industry to improve its environmental performance. In 2010, 7.2% of virgin raw materials were replaced by waste materials (MPA Cement, 2011). The industry only selects wastes that are safe and compatible with the cement manufacturing process and hence having no adverse effect on product quality or public health.

2.3.1.3   Industrial ecology

The science of industrial ecology emerged in the late 1980s and refers to the study of the physical, chemical and biological interactions and interrelationships within and among industrial and ecological systems. Applications of industrial ecology involve identifying and implementing strategies for industrial systems to more closely emulate harmonious and sustainable ecological systems. Industrial ecology can be considered a comprehensive approach to implementing sustainable, industrial behaviour; it is the shifting of industrial processes from linear (open loop) systems, in which resource and capital investments move through the system to become waste, to a closed loop system where wastes become inputs for new processes.

'Why would our industrial system not behave like an ecosystem, where the wastes of a species may be resource to another species? Why wouldn't the waste outputs of an industry be the inputs of another, thus reducing use of raw materials, pollution, and saving on waste treatment?' (Frosch & Gallopoulos, 1989). Industrial ecology proposes not to see industrial systems (for example a factory, an eco-region, or national or global economy) as being separate from the biosphere, but to consider it as a particular case of an ecosystem – but based on infrastructural capital rather than on natural capital. It is the idea that if natural systems do not have waste in them, we should model our systems after natural ones if we want them to be sustainable. Industrial ecology is practiced throughout the concrete supply chain.

Figure 2.2   Spinnaker Tower, Portsmouth.

Secondary materials are useful by-products of other industrial processes, notably fly ash and Ground Granulated Blastfurnace Slag (GGBS) which would potentially otherwise be sent to landfill. Apart from the obvious attractions of creating a use for these materials, their incorporation in factory made cements or as concrete mixer additions translates into direct reductions in quarrying, energy consumption and emissions.

GGBS is a useful by-product recovered from blast-furnaces used in the production of iron and can be used un-ground as a coarse aggregate or as a supplementary cementitious material where it can replace up to 70% of cement in a concrete mix. Fly ash is a useful by-product from coal-fired power stations. All cementitious additions including GGBS and fly ash account for around 30% of total UK consumption of cementitious material (TCC, 2013). Extensive use of industrial ecology has been the norm for decades. For example 10 years ago the UK annually used approximately 1.5 million tonnes (Mt) of GGBS and fly ash as cementitious replacement every year, (approximately 10% of total cementitious use) with the following environmental benefits (Higgins et al., 2002).

- Reduction in annual CO_2 emissions of 1.5Mt.*
- Reduction in primary energy use by 2,000 million kilo Watts per hour.*

- Saving of 1.5Mt of quarry material.
- Saving of 1.5Mt of landfill.

*(Improved efficiency of cement production has reduced CO_2 and energy savings per unit produced).

The advantages of these materials do not stop there. Their beneficial chemical properties in conjunction with Portland cement produce workable and durable concretes that are highly resistant to penetration by chloride ions, sulphates and other chemicals. The Spinnaker Tower in Portsmouth (Figure 2.2) is a prestigious example, where a 50% GGBS replacement concrete mix was used in its construction (Swamy, 2000).

Another example of industrial ecology is the use of waste tyres by the cement manufacturing industry. Every year the UK produces 400,000 tonnes of waste tyres, posing a significant environmental problem. Legislation prevents the dumping of tyres in landfill. Used tyres make an ideal kiln fuel for the production of cement, without any adverse environmental effects. Kiln temperatures are so high that tyres burn without fumes or flame – and what's more the residue from burning tyres can be chemically treated and reused again as fuel. The obvious pay-off from burning tyres is the fossil fuel and carbon emissions saved. It is estimated that the UK cement industry currently consumes 5.6 million waste tyres. Trials are also underway with other alternative fuels in cement making, such as recycled liquid fuel, inert Processed Sewage Pellets (PSP) and packaging waste. Used tyres have also even been recycled into concrete as they contain steel fibres. Recent research found that recycled steel fibre (which is cheaper than conventional steel fibre) leads to an increase in concrete's strength, ductility and toughness, making it suitable for a range of specialised applications such as impact and acoustic barriers.

2.3.2   *Emissions reduction*

One of the most important aspects of sustainability is 'do not pollute'. This is normally defined as 'to minimise and, where possible, eliminate emissions to the atmosphere, land and water'. To do this, civil engineering projects have to take positive steps to protect against pollution and reduce emissions such as dust, contaminated water or noise.

Like all activities with the potential to impact on people and the environment around them, cement and concrete operations are, quite rightly, closely monitored and carefully regulated. In Europe, the Integrated Pollution Prevention & Control (IPPC) Directive requires industrial and agricultural activities with a high pollution potential to have a permit. This permit can only be issued if certain environmental conditions are met, so that the companies themselves bear responsibility for preventing and reducing any pollution they may cause (IPPC, 2008). The implementation of IPPC in the UK is carried out by the Environment Agency, whose job it is to ensure that all emissions to land, air and water are avoided or controlled within safe limits. The Environment Agency is the main regulator of the UK cement industry. For example, in England and Wales, the result is the Pollution Prevention and Control (PPC) regulatory regime. Other parts of the concrete industry are subject to regulation by local authorities under Part B of the PPC regulations and many other pieces of legislation. Equivalent bodies and regulations exist in other industrialised countries and many economies in transition.

In this section the emissions from both the construction and the cement industries are considered under each of the headings; Carbon Dioxide CO_2 and Noise Pollution.

2.3.2.1 Carbon Dioxide CO_2

CHALLENGE

In producing concrete the main emissions to air are associated with the cement-making process. Cement production involves the heating of blended and ground raw materials which may consist of: limestone or chalk, clay or shale, sand, iron oxide and gypsum. During the cement-making process, and specifically the clinker formation process, gases with global warming potential (i.e. a relative measure of how much heat a greenhouse gas traps in the atmosphere) are emitted. CO_2 accounts for the main share of these gases. Other climatically-relevant gases, such as dinitrogen monoxide (N_2O) or methane (CH_4), are emitted in very small quantities only. CO_2 emissions are both raw material-related and energy-related. Raw material-related emissions are produced during the thermal decomposition of calcium carbonate ($CaCO_3$) or limestone decarbonation and account for about 60% of total CO_2 emissions from efficient dry plant cement manufacture. These emissions are not only distinct in terms of the process that generates them; they are also partly reversible through the process of carbonation – see section on responses. Energy-related emissions are generated both directly through fuel combustion to heat the 1400° kilns and indirectly through the use of electrical power. The manufacture of one tonne of UK cementitious materials generates approximately 0.719 tonnes of direct CO_2 emissions (2011 data).

Almost 3 billion tonnes of CO_2 were emitted globally in producing 3.6 billion tonnes of cement in 2011 (Figure 2.3) (CEMBUREAU, 2012).

Owing to growing demand for cement in developing economies it is estimated that cement production will follow population growth, that is, it will almost double in the next 40 years. Society, however, requires that global CO_2 emissions are halved by 2050 – see section on global responses – and this presents a great challenge for the cement manufacturing industry.

Additional CO_2 emissions are associated with the transport of materials, fuels and final product (within the industry and to customers), the crushing of rock to form aggregate, the production of steel reinforcement and the energy used to process the other raw materials or to power other manufacturing operations.

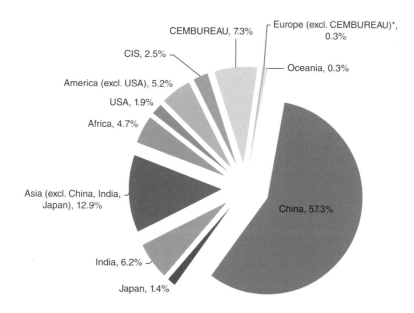

* Including EU27 countries not members of CEMBUREAU

Figure 2.3   World cement production 2011 by region and main countries (CEMBUREAU, 2012). Reproduced by permission of CEMBUREAU.

In the UK the construction of our built environment accounts for 10% of CO_2 emissions. Of this, the manufacture and delivery of concrete, as the most widely used material in construction, accounts for 2.6% of our CO_2 emissions (TSCTG, 2003). This should be compared to the use of the built environment – energy consumed to heat, cool and light buildings – which accounts for 50% of our CO_2 emissions and the 26% of our CO_2 emissions that arise from transport (NETCEN, 2006). These figures show how important the in-use impacts of our built environment are compared to the embodied impacts. The in-use impact is normally measured with operational CO_2 (OCO_2) emissions.

Embodied CO_2 (ECO_2) is considered a useful metric for comparing the global warming potential of different construction materials. Based upon the extraction and transportation of raw materials and their manufacture into the final product, ECO_2 is expressed as CO_2 per unit mass ($kgCO_2$/tonne) or CO_2 per unit area for a completed building ($kgCO_2$/m²). Interestingly, once issues such as raw material transportation are taken into account, the misconceptions about the ECO_2 of different construction materials are made apparent – see Table 2.4 (TCC, 2011).

RESPONSE

As seen in section 2.3.1.1, alternative fuels and waste materials are used extensively in the production of cement in the UK. Despite being fundamental to the built environment and widely used, cement production contributes less

Table 2.4   Embodied carbon dioxide (ECO$_2$) and construction materials.

Concrete	Concrete Type	ECO$_2$ (kgECO$_2$/m³)	ECO$_2$ (kgECO$_2$/tonne)
Blinding, mass fill, strip footings, mass foundations[1]	GEN1 70mm (CEM I only)	177	75
Reinforced Foundations[1]	RC30 70mm** (CEM I only)	316	131
Ground floors[1]	RC35 70mm* (CEM I only)	316	133
Structural: in situ floors, superstructure, walls, basements[1]	RC40 70mm** (CEM I only)	369	152
High strength concrete[1]	RC50 70mm** (CEM I only)	432	174
Dense concrete aggregate block[2]	Precast block	147	75
Aerated concrete block[2]	Precast block	121	240
Generic lightweight aggregate block[3]	Precast block	168	120
TIMBER			
Timber, UK Sawn Hardwood[4]		369	470
Timber, UK Sawn Softwood[4]		185	440
Plywood[4]		398	750
STEEL			
UK Produced Structural Steel Sections[5]		15,313	1,932

*includes 30kg/m³ steel reinforcement
**includes 100kg/m³ steel reinforcement

Notes
1. The figures for GEN 1, RC32/40 and RC40/50 were derived using industry agreed representative figures for cementitious materials, aggregates, reinforcement, admixtures and an appropriate figure for water. They take into account other greenhouse gas emissions and therefore are ECO$_2$ equivalent (ECO$_2$e) figures.
2. BRE Environmental Profiles database, Building Research Establishment (BRE), 2006.
3. Communication from The Environment Division, BREEAM Centre, Building Research Establishment (BRE), 2005.
4. Hammond, G. and Jones, C. (2006) Inventory of Carbon & Energy (ICE) version 1.5 Beta, Department of Mechanical Engineering, University of Bath, UK.
5. Amato, A. and Eaton, K.J., (1998) A Comparative Environmental Life Cycle Assessment of Modern Office Buildings, Steel Construction Institute.

NOTE: ECO$_2$ must be considered in the context of longevity. For example, if element A lasts twice as long as element B, the ECO$_2$ of element A is effectively half of that of element B.

than 2% of the country's total carbon dioxide production. A practical example of progress being made in the UK is the kiln at Hanson Cement's Padeswood plant in North Wales. This opened in 2005, and replaces three older and less efficient kilns at the site. There has been a 60% increase in output of clinker compared to production from the old kilns with significant amount of energy savings and the new kiln achieves some outstanding reductions in emissions per tonne produced including a 43% reduction in dust, 57% reduction in nitrogen oxides and a 91% reduction in sulphur dioxide in comparison with emissions from the old kilns (BCA, 2006b).

Concrete carbonation can also be taken into account thereby crediting concrete as a CO_2 sink. Carbonation is the process by which the pH of concrete is reduced from around 12 to below 9 to 10 through the absorption of atmospheric CO_2. With no carbonation, Portland cement concrete has a pH level of at least 12.6 and this minimises the potential for corrosion of steel reinforcing bar; at a pH above 9 to 10 a protective oxide layer forms on the surface of reinforcing bars. It is therefore important that through concrete specification, carbonation is limited to the surface of reinforced concrete and prevented from reaching depths where reinforcing bars are located. Standard(s) for specifying concrete ensures that this can be achieved across a broad range of applications. Whilst carbonation during the service life of reinforced concrete is intentionally kept to a minimum, there is a much greater uptake at the end of its life when it is crushed and CO_2 is more readily absorbed due to the significant increase in surface area. In unreinforced concrete used in blocks, and cementitious materials such as mortar, carbonation is more rapid as CO_2 can permeate the material more easily. This does not present a problem since no reinforcing bars are present.

Preliminary calculations examining the key UK cement markets/applications show that around 20% of the direct CO_2 emissions from the manufacture of cement are reabsorbed over its life cycle, that is, during its service life and secondary life following crushing and reuse. Whilst the carbonation process cannot be said to diminish the CO_2 emission to air during the manufacture of cement, a 20% uptake will ultimately reduce its environmental impact from an initial 822kg of CO_2 per tonne (2005 direct emissions) to around 670kg/t over its life (Clear & De Saulles, 2007).

The long-term solution would be to capture CO_2 emissions and lock them away in geological formations forever. Carbon Capture and Storage (CCS) is an emerging technology that is not yet proven at an industrial scale in cement manufacture. The electricity generation industry is pioneering the development of CCS because of the scale of their emissions in comparison with other industrial processes such as cement production. Nevertheless, the cement industry does consider CCS to be a long-term possibility and is investing in research and development to see if, how and when the technology can be applied to clinker production. It is important to note, however, that capture technologies can only be useful when the full chain of CCS is available, including transport infrastructure, access to suitable storage sites and a legal framework for CO_2 transport and storage, monitoring and verification, and licensing procedures.

In the short term, other ways of reducing the CO_2 impact of cement in producing concrete is through the use of cementitious additions (also referred to as cement replacements) such as GGBS, fly ash and silica fume that are covered in Chapter 4.

2.3.2.2   Noise pollution

CHALLENGE

The World Health Organisation suggests that noise can affect human health and well-being in the following ways:

- Creating feelings of annoyance.
- Disturb sleep.
- Interfere with communication particularly listening.
- Interfere with learning.
- Cause anti social or aggressive behaviour.
- Cause hearing loss.

Quarrying activities are potentially very noisy.

RESPONSE

There have been major advances in recent years in the reduction of noise from quarries and factories. The industry makes strenuous efforts to reduce the noise produced by its activity and mitigate the effects on workers and neighbours of the noise produced. The rock faces within a quarry can often provide a barrier to protect neighbours from noise pollution. Many of the potentially noisy quarrying operations such as crushing and sieving are carried out on the floor of the quarry to make use of the 'rock face barrier'.

Noise baffles or screens are usually constructed around the perimeter of quarries. If there is sufficient space these can take the form of wide mounds built from top soil and quarry waste. These can be planted with native species to increase their noise screening effectiveness, act as a natural filter for quarry dust and provide a habitat for wildlife.

If space around the quarry perimeter is limited then noise limiting fences may be constructed.

Within the quarry many strategies are used to reduce the amount of noise produced. These include:

- Restricting the speed of vehicles.
- Using noise-absorbing rubber matting on the floor of rock transporting vehicles.

- Reducing the volume of audible vehicle alarms (reversing etc.) particularly at night.
- Using new sound absorbent materials in machinery such as screens and sieves, for example, polypropylene.
- Ensuring workers are properly protected from noise, for example, sound insulation in vehicle cabs and providing appropriate ear protection.

In terms of cement making in the UK, all operations are controlled by the Environment Agency and potential noise pollution carefully monitored. Factory plant is generally fully enclosed and specific pieces of equipment further sound-proofed as necessary. Factory working and vehicle movement times are controlled by planning permissions to minimise potential noise nuisance and changes to blasting practices in quarries have reduced vibration and noise.

Off site manufacturing such as precast concrete and increased use of self compacting concrete on site (no need for vibration compacting) help reduce noise pollution on construction sites (see Chapter 4).

2.3.3 *Transport of construction materials*

CHALLENGE

A product should be consumed as near to the place of its production as possible to:

- Minimise the need for transport and the associated environmental, economic and social impacts of transportation.
- Support the local economy and hence local society.
- Prevent the export of the associated environmental impacts of production to another location with less stringent environmental and social protection legislation.

If transport is needed efforts should be made to ensure the most sustainable method of transportation.

RESPONSE

The UK is almost completely self-sufficient in the materials needed for the manufacture of concrete. The concrete sector roughly comprises:

- 13 cement plants.
- 1,300 aggregate sites.
- 1,000 ready-mix concrete sites.
- 850 precast concrete sites.

About 99.99% of aggregates are extracted from the UK's soil. Approximately 90% of cement is manufactured in the UK from UK constituents and the average distance of ready-mixed concrete to site is in the region of 10 miles. This is very different from other materials that are imported, such as timber (see Appendix B). More than 61% of the timber used in Britain for construction in 2011 was imported from places around the world (Forestry Commission, 2011).

The UK concrete sector uses non-road transport when the economic cost is not prohibitive. For example, rail is currently the primary transport mode for over 15 million tonnes of aggregates and over 2 million tonnes of cement. The transport within the concrete supply chain has the following distribution: 90% road, 9% rail – increased from 7% in 2008 – and 1% water (TCC, 2013).

2.3.4 *Preserving biodiversity*

CHALLENGE

The term biodiversity refers to the variety of life on Earth and measures the ecological well-being of the environment. Biodiversity is a challenge for material manufacturing industries. The challenge is most difficult for forestry which has a mono culture of single species trees. The protection of natural habitats, features and species is a vital component of sustainable civil engineering projects, biodiversity is part of Environmental Impact Assessment (EIA) which is a statutory requirement and most responsible projects have clear action plans to address the particular conditions of a site. The Highways Agency also has an action plan for its 'soft' estate.

The concrete industry should look for opportunities to provide and protect habitats. For civil engineering projects this means locating new development appropriately, preserving and enhancing natural features and biodiversity, and also ensuring that land use is integrated with transport and infrastructure plans.

RESPONSE

It is common for civil engineering projects to address the needs of local, sometimes rare, species of flora and fauna, particularly in areas of wetland or ancient forest. Botanists and zoologists are consulted to identify the species, discuss its habitat and liaise with the project team to devise the best solution to minimise disturbance, whether this is diverting the route of a road or physically relocating the species. There are a number of applications in which concrete can be used to respond to the biodiversity issue – including precast concrete units being used as artificial reefs, providing a habitat for fish and other marine creatures.

Road developments that cross established wildlife corridors must respect the needs of the local species and there are several examples of concrete pipes being used as underpasses, for wildlife crossings. An example is a relief road serving Bolnore village, near Haywards Heath, where the needs of the travelling community were met, while protecting the habitat of the protected species – in this case providing a safe route via a pipe under the road for the eventual return of otters to Foundry Brook, part of River Ouse.

One of the Mineral Products Association's (MPA) 'Core Values' in its Sustainable Development Strategy is a commitment to 'improving our management of biodiversity and geodiversity'. For example, developing site restoration plans and biodiversity action plans is also a key objective for the UK cement industry and is featured in its cement industry sector plan. Fortunately in the UK the aggregates required to produce concrete are ubiquitous and plentiful which allows for suitable sites to be selected.

In an attempt to quantify the efforts that are being put in to manage and improve biodiversity throughout the quarrying industry the members of MPA have developed the indicators representing the provision of habitat as follows:

- Trees planted = 139,392
- Hedgerows planted (km) = 17,64
  (All figures are for 2010)

The MPA are also developing another indicator, which is Designated Sites of Specific Scientific Interest (SSSIs) in each condition category. Many of the UK's nature reserves have been created on the sites of former quarries, including over 700 of the almost 7,000 SSSIs and many of them are still supported and maintained by the quarrying companies. SSSIs are the finest sites for wildlife and natural features in the UK, supporting many rare and endangered species, habitats and natural features. The purpose of SSSIs is to safeguard for present and future generations sites of high natural importance and they therefore make a vital contribution to the ecological processes upon which we all depend.

2.3.5   Site restoration

Recycling land for beneficial use is an important opportunity for sustainable development and, especially in the UK, building on brownfield land, that is, land, sometimes contaminated, used by industry in the past is well established since 1998 – see Chapter 3.

Quality restoration and aftercare of industry operations, sensitive to local requirements, is an essential part of responsible stewardship in the UK concrete, aggregates and cement industry. It is estimated that 0.11% of the UK land area is currently being quarried.

The members of the Mineral Products Association measure and report upon the following information, per annum:

- Proportion of UK land area being quarried (aggregates) = 0.10%
- Ratio of land restored, to land prepared for quarrying = 5:4
  (All figures are for 2010)

Quarrying is in fact only a temporary land-use and a quarry's environmental restoration after use effectively means the site has been borrowed from, rather than permanently lost, to nature. For a sand and gravel quarry, mineral extraction will usually take place for 10-15 years, while for a rock quarry, a 40-year life is typical. Restoration is already planned before work starts in the quarry and environmental restoration follows closely behind extraction on a progressive basis.

The industry has a very strong track record when it comes to quarry restoration. Quarries are restored to be: farmland; nature reserves; water sport parks; fishing lakes; and even shopping centres. Restoration of quarries is tightly controlled by planning permissions in terms of both the end use and speed of delivery and there are also annual awards for the best restorations given by the Mineral Products Association.

As well as restoring quarries after they have been used, restoration of quarries during their useful life is also an important issue to the industry and local communities. For instance, both Hanson Cement and Lafarge Tarmac Cement are working on the restoration of quarry faces to reduce visual impact and to introduce new habitats while the site is operational. Seeding and tree planting is carefully planned so that indigenous species are used.

Furthermore, all the cement works also have formal restoration plans under their existing planning permissions and under the Environment Agency Pollution Prevention Control permits. However, cement manufacturing operations have very long lives so definitive after-use plans for these areas are not practical.

2.4 Social progress

Sustainability is not just about environmental issues, it also encompasses social progress and this is core to the government's, as well as, institutional and executive agencies' strategic responses to the sustainability agenda. Social concern covers issues both within the business (e.g. employees) and outside of the business (e.g. local communities). The government's sustainable construction strategy asks the industry to 'respect people and their local environment – be responsive to the community in planning and undertaking construction' and to 'deliver buildings and structures that provide greater satisfaction, well-being and value to customers and users' (BERR, 2008).

In developing countries there is often greater emphasis on poverty reduction and access to safe and affordable shelters although in developed countries social sustainability frequently focuses on social equity and healthy environment. As demonstrated by the United Nations Commission on Sustainable Development with the Indicators of Sustainable Development, basic social aspects such as child labour that are taken for granted in developed countries are relevant and important components of sustainability in developing countries (CSD, 2009).

Providing society with the transport, utilities and facilities that it needs is of course the mainstay of civil engineering, but the term 'respect for people' does go further than this. It is also about addressing the needs of stakeholders, employees and local communities; it includes health and safety, welfare and employment. Further information on addressing respect for people issues within one's own business is available through the UK Constructing Excellence website (Constructing Excellence, 2011).

All building and infrastructure projects are driven by a clear social need – for example to provide a hospital for patients or a road for commuters – and, in this way, they satisfy the social strand of sustainability. However, they also interact with local communities in many intended or unintended ways having sometimes positive but also negative social impacts.

The challenge for the construction industry is to provide buildings and infrastructure that are functional, safe, durable, secure and robust in support of social progress. In this section the 'concrete' response to this challenge is presented under the headings Functionality, Safety, Durability, Robustness and Security, Aesthetics, Archaeology and Community Involvement.

2.4.1 *Functionality*

The use of exposed concrete to maximise thermal mass allows us to use natural environmental systems to cool and heat our built environment. In naturally ventilated concrete buildings, the provision of openable windows can provide good airflow and a degree of occupant control, which has a positive effect on the occupants 'comfort'. The bonus of concrete is that, when used in naturally ventilated buildings, it provides a healthier indoor air quality and can help to reduce the incidence of sick-building syndrome in commercial buildings. The exposed concrete surfaces also reflect light into a building's interior. This can reduce the need for artificial lighting, improving the quality of light for the occupants and helping to prevent eye strain.

Furthermore, as concrete is naturally inorganic and inert it does not need treatment with additional toxic chemical treatments, such as the Volatile Organic Compounds (VOCs) used to preserve timber (see Appendix B). Physical proof of concrete's inherent inert properties is its use in the London ring main, a vast engineering undertaking, 2.5m diameter pipe 50 miles long – twice as long as the Channel Tunnel, which supplies 50% of London's water supply.

Concrete's acoustic performance makes it suitable for noise barriers such as Gatwick airport (Figure 2.4). With inherent properties of strength, durability

Figure 2.4   The wave wall at Gatwick contains noise from manoeuvring aircraft. Reproduced by permission of Buchan Concrete.

and versatility, concrete acoustic barriers provide low cost, low maintenance and effective solutions to unwanted noise.

The sound insulation and acoustic performance of buildings has grown in importance too, primarily due to the growing demand from government for increased density of dwellings. The number of complaints about noise has increased both due to closer proximity and the new demands placed on housing (e.g. entertainment systems). For this reason, the UK Building Regulations sound insulation requirements within all types of buildings, especially dwellings have been made more stringent over recent years.

In general, increasing the mass of a wall or floor improves the sound insulation of a room; hence concrete and masonry offer a good barrier to airborne sounds, while impact sound is additionally controlled with appropriate floor and ceiling finishes. A range of 'Robust Details' (RDs) for both masonry and concrete walls and concrete floors has been agreed by the Building Regulations Advisory Committee (Robust Details, 2011). These offer approved construction choices for both party walls and separating floors and include aspects of the external wall in controlling sound between dwellings (TCC, 2010). Good acoustic properties can also be achieved for multi-occupancy residences such as hotels, prisons, student accommodation and so on, using a range of concrete options. One example is tunnel form construction (in which the walls, floors and ceilings are made from cast in-situ concrete using high quality reusable formwork).

2.4.2 Safety

The protection of human life and livelihoods is a vital requirement for any structure. Concrete's mass, strength, stiffness and ductility – the latter enhanced via appropriate reinforcement detailing – are vital for the construction of buildings and infrastructure. Reinforced concrete framed buildings and infrastructure perform well in natural disasters such as earthquakes and can withstand impact loads, making concrete suitable for applications such as motorway crash barriers – see section 3.3.3 – and protection of facilities against explosions.

Concrete's performance when subjected to fire is second to none. Concrete does not burn, has a slow rate of heat transfer (which keeps the reinforcement below critical temperature) and excellent fire resistance. In accordance with 'EN13501-1:2007 Fire Test to Building Materials' concrete is classified as A1 because it is effectively non-combustible. It does not emit hazardous substances (even in the hottest fires) or drip molten particles. Fire resistance is a major consideration in the construction of tunnels. Concrete surfaces and pavements in road tunnels will stand up to extreme fire conditions such as temperatures up to 1350° for long periods of time as encountered in road tunnels – the Mont Blanc tunnel fire in 2001. For some time explosive spalling at high temperatures has been seen as a hazard when using high strength concrete. This problem has been addressed by the use of polypropylene fibres in the concrete mix that reduces spalling and offers a cost effective solution (ECP, 2007).

Health and safety is the concrete industry's top priority. The reportable injuries have been reduced by 39% in the period 2008 to 2012. (TCC, 2013)

2.4.3 Durability

Durability is the ability of a material to maintain its designed function in service and last a long time without significant deterioration. This of course partly depends on design, quality of construction and maintenance. A durable material helps the environment by conserving resources and reducing waste and the environmental impacts of repair and replacement. Refurbishment and demolition waste contributes to solid waste going to landfill. The production of new building materials depletes natural resources and can produce air and water pollution.

The design service life of buildings is often 50 years and bridges 120 years, although concrete buildings often last over 100 years and bridges a lot longer. Tests have shown that concrete infrastructure such as pipes over 100 years old still perform perfectly well. Most concrete and masonry buildings are demolished due to obsolescence rather than deterioration. A concrete shell can be left in place if a building use or function changes or when a building interior is renovated. Concrete, as a structural material and as the building exterior skin, has the ability to withstand nature's normal deteriorating mechanisms as well as natural disasters.

Durability of concrete may be defined as the ability of concrete to resist weathering action, chemical attack and abrasion while maintaining its desired engineering properties. Different concretes require different degrees of durability depending on the exposure environment and properties desired. For example, concrete exposed to tidal seawater will have different requirements than an indoor concrete floor. Concrete constituents, their proportioning, interactions between them, placing and curing practices and the service environment determine the potential durability and life of concrete.

Concrete construction provides dwellings that are durable and resistant to weather, vermin and pests. These houses are tried and tested and may be assumed to offer a minimum 100 year service life with little or no maintenance, but in reality many will last for centuries. As concrete is inorganic by nature there is no process of decay in concrete and masonry and these materials are also able to cope with environmental shifts, which is particularly important in view of the predicted long-term weather variations due to climate change in the UK. Marine Crescent (Figure 2.5) was originally built in 1870; the seaside buildings only required minimal repairs to their original concrete structure to convert for new occupants in 2004.

Another example of concrete's longevity is the refurbishment of the UK's oldest concrete building, the two-storey Grade II Victorian Gothic house on Lordship Lane in south London. The Concrete House originally completed in 1873, was converted into five flats in 2013.

Resistance to chemical damage

Concrete is resistant to most natural environments and many chemicals. Concrete is virtually the only material used for the construction of wastewater transportation and treatment facilities because of its ability to resist corrosion caused by the highly aggressive contaminants in the wastewater stream as well as the chemicals added to treat these waste products. However, concrete is sometimes exposed to substances that can attack it and cause deterioration. Chemical manufacturing and storage facilities are, not surprisingly, a good example. The effects of sulphates and chlorides are discussed below. Acids attack concrete by dissolving the cement paste and calcareous aggregates. In addition to using concrete with a low

Figure 2.5   Marine Crescent, Folkestone. Reproduced by permission of The Concrete Centre.

permeability, surface treatments can be used to keep aggressive substances from coming in contact with concrete.

Resistance to sulphate attack

Excessive amounts of sulphates in soil or water can attack and destroy a concrete that is not properly designed. Sulphates (for example calcium sulphate, sodium sulphate and magnesium sulphate) can attack concrete by reacting with hydrated compounds in the hardened cement paste. These reactions can induce sufficient pressure to cause disintegration of the concrete. Like natural rock such as limestone, porous concrete (generally with a high water-cementitious material ratio) is susceptible to weathering caused by salt crystallisation. Examples of salts known to cause weathering of concrete include sodium carbonate and sodium sulphate. Sulphate attack and salt crystallisation are more severe at locations where the concrete is exposed to wetting and drying cycles, than continuously wet cycles. For the best defence against external sulphate attack, concrete is designed with a low water to cementitious material ratio and use cements specially formulated for sulphate environments.

Resistance to seawater exposure

Concrete has been used in seawater exposures for decades with excellent performance. However, special care in mix design and material selection is necessary for these severe environments. A structure exposed to seawater or seawater spray is most vulnerable in the tidal or splash zone where there are repeated cycles of wetting and drying and/or freezing and thawing. Sulphates and chlorides in seawater require the use of low permeability concrete to minimise steel corrosion and sulphate attack. A cement resistant to sulphate exposure is helpful, as is adequate concrete cover over reinforcing steel.

Resistance to corrosion

Chloride present in plain concrete that does not contain steel is generally not a durability concern. Concrete protects embedded steel from corrosion through its naturally high alkalinity. The high pH environment in concrete (usually greater than 12.5) causes a passive and non-corroding protective oxide film to form on steel. However, the presence of chloride ions from de-icing salts or seawater can destroy or penetrate this film. The resistance of concrete to chloride is good; however, for severe environments, it can be increased by using a low water-cementitious material ratio and supplementary cementitious materials such as fly ash and GGBS, to reduce permeability and improve the concrete-steel interface structure. Increasing the concrete cover over the steel is the traditional way to protect reinforcement from corrosion. Other methods of reducing steel corrosion include the use of corrosion inhibiting admixtures, epoxy-coated reinforcing steel, stainless steel reinforcement, surface treatments, concrete overlays and cathodic protection.

Resistance to Alkali-Silica Reaction (ASR)

ASR is an expansive reaction between reactive forms of silica in aggregates and potassium and sodium alkalis, mostly from cement, but also from aggregates, pozzolans, admixtures and mixing water. The reactivity is potentially harmful only when it produces significant expansion. Indications of the presence of alkali-aggregate reactivity may be a network of cracks, closed or spalling joints, or movement of portions of a structure. ASR can be controlled through proper aggregate selection and/or the use of supplementary cementitious materials (such as fly ash or GGBS) or blended cements proven by testing to control the reaction.

2.4.4   Robustness and Security

Design codes, government documents and other standards and specifications such as those issued by the Highways Agency give clear and effective requirements and guidance on the robustness of structures, that is, ensuring that structures will not succumb to progressive collapse if one part becomes compromised. This benefit is understandably important: people need to be able to rely on a structure to maintain its robustness even, to a reasonable degree, during extreme events. Reinforced concrete structures are particularly robust as the reinforcement provides continuity between elements.

For example Building Regulations in the UK require buildings to be designed against disproportionate collapse, that is, any damage resulting from an accidental loss of a supporting element such as a column should not be disproportionate to the cause – for example, the loss of a column should not result in the loss of the whole building. Concrete (in-situ) framed buildings often satisfy this requirement and without significant additional reinforcement and ties/connectors in precast frames are easily accommodated.

Personal safety is an increasing concern, not only in relation to crime on the streets but also intrusions into our buildings. Security has been improved by way of locks and alarm systems to windows and doors, but what of the structure itself? Concrete and masonry walls are accepted as being solid and robust and this benefit should not be underestimated. It cannot be assumed that all other forms of construction offer the same degree of robustness and security.

2.4.5 *Aesthetics*

The versatility of concrete enables designers to deliver solutions that can satisfy the aesthetic requirements of a project. For more information on visual concrete see Chapter 3.

The aesthetic impact of a quarry or a manufacturing facility is important to a local community. Whilst a manufacturing facility may be an economic blessing for a community, it still needs to have as negligible an impact on the aesthetics of the local area as possible. With quarries, there is a similar concern.

Screening (either natural or man-made) is often used to negate any negative visual impact. In the case of quarries, progressive restoration can be undertaken to reduce the visual impact. Quarry waste is used for screen banks and for banking up against steep faces. These banks are often carefully graded and planted to give a natural feel.

In sensitive areas, such as Special Landscape Areas, a conventional quarry would be an alien landform and can be visually intrusive – for instance, if it broke the skyline. In such circumstances quarries can be designed to blend into the natural environment. For instance, in Hafod, South Wales, the rock quarry is an extension of the existing valley. The aim is the establishment of a restored slope identical to the natural valley sides.

Figure 2.6 Bluewater shopping centre built on an old chalk quarry (before and after), Kent. Reproduced by permission of Gordon Edgar. Photo by DAVID ILIFF. License: CC-BY-SA 3.0.

Quarries can also be returned to beneficial uses such as shopping centres, which not only support the local community, but also improve the aesthetics of the countryside (Figure 2.6).

2.4.6 Archaeology

Many of Britain's most significant archaeological finds have come about as a direct result of quarrying. Such was the significance of a woolly mammoth discovery in the Cotswold Water Park that media right across the world took notice. The fossilised skull was only the second to have been found in Britain in 200 years. At Wareham in Dorset, an entire town has been uncovered at a 55-hectare site owned by Aggregate Industries. The slow process of uncovering more than 7,000 years of history began in 1992. It has become one of the largest areas of Middle Bronze Age landscape ever to be excavated and has brought to light one of the most substantial ranges of pottery from that era yet discovered.

2.4.7 *Community involvement*

At its most effective, community involvement is an inclusive process involving all interest groups that have a concern about the outcome. This includes the decision makers, those directly affected by the decision and those who could support or obstruct its implementation. Engagement will often include those who are usually excluded.

The process really works when responsibility for the agenda and the process is shared among all stakeholders.

The cement and concrete industries are fully involved with local communities as evidenced throughout this chapter. Individual companies are involved in local, national and global initiatives and these are well documented on their websites and publications with partners such as RSPB, Wildlife Trusts and local conservation groups. There are also programmes of site visits, including school groups. Collective action is via the significant work of trade associations and The Concrete Centre. Educational activities are aimed at a variety of audiences, including school children, students in higher education, architects, designers and all those involved in the design, construction and use of cement and concrete. Initiatives include teaching resources, websites, visits to cement plants and/or quarries, student design competitions, support for research, technical guidance documents, free advice and helpline, CPD presentations and courses, conferences and events.

2.5 Economic growth

Although there are environmental impacts associated with cement and concrete production, we must not lose sight of the role that concrete and cementitious materials play in our built environment and the value of this built environment in our quality of life. New research from leading economic consultancy Capital Economics has highlighted the critical role of the mineral products industry that includes cement and concrete to the UK economy as follows (Capital Economics, 2012):

- Makes a Gross Value Added contribution to the UK economy of over £4 billion pa - greater than creative industries such as film and video and not far short of motor vehicles and aerospace.
- Generates an annual turnover of £9 billion.
- Has labour productivity 2.5 times higher than the national average.
- Supplies industries with a turnover of £400 billion.
- Is the largest supplier to the £120 billion construction industry.
- Pays over £1 billion of taxes annually.
- Employs over 70,000 people.
- Makes significant economic contributions throughout the UK.

These findings highlight the importance of approaching sustainability holistically; all facets, social, environmental and economic should be considered equally. To consider only one element skews the perception of the overall performance; embodied and in-use or upstream and downstream facets must be considered if we are to achieve real sustainability.

In the next section the contribution of the cement and concrete industry to the UK economy at national, local and household levels is examined.

2.5.1   National economy

Concrete is the 'backbone' of the UK construction industry. Whether a building's super-structure is made of concrete, steel or timber, it will almost always be built on concrete foundations. The floors of commercial or industrial premises are also typically concrete.

As the UK economy grows, so does the construction sector, and within that, the demand for concrete. Since 1999, the country's GDP has grown by an average annual percentage of just over 5%, translating into a growth for the construction and building materials industries. In 2004, the construction industry employed 6.6% of Britain's total workforce and generated around 10% of its GDP. Notwithstanding the economic downturn in recent years, concrete's economic significance as an essential supplier to the UK's construction industry is considerable.

Concrete and many of its components are produced in the UK from local materials. This insulates the country from the international volatility in the oil and iron markets and helps the balance of payments contributing to national wealth.

The UK's self-sufficiency in concrete compares favourably to the situation for construction's other main building materials such as timber (see Appendix B); more than 61% of the timber used in Britain for construction in 2011 was imported (Forestry Commission, 2011).

2.5.2   Local economy

The concrete sector is a vital component in the UK economy. It directly employs over 40,000 people and has a turnover of around £5 billion. Because its manufacturing plants and quarries are scattered throughout the UK, the people it employs are spread through many communities. A large facility, as in the case of cement works, is often the major employer in an area (which, in the case of cement, is generally rural) as well as contributing significant sums into the local community through sub-contracting or buying local services.

The cement industry provides jobs at both skilled and semi-skilled levels for some 3,500 people and supports about 15,000 indirectly. About 200 people are employed directly in the manufacturing of GGBS, with a further 150 employed indirectly. The precast industry, which manufactures concrete products offsite, employs around 22,000 people. Around 6,500 are directly employed in the manufacture of ready-mixed concrete, which is delivered in the familiar concrete mixing transportation truck. A further 13,000 are employed in the quarrying industry, which supplies the concrete industry (and others) with materials. Once associated workers have been taken into account, such as hauliers, those employed in the mortar industry and other induced local employment, the total number employed indirectly is likely to be closer to 100,000 although this figure has reduced by 20–30% after the recent economic downturn.

2.5.3 Household Economy

Due to our dependence on fossil fuels and the dwindling UK reserves we must face up to increasing energy costs and the real risk of fuel poverty which will potentially impact the most vulnerable groups of our society.

In all buildings, heat is generated by people, cooking, electrical equipment, computers, lighting and passive solar gain which means that buildings can overheat during the summer. A particular benefit of concrete is its high thermal mass – see section 2.2.1 – that minimises the need for air-conditioning in the summer and reduces heating bills in the winter. Excellent air tightness is also easily achieved with concrete construction; this results in better managed air change rates, reduced energy consumption for space heating and financial savings for the occupant – for details see Chapter 3.

Another benefit of utilising concrete's thermal capacity and introducing natural ventilation is the improvement in natural light. Exposed concrete can reflect light far into a building's interior and this can reduce the need for artificial lighting, saving energy and therefore money.

2.6 Regulatory responses

It is generally accepted that tomorrow's world will be within two extreme scenarios as follows:

The carbon-constrained world: Energy is primarily from low and zero-carbon sources; lifestyles are highly efficient in resource terms, with all the precious zero-carbon energy, every kilogram of damaging CO_2 from carbon-based fuels, and every drop of water accounted for; buildings do not rely on mechanical heating and cooling.

The climate-constrained world: Life continues as it is; economy grows primarily through the use of fossil fuels and the ensuing climate change has lead to wide spread environmental degradation; 60% of species existing at the turn of the millennium are lost, many of the worlds coastal cities are abandoned; the last wild fish stocks are gone.

An important influence on how humans will impact on tomorrow's world is government regulations and their implementation.

2.6.1   Global

In 1992 in Rio, at a meeting commonly called the Earth Summit, the United Nations Framework Convention on Climate Change (UNFCCC) was established. The UNFCCC currently has 192 Parties (countries) as members. Parties to the UNFCC were categorised as:

- Annex I countries (industrialised countries and economies in transition).
- Annex II countries (a sub-group of Annex I - developed countries which pay for costs of developing countries).
- Developing countries (not required to reduce emission levels unless developed countries supply enough funding and technology).

UNFCCC has met annually at its Conference of the Parties (COP).

The first global initiative towards sustainable development, and specifically climate change, was the outcome of COP3 in Kyoto in 1997. The Kyoto Protocol was adopted, which sets out mechanisms for emissions reduction and carbon trading, that is, the ability of a company to buy emissions from the market, if its own emission cut is insufficient, or to sell surplus emissions to the market if its cut exceeds its allocation. A major achievement at Kyoto was the political agreement from 191 states including the world's leading economies to reduce greenhouse gas emissions by 8 to 10% below existing 1990 levels with the view to reducing their overall emissions of such gases by at least 5% below existing 1990 levels in the first commitment period 2008 to 2012. Commitments under the Protocol vary from nation to nation. For example an 8% average in the European Union ranges between 28% reduction by Luxemburg to 27% increase by Portugal. Major polluters such as the United States (accounting for approximately 15% of global emissions) initially agreed with a 7% reduction to later withdraw their support of the Protocol.

Following Kyoto COP15 took place in Copenhagen in 2009 but did not live up to its expectations as the politicians failed to reach an agreement. Parties committed to implement individually or jointly the quantified economy-wide mid-term emissions targets for 2020. This means that for the US, it is a weak 14-17% reduction on 2005 levels (equivalent to 3-5% on 1990 levels); for the EU (accounting for approximately 15% of global emissions), a still-to-be-determined goal of 20-30% on 1990 levels; for Japan, 25% and Russia 15-25% on 1990 levels; China (accounting for approximately 25% of global emissions) did not agree to reduce emissions but agreed to reduce the rate of increase by 40%. It has been estimated that more than 15% of emissions are attributed to the clearing of forests but there are no safeguards attached to the COP15 commitment to reduce deforestation – at the current rate of destruction forests will have vanished by 2027!

The COP17 conference was held in Durban in 2011 to establish a new treaty to limit carbon emissions. The conference agreed to a legally binding deal comprising all countries, which will be prepared by 2015, and to take effect in 2020. There was also progress regarding the creation of a Green Climate Fund (GCF) for which a management framework was adopted. The fund is to distribute US$100 billion per year to help poor countries adapt to climate impacts. In reality, the only COP agreement so far has been that rich nations are to continuously increase their financial support to developing nations. The outcome of latest conference, COP18 in Doha in 2012, was the same.

There is some progress, for example the European Union (EU) is on track to meet its Kyoto target for greenhouse gas (GHG) emissions despite an overall 2.4% increase in 2010, according to new figures released by the European Environment Agency (EEA) in June 2012. Also many companies and organisations recognise the imperative to act and are adopting carbon reduction strategies. The development of low carbon solutions is now a standard requirement in clients' briefs and engineers are asked to meet the challenge of providing sustainable buildings and infrastructure.

2.6.2 *European*

The European Commission began the practice of periodically issuing Environmental Action Programmes in the early 1970s. These programmes set out forthcoming legislative proposals and discussed broader perspectives on EU environmental policy.

The Sixth Community Environment Action Programme (6EAP) was adopted in July 2002 and was the first such programme to be jointly adopted by the Council and the European Parliament. The 6EAP provides a 10-year framework for EU action on the environment, setting out key environmental objectives to be achieved in four priority areas: climate change, nature and biodiversity, environment and health, and natural resources and waste. More detailed measures to meet the environmental objectives of the 6EAP were to be set in seven 'Thematic Strategies': on soil protection, marine environment, pesticides, air pollution, urban environment, natural resources and waste.

An independent evaluation of 6EAP concluded in 2011 that it served as a reference for Member States and local authorities in defending environmental policy against competing policy demands, securing appropriate funding and providing predictability for business. Nevertheless there was no evidence that

6EAP was a dominant factor behind the adoption of environmental legislation during the last decade.

In accordance with the European Environmental Bureau, Federation of Environmental Citizens' Organisations, the 6EAP was important in keeping environment on the EU agenda, but the implementation has been un-ambitious and partly a failure. The new 7EAP needs to define in an un-ambivalent manner the environmental challenges the EU is faced with, including accelerating climate change, deterioration of eco-systems and increasing overuse of natural resources and, set ambitious environmental framework conditions such as 'halving the EU's ecological footprint by 2030' for the implementation of economic, research and innovation, industrial and employment policies (EEB, 2010).

The EU Emissions Trading System (EU ETS) is a cornerstone of the European Union's policy to combat climate change and its key tool for reducing industrial greenhouse gas emissions cost-effectively. Being the first and biggest international scheme for the trading of greenhouse gas emission allowances, the EU ETS covers some 11,000 power stations and industrial plants in 30 countries. The installations regulated by the EU ETS are collectively responsible for close to half of the EU's emissions of CO_2 and 40% of its total greenhouse gas emissions. The second trading period began in January 2008 and spans a period of five years, until December 2012. The third trading period will run from January 2013 to December 2020. In 2020 emissions will be 21% lower than in 2005.

2.6.3   United Kingdom

The top level framework in the UK is the Climate Change Act 2008. This contains a legally binding long-term framework to cut carbon emissions – mitigation – and to deal with the impacts of climate change – adaptation. The Climate Change Act introduced a Climate Change Committee (CCC) to provide expert advice and scrutiny on the government's climate change work and emissions targets. The UK's Strategy for Sustainable Construction was also re-issued in 2008. Chapters 5 and 8 deal with design for mitigation and Chapter 9 deals with design for adaptation (BERR, 2008). The strategy states that no building or piece of infrastructure can be considered genuinely well designed or sustainable if it is not fit for purpose, resource efficient, adaptable and resilient to climate change and does not contribute to the triple bottom line of environmental, social and economic sustainability.

Under the Climate Change UK Programme the UK plans to deliver the Kyoto Protocol targets of reducing the full basket of greenhouse gases by 12.5% below the 1990 levels. The long term goal is to reduce CO_2 and other greenhouse gas emissions by at least 80% of their 1990 level by 2050 with real progress of 37% by 2020 (CCC, 2010).

Buildings are responsible for approximately 50% of the UK's total greenhouse gas emissions and, as domestic properties constitute a major portion of UK construction activity, the government has set the ambitious target to reduce carbon emissions for new homes to zero by 2016. The Code for Sustainable Homes has been developed by the Building Research Establishment and its use has been made compulsory in the design of all new social housing which must achieve code level 5 by 2013 and code level 6 – zero carbon – by 2016.

The Communities and Local Government 'Green Commercial Buildings Task Group' commissioned the UK-GBC to investigate the costs and benefits of raising the energy performance standards in new non-domestic buildings above those currently set out in the building regulations all the way to zero carbon. A key finding was that a challenging yet achievable timeframe for achieving zero carbon new non-domestic buildings along the lines set for housing is needed and a deadline of 2020 could be feasible.

Each English region has already established an Independent Regional Climate Change Partnership (RCCP) made up of local stakeholders, ranging from regional development agencies through to small local charities, and working very closely with UKCIP. These partnerships investigate, assess and advise on the impacts of climate change regionally, share experiences and work together on joint projects.

The UK's planning system and building regulations play a pivotal role in ensuring sustainable development. Planning guidance on climate change has been available via a number of planning policy statements since 2005. In many planning authorities in the UK a sustainability statement has to be submitted with planning applications for all except the smallest buildings, such as an individual house. The sustainability statement summarises how the proposed development will meet the sustainability aspects of the planning policies. Building regulations keep increasing the minimum performance of building design for energy efficiency. There is also considerable guidance available from bodies such as the Construction Industry Research and Information Association (CIRIA) to help engineers design and construct for climate change.

Ongoing innovations in concrete technology mean that concrete can and should make a significant contribution to the achievement of the government's emission targets (Swamy, 2000). Furthermore, using GGBS or fly ash concrete, either as a mixer addition or through a factory made cement, significantly reduces the overall greenhouse gas emissions associated with the production of concrete. The reduction in overall greenhouse gas emissions can be as high as 60%, depending on the concrete mix design and the application. For further information see Chapter 4.

The Aggregate Levy and the Landfill Tax are mechanisms to provide economic incentives to the construction industry to use recycled aggregates and the Climate Change Levy provides an incentive to the energy-intensive manufacturing industries to increase energy efficiency and to reduce carbon emissions.

Aggregate levy

The UK government announced in the March 2000 budget that an aggregates tax of £1.60 per tonne would be introduced in April 2002. The Chancellor of the Exchequer announced in his budget of March 2007 that the Aggregates Levy would rise to £1.95 per tonne from April 2008, amounting to an increased tax burden of between £70m and £80m.

The tax applies to crushed rock and sand and gravel extracted or dredged in the UK for aggregates use. Aggregates exports are not taxed, but imports of aggregates are taxed at the first point of sale in the UK. Imports of products manufactured with aggregates, such as concrete blocks, are also not taxed.

The Waste & Resource Action Programme (WRAP) is entirely funded by the Department of Environment Food and Rural Affairs (DEFRA) from the Aggregates Levy Sustainability Fund, and, since its inception, it has invested over £10 million in total with £2.2 million in reprocessing infrastructure. This investment will secure the supply of almost one million extra tonnes of recycled and secondary aggregates. Having secured continuing funding from DEFRA and the Scottish Executive, WRAP has set its sights on delivering a 10% increase in the use of non-primary aggregates in higher-value applications such as the manufacture of concrete (TCC, 2007).

Concrete is a recyclable material. Most people do not stop to think of what happens to the rubble when a structure is demolished, but perhaps assume it all goes to landfill. In fact anything up to 95% of a building's components can be recycled, including the most heavily reinforced concrete.

Landfill tax

Land filling is discouraged due to a number of key reasons:

- Climate change caused by landfill gas from biodegradable waste.
- Loss of resources.
- Constraints on areas suitable for landfill sites.
- Loss of recyclable components of waste land filled.

Landfill tax – introduced in 1996 – is seen as a key mechanism in enabling the UK to meet its targets set out in the European Landfill Directive. Through increasing the cost of landfill, other advanced waste treatment technologies with higher gate fees become more financially attractive.

Following the 2007 budget the standard rate of landfill tax was increased from £21 per tonne to £24 per tonne on 1 April 2007. From 1 April 2008 onwards it was increased annually by £8 per tonne until 1 April 2010. In 2013 the standard rate is £72 per tonne. The lower rate, which applies to specific inactive wastes, was increased from £2 to £2.50 per tonne from 1 April 2008.

The landfill tax encourages innovative re-use and recycling of construction materials and drives the economics of recycling concrete out of the waste stream.

Climate change levy

The Climate Change Levy (CCL) – introduced in 2001 – is a tax on energy delivered to users in the United Kingdom. Its aim is to provide an incentive to increase energy efficiency and to reduce carbon emissions. When CCL was introduced in the UK, the position of energy intensive industries was considered, given their energy usage, the requirements of the Integrated Pollution Prevention and Control regime and their exposure to international competition. As a result an 80% discount from the levy was allowed for those sectors that agreed targets for improving their energy efficiency or reducing carbon emissions.

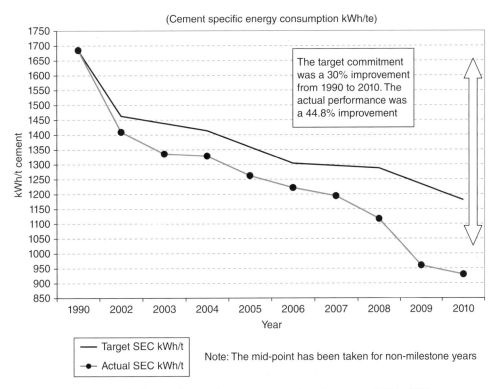

Figure 2.7   UK cement industry climate change agreement performance 1990 to 2010. Reproduced by permission of MPA Cement.

The regulations cover the ten main energy intensive sectors of industry: aluminium, cement, ceramics, chemicals, food & drink, foundries, glass, non-ferrous metals, paper and steel; and over 30 smaller sectors, and, in agriculture, livestock units for the intensive rearing of pigs and poultry.

The cement industry uses energy efficiently as it represents around 35% of its production costs and the industry is working hard to reduce the carbon dioxide it generates through its manufacturing process. The industry is committed to invest in new plant and increased use of alternative fuels. Three new kilns at Rugby (Cemex UK Cement), Padeswood (Hanson Cement) and Tunstead (Hope Construction Materials) have replaced older, less efficient processes.

UK cement manufacturers signed a Climate Change Levy Agreement with government to deliver an overall energy efficiency improvement across their sector of 26.8% by 2010 against a base year of 1990. The industry had already achieved a better improvement in energy efficiency in 2006 and has been working to achieve a target greater than 30% (Figure 2.7).

The UK cement companies are also among over 160 companies worldwide that have signed up to the Cement Sustainability Initiative (CSI) of the World Business Council for Sustainable Development. There are numerous targeted joint projects and individual company actions arising from this initiative (WBCSD, 2002).

2.7 Summary

Measuring sustainability is a challenge for engineers as they are required to think holistically based on modern qualitative non-measurable values rather than traditional quantitative measurable criteria. In this chapter the main challenges of implementing sustainability are presented, each followed by example responses drawn from the cement and concrete industries.

Anthropogenic CO_2 emissions have reached unprecedented levels in the last 50 years and have been implicated as the primary cause of global warming. Climate change is the biggest challenge within sustainability and is causing temperature rise and increased risk of flooding and wind damage. Concrete's inherent property of thermal mass provides a sustainable solution for rising temperatures in buildings, concrete is the preferred material for river and sea flood defence systems and concrete buildings perform better under extreme wind and other natural disasters.

With the world population doubling every 40 years and resource consumption doubling every 20 years there is a pressing need for environmental protection. Concrete's environmental impacts mainly consist of embodied impacts attributed to cement production. In putting these impacts into perspective, embodied impacts are very small in comparison with in-use impacts. With respect to resource depletion, the cement industry is making strides in reducing both natural materials and the amount of fossil fuel used in manufacturing cement and, the aggregates industry is maximising the replacement of natural aggregates with recycled ones. With regard to emissions reduction, the cement industry is reducing the embodied impact of cement with the use of alternative fuels and the concrete industry by replacing cement in the mix with waste materials and by-products such as GGBS and fly ash. All materials needed for producing concrete are local with minimum transportation impact. Restoring quarries to preserve biodiversity is a success story in the UK.

Functionality, safety, durability, robustness and security, aesthetics, archaeology, and community involvement are key parts of social sustainability. Concrete functions well and is fit-for-purpose, for example, as exposed concrete saving energy via thermal mass for buildings or as a noise barrier for its acoustic performance. Concrete saves lives with its performance to fire that is second to none. Concrete buildings are durable, able to resist weathering actions and often last over 100 years. Concrete structures are very robust satisfying progressive collapse requirements and ensuring minimum accidental damage to non-structural elements. The versatility of concrete enables designers to deliver solutions that can satisfy the aesthetic requirements of a project. Many of Britain's most significant archaeological finds have come about as a direct result of quarrying. The cement and concrete industries are fully involved with local communities.

Economic growth is examined at national, local and household levels. The cement and concrete industries are the 'backbone' of the UK construction industry and make a substantial contribution to the UK economy by generating an annual turnover of £9 billion and employing over 70,000 people. Local cement works are often the major employer in an area. Concrete's thermal mass and airtightness reduces household energy bills.

Perhaps the most important influence on how humans will impact on tomorrow's world is government regulations and their implementation. A global landmark agreement that set legally binding targets for carbon emissions was the Kyoto Protocol in 1997. The latest event, COP18, in 2012 did not manage to take it far enough. At European level, the Sixth Community Environment Action Programme (EAP) was adopted in 2002. Unfortunately 6EAP did not really influence environmental legislation in the member states in the last decade. In the UK, the top framework is the Climate Change Act 2008 and the commitment to reduce greenhouse gas emissions by at least 80% of their 1990 level by 2050. The Climate Change Levy provides an incentive to the energy-intensive manufacturing industries to increase energy efficiency and to reduce carbon emissions. The UK cement manufacturers signed a Climate Change Levy Agreement with government to deliver an overall energy efficiency improvement across their sector of 26.8% by 2010 against a base year of 1990. The industry had already achieved a better improvement in energy efficiency in 2006 and delivered a 44.8% improvement by 2010.

References

Allwood, J. & Cullen, J. (2011) *Sustainable Materials with both eyes open* On-line at http://withbotheyesopen.com/

BCA & Forum for the Future (2005) *The UK Cement Industry: Benefit and cost analysis*, British Cement Association (BCA) & Forum for the Future, UK.

BCA (2006b) *Key Issue: Climate change*, British Cement Association (BCA), UK.

BCA (2008) *Using wastes as fuel and replacement raw materials in cement kilns: Cement quality and concrete performance.* Fact Sheet 7, BCA (British Cement Association), UK.

BERR (2008) *Strategy for Sustainable Construction* BERR (Department for Business Enterprise & Regulatory Reform), UK.

Capital Economics (2012) *The Foundation for a Strong Economy, Initial Assessment of the Contribution of the Mineral Products Industry to the UK Economy*, Capital Economics, UK.

CCC (2010) *The Fourth Carbon Budget – Reducing Emissions Through the 2020s CCC* (Committee on Climate Change), London, UK.

CEMBUREAU (2012) *The European Cement Association*, CEMBUREAU, Brussels, Belgium.

Clear, A.S. and De Saulles, T. (2007) *BCA Recarbonation Study*, British Cement Association, UK.

Constructing Excellence (2011) UK (www.constructingexcellence.org.uk)

CSD (2009) *Indicators of Sustainable Development*, United Nations Commission on Sustainable Development (CSD) http://www.un.org/esa/dsd/

DEFRA (2012) *UK Climate Change Risk Assessment: Government Report*, Department of Environment, Food & Rural Affairs (DEFRA), UK.

DEFRA (2013) *Sustainable Development Indicators*, Department of Environment, Food & Rural Affairs (DEFRA), UK.

ECP (2007) *Comprehensive Fire Protection and Safety with Concrete*, European Concrete Platform (ECP), Brussels, Belgium.

EEB (2010) *Future of EU Environmental Policy: Towards the 7th Environmental Action Programme – Sustainability.* EEB (European Environmental Bureau), Brussels, Belgium.

Fenner, R.A., Ainger, C.A., Cruickshank, H.J., Guthrie, P. (2006) *Widening horizons for engineers: addressing the complexity of Sustainable Development.* Proceedings of the Institution of Civil Engineers, Engineering Sustainability, UK, 159 ES4 pp. 145-154, UK.

Fleming, R. (1998) *Historical Perspectives on Climate Change*, Oxford University Press, New York and Oxford.

Forestry Commission (2011) UK Wood Production and Trade, 2011 Provisional Figures, Economics and Statistics, Forestry Commission, Edinburgh, UK.

Frosch, R.A. & Gallopoulos, N.E. (1989) *Strategies for Manufacturing, Scientific American*, USA, 261(3) pp. 144–152, USA.

GWA (2007) Global Warming Art (GWA) www.globalwarmingart.com

Hacker, J., De Saulles, P.T., Minson, J.A. and Holmes, J.M. (2008) *Embodied and Operational Carbon Dioxide Emissions from Housing: A case study on the effects of thermal mass and climate change*, Elsevier, *Energy and Buildings*, 40, 375–84.

Higgins, D., Parrott, L. and Sear, L. (2002) *Effects of ground granulated blast furnace slag and pulverised fuel ash upon the environmental impacts of concrete.* Available from ConCemSus, UK (http://www.concemsus.info)

HM Treasury (2006) The Stern Review Report: The economics of climate change, HM Treasury, UK.

IPCC (2012) *Managing the Risks of Extreme Events and Disasters to Advance Climate Change Adaptation. A Special Report of Working Groups I and II of the IPCC* (Intergovernmental Panel on Climate Change), Cambridge University Press, Cambridge, UK, and New York, USA.

IPPC (2008) Integrated Pollution Prevention and Control (IPPC), Directive 2008/1/EC of the European Parliament and of the Council, EU.

McLaren, D., Bullock, S., & Yousuf, N. (1998) *Tomorrow's World Britain's Share in a Sustainable Future*, Friends of the Earth, Earthscan Publications Ltd., UK.

Met Office (2010) *Evidence The State of the Climate.* Met Office, UK.

MPA Cement (2011) *Performance 2010 A sector plan report from the UK cement industry*, Mineral Products Association (MPA) Cement, UK.

NETCEN (2006) *UK Greenhouse Gas Inventory 1990–2004 Annual Report for submission under the Framework Convention on Climate Change* (issue 1.1), NETCEN (National Environmental Technology Centre), UK.

NRMCA (2012) Concrete CO_2 Fact Sheet, National Ready Mixed Concrete Association (NRMCA), February 2012, USA.

Robust Details (2011) UK (www.robustdetails.com)

Swamy, R. (2000) *Designing Concrete and Concrete Structures for Sustainable Development* CANMET/ACI International Symposium on Concrete Technology for Sustainable Development, Vancouver, Canada.

TCC (2005) *Thermal Mass – A concrete solution for changing climate*, The Concrete Centre (TCC), UK.

TCC (2007) *Sustainable Concrete*, The Concrete Centre (TCC), UK.

TCC (2010) *How to Achieve Acoustic Performance in Masonry Homes*, The Concrete Centre (TCC), UK.

TCC (2011) *Specifying Sustainable Concrete Understanding the role of constituent materials*, MPA - The Concrete Centre (TCC), UK.

TCC (2013) *Concrete Industry Sustainability Performance Report*, 6th report: 2012 performance data, MPA - The Concrete Centre (TCC), UK.

The Structural Engineer (2011) Sustainability briefing climate change and wind speeds, *The Structural Engineer* 89(10).

TSCTG (2003) *The UK Construction Industry: progress towards more sustainable construction 2000–2003.* TSCTG (The Sustainable Construction Task Group), UK.

UKCIP09 (2009) *UK Climate Projections Science Report: Climate change projections*, UKCIP, Department for Environment, Food and Rural Affairs, UK.

UN (1998) *Kyoto Protocol to the United Nations Framework Convention on Climate Change.* UN (United Nations), Kyoto, Japan.

Wayne, B. (1994) *Assessing the Relative Ecological Carrying Capacity Impacts of Resource Extraction*. Trusty & Associates Ltd. in association with Environmental Policy Research, submitted to Forintek Canada Corp. for its Sustainable Materials Project, Canada.

WBCSD (2002) The Cement Sustainability Initiative: Our Agenda for Action, World Business Council for Sustainable Development (WBCSD), Geneva www.wbcsd cement.org

WRAP (2012) *Waste and Resources Action Programme* (WRAP) UK (www.wrap. org.uk)

3 Conceptual Design of Buildings and Infrastructure

3.1 Introduction

The built environment – buildings and infrastructure – are fundamental for the health of the economy, for the maintenance and progress of society and can have both benefits for and impacts on the environment.

Construction itself represents 9% of the UK economy (BIS, 2010) and underpins all other economic activity. For example the functions within commercial and industrial buildings are fundamental to the economy, as are roads, railways and ports.

Public buildings (non-housing) representing education, health, justice and other public functions together with housing and other residential accommodation are essential to our society. Furthermore the quality of these buildings is a determining factor of the well-being within society. Their functions rely on transport, energy, water and communication infrastructure.

Buildings can provide environmental benefits. Examples of this, each related to reducing transport impacts, include:

1. Inter-modal transport hubs for goods distribution (e.g. warehouse distribution centres can reduce total freight transport impacts);
2. buildings associated with public transport (e.g. car parks at bus/train stations reduce private car journeys);
3. computer server centres enable greater use of IT, thereby increasing home working and reducing commuter journeys as well as reducing business travel.

Sustainable Concrete Solutions, First Edition. Costas Georgopoulos and Andrew Minson.
© 2014 John Wiley & Sons, Ltd. Published 2014 by John Wiley & Sons, Ltd.

Infrastructure projects can also provide environmental benefits, such as:

1. guided bus-ways to provide an alternative to private car journeys;
2. waste incinerators to replace land fill with power generation;
3. sewerage infrastructure to ensure water quality in rivers and coastal areas.

However, the built environment also has environmental impacts, for example:

1. Energy use associated with buildings and infrastructure in the UK represents approximately 45% and 27% of the total UK energy consumption respectively.
2. Natural resources are required to construct the built environment. For example in the UK annual construction related consumption is approximately 200 million tonnes of aggregate, 10 million tonnes of cement (MPA, 2011) and 17% of the total UK steel demand of 10 million tonnes (EEF, 2011).
3. Waste arising from construction and maintenance of buildings and infrastructure, let alone the operations within, is significant – around one third of all waste in the UK (WRAP, 2010).

The challenge for construction professionals, together with their clients, is to deliver built environment projects that maximise the economic, societal and environmental benefits whilst minimising the environmental impacts.

The scope for meeting this challenge is maximised when the concept for new towns and cities is developed so that the inter-relationship between projects within can be harnessed simultaneously. For example the locations for living, working and shopping together with transport infrastructure can be optimised.

Case Study: Masdar City, Abu Dhabi

Masdar City aims to become one of the most sustainable cities in the world by being carbon-neutral, zero-waste, powered by renewable energy and built with innovative green technologies. Abu Dhabi, part of the United Arab Emirates, began building Masdar in 2008 and expects to complete it by 2025. When completed, the 6.5 square kilometre city could be home to 40,000 people and a host of cultural institutions, educational and research facilities and green-tech companies.

The design of Masdar seeks to facilitate energy generation and reduce consumption of electricity and water. These are achieved with optimal orientation of buildings and infrastructure, integration of industrial/cultural/residential areas, adoption of low-rise/high density development and by providing a high quality pedestrian friendly way of life with the lowest environmental impact.

Figure 3.1   Masdar Institute Campus; Building (right) – Close up on the glass-reinforced concrete façade (left). Reproduced by permission of Gavrilis Ioannou.

Masdar's sustainability objectives influence material choices. Concrete, being a local material, is the preferred option for buildings and infrastructure. For example, low carbon ready-mix concrete and recycled reinforcement was used for the construction of 'Masdar Institute Campus' that was the first fully solar powered building in Masdar. GGBS replaced a significant portion of Portland cement in the concrete mix — up to 80% in some places. The use of GGBS reduced the carbon footprint associated with the structure and also improved constructability by slowing the concrete's hydration and reducing the heat generated in the process. The building also features a perforated façade made of glass-reinforced concrete coloured with local sand and detailed with patterns commonly found in traditional Islamic architecture (Figure 3.1). The interior is fair-faced concrete offering the benefit of thermal mass that further reduces energy demands.

Conceptual design follows a positive project feasibility assessment. General concepts and ideas are generated from a range of known possible solutions. The design team carries out an appraisal of each alternative solution by considering all relevant design constraints and selects a limited number of solutions to be carried forward to the preliminary design stage.

Decisions taken during the conceptual design stage of a project are likely to have more significant impact on the total cost and construction programme of the project (Figure 3.2) – as well as the project's sustainability credentials.

It is therefore essential that these crucial decisions at conceptual design stage are appropriately informed with the latest research and development on materials, design methods and construction techniques.

The reader at the end of this chapter should be able to take informed decisions on key sustainability issues during the conceptual design stage of buildings and infrastructure.

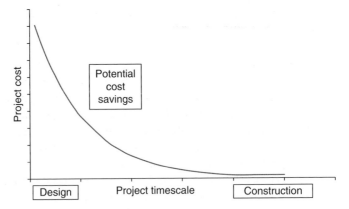

Figure 3.2   Potential cost savings over time of a project.

3.2   Conceptual design of buildings

3.2.1   Introduction

The sustainability of buildings is not just about 'what materials are used in its construction' or 'how it is operated by occupants'. Firstly, the client must establish an outline brief (section 3.2.2) so as to enable a sustainable building to be developed by the design team. Then the project team has a critical role in how the whole building is designed (section 3.2.3) before considering each component in turn and ensuring that each positively contributes to the challenge of minimising impacts and maximising performance benefits. Sections 3.2.4 to 3.2.8 cover substructures, lateral stability, frames and flooring, cladding and roofs respectively. Finally in sections 3.2.9 to 3.2.11, innovations are considered, sustainability assessment methods explained and life cycle carbon results presented.

3.2.2   What are sustainable buildings?

A building can be designed to be more sustainable through firstly developing the right brief – ensuring the right scope, purpose, size and location – and secondly, once the brief has been determined on behalf of the client, the design team will deliver the most sustainable design by optimising the balance between minimising impacts and maximising the performance.

It is never the case that one building or design solution is not sustainable and an alternative is sustainable. This is because sustainability represents such a wide range of issues.

3.2.2.1   The right brief

The Green Overlay to the RIBA Outline Plan of Work (RIBA, 2011) gives the following sustainability check point at Stage A (the preparation appraisal stage for a project):

'Strategic sustainability review of client needs and potential sites, including re-use of existing facilities...'

Strategic decisions at this earliest stage can arguably have the greatest influence on how sustainable the ultimate project is or is not. For example, siting a new office away from any public transport gives no alternative to private travel, but may be justified on sustainability grounds because it may enable the office to be naturally ventilated with openable windows in an out of town environment, conducive to low energy performance and an enhanced working environment.

At stage B (the preparation: design brief stage) the building lifespan, parameters for climate adaptation and key requirements (such as areas for different functions) should be decided. These decisions once again will dictate boundaries to how the designer can minimise impacts and maximise performance benefits.

3.2.2.2 Impacts

To construct a new building there inevitably will be impacts. Impacts from all the stages leading up to the building opening:

- extraction/production of materials;
- transport;
- manufacture (at potentially multiple sites with transportation impacts between each);
- transport again;
- installation.

And these environmental impacts can be grouped under:

- energy consumed during extraction, manufacture and installation;
- energy consumed in transport;
- CO_2 and greenhouse gasses emitted in extraction, manufacture and installation;
- CO_2 and greenhouse gasses emitted in transport;
- impacts on hydrological cycle during extraction, manufacture (and installation) e.g. surface run off and water extraction;
- water consumed during extraction, manufacture (and installation);
- extraction of non renewable mineral resources required for manufacture of construction products;
- land required for production of materials (e.g. biomass);
- ecological and biodiversity impacts of mineral extraction and land use;
- solid waste requiring disposal;

- pollution associated with extraction, manufacture and installation leading to:
  - ozone depletion;
  - photochemical oxidation;
  - acidification;
  - eutrophication;
  - toxicity for man, freshwater or terrestrial;
  - radioactivity.

For each material used, these impacts should be minimised through improvements made by the construction materials and products supply industry.

For each building these impacts should be minimised by design teams by:

1. minimising material use (but not at undue expense of building performance) through:
   - efficient design (e.g. structural engineers optimising structural elements);
   - efficient integrated design (e.g. design professionals gaining efficiency by developing solutions together);
   - maximising performance such that components and whole buildings last longer.
2. using the right materials in the right place to minimise whole life impacts – balancing the impacts at construction stage with operational impacts.

3.2.2.3 Maximising performance benefits

The building must perform according to the client brief. For some aspects a minimum performance is sufficient. If a better performance can be achieved at minimal cost (financial and/or environmental) then the benefit may outweigh the cost. Performance benefits include: energy, ventilation, daylight (glare), day-lighting, acoustics (internal and external), robustness/low maintenance, flood resistance, fire resistance, security, future climate adaptation, long life/loose fit in terms of alternative uses of building or elements/components.

For those performance parameters listed above that affect occupant comfort, there is evidence that improvement on these parameters leads to improved productivity in the business environment, better learning in educational facilities and enhanced recovery in healthcare facilities.

3.2.3 *Whole building design*

In section 3.2.2 the parameters for assessing a building's sustainability credentials are explained. Also the impact of the outline brief on sustainability is covered. (The outline brief answers which location? what function? new build or not? etc.).

This section, 3.2.3, considers how designers can work with the outline brief to deliver sustainable buildings when considering the whole building whilst sections 3.2.4 to 3.2.8 consider component parts.

3.2.3.1 Design life and future flexibility

Some buildings are temporary and this is a clear requirement from the client. However, for the remainder, the client and design team may determine a design life by balancing the:

1. expected life of building components (BCIS, 2006);
2. confidence in knowledge of new future functions and their requirements;
3. risks that present functions will in the future need different spaces and specifications;
4. risks that the building location will be economically suited for a different function in the future.

A typical school, hospital or office building is designed for a 50 or 60-year life. A retail sector distribution centre would be half this, a consequence of likely future change in functional requirements, functions themselves and locations. For most buildings the final three points are difficult to assess and if they are accounted for it is in terms of designing for future flexibility – flexibility to:

1. accommodate new functions;
2. accommodate different demands from the same functions;
3. accommodate change of use.

If the future function is well defined, for example, transforming an Athletes Olympic Village into long-term residences, then it is just part of the client brief! During the 2012 Olympic Games in London the Olympic and Paralympic Village housed more than 17,000 athletes and officials, following the Games it was converted to provide 2800 homes. If future functional requirements are completely unknown, flexibility is delivered through considering the following issues beyond the confines of the intended first use of the building:

*   structural live loads;
*   column spacing/floor spans;
*   floor to ceiling heights;
*   deflection and vibration limits;
*   provision of voids in planning, circulations and services;
*   provision for changing the building envelope;
*   provision for exposing the structure;
*   provision for expansion/extension;

- a future amended services strategy (i.e. separate services from structure);
- provision for climate adaptation (increased risk of extreme weather, higher design temperatures).

There is an increased cost for increased flexibility so judgement must be exercised as to how much to invest for an unknown future. There is little guidance available in this difficult area. Whatever the level of investment, good information is critical to being able to capitalise on inbuilt flexibility. Future owner occupiers must know what has been provided so that it can be taken into account in future decisions regarding rebuild/refurbish.

A further consideration for design life is life time energy demands and this is addressed in section 3.2.3.2.

3.2.3.2 Life time energy/CO_2

In terms of utilisation of building material resources the ideal scenario is for buildings to remain functional for a very long time. However, as buildings become more energy efficient, at what point is it best to demolish an existing high operational CO_2 (OCO_2) building and replace it with a new, low OCO_2 alternative. When considering a new project, should we expect future replacement by a more energy efficient one before the structure itself needs replacement?

To address such questions the following should be considered:

- ECO_2/energy of new build and future replacement/refurbishment;
- OCO_2/energy now and in the future of today's building;
- OCO_2/energy now of a future replacement or refurbished building;
- the relative impact or cost of CO_2 emitted/energy used over the remainder of the twenty-first century. Does CO_2 emitted in 2015 have a higher impact or cost than CO_2 emitted in 2055, or 2095?

Given that sustainability is more than just CO_2/energy, the above considerations could/should also be framed in terms of other parameters such as use of resources, disruptions to communities, and so on. However, this level of complexity is rarely entered into.

The table of values (Table 3.1) provides the data with which comparison of different scenarios (Tables 3.2 and 3.3) can be made. The two scenarios considered in tables 3.2 and 3.3 are single build for a 60-year life and rebuild after 30 years. The 60-year whole life emissions excluding Cat B fit outs for the two scenarios are 6280 and 5880 $kgCO_2e/m^2$ respectively. It must be noted that this difference is well within the sensitivity of the input data and is less than 10% of operational emissions.

However, given the other impacts associated with rebuild and the significant impacts associated with fitout, a good case can be made for long lasting structures with minimal and robust finishes.

Table 3.1   Indicative Embodied and Operational Carbon Values (Clark, 2013). Reproduced by permission of RIBA Publishing.

Indicative Embodied and Operational Carbon Values with range bracketed (kg CO_2e/m^2 of gross internal area)		
New build (shell and core)	600 (400 to 900)	(60 yr life)
Fitout (Cat A)	100 (70 to 150)	(every 15 years)
Fitout (Cat B)*	200 (100 to 300)	(every 7.5 years)
New Build Total	**900 (570 to 1350)**	
Minor Refurbishment (excl. fitout)	25 (15 to 40)	(every 15 years unless a major refurbishment)
Major Refurbishment (excl. fitout)	100 (70 to 150)	(every 30 years)
Demolition and Disposal	30	
Annual Operating Energy Emissions (now)	100	
Annual Operating Energy Emissions after a Major refurbishment in 30 years time	70	
Annual Operating Energy Emissions after a rebuild in 30 years time (low energy case)	40	

*high degree of uncertainty due to minimal available data.

Table 3.2   Example for 60-year lifetime scenario (adapted from Clark, 2013).

Year		kg CO_2e/m^2 of gross internal area	
		Embodied	Operational
1	New Build + Fitout Cat A and B	900	
7.5	Fitout Cat B	200	
15	Minor refurb, Fitout Cat A and Cat B	325	
22.5	Cat B	200	
1–30	Operational		3000
30	Major Refurb, Fitout Cat A and Cat B	400	
37.5	Fitout Cat B	200	
45	Minor refurb, Fitout Cat A and Cat B	325	
52.5	Cat B	200	
31–60	Operational		2100
60	Demolish	30	
	Total	1180 excl Cat B 2780 incl Cat B	5100

3.2.3.3   Design for deconstruction

To minimise waste and maximise re-use of building elements the following should be considered:

1. Ensure that buildings are conceived as layered according to their antici-pated life spans.
2. Ensure all components can be readily accessed and removed for repair or replacement.

Table 3.3   Example of 2 × 30-year lifetime scenario (adapted from Clark, 2013).

Year		kg CO_2e/m^2 of gross internal area	
		Embodied	Operational
1	New Build, Fitout Cat A and B	900	
7.5	Fitout Cat B	200	
15	Minor refurb, Fitout Cat A and Cat B	325	
22.5	Cat B	200	
1–30	Operational		3000
30	Rebuild Fitout Cat A and Cat B	900	
37.5	Fitout Cat B	200	
45	Minor refurb, Fitout Cat A and Cat B	325	
52.5	Cat B	200	
31–60	Operational		1200
60	Demolish	30	
	Total	1680 excl Cat B	4200
		3280 incl Cat B	

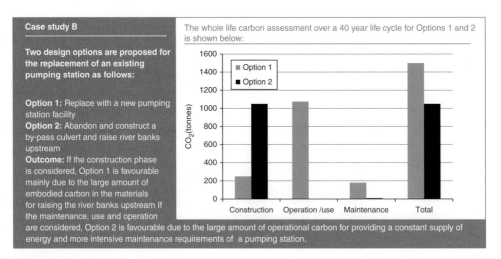

Case study B

Two design options are proposed for the replacement of an existing pumping station as follows:

Option 1: Replace with a new pumping station facility
Option 2: Abandon and construct a by-pass culvert and raise river banks upstream
Outcome: If the construction phase is considered, Option 1 is favourable mainly due to the large amount of embodied carbon in the materials for raising the river banks upstream If the maintenance, use and operation are considered, Option 2 is favourable due to the large amount of operational carbon for providing a constant supply of energy and more intensive maintenance requirements of a pumping station.

The whole life carbon assessment over a 40 year life cycle for Options 1 and 2 is shown below:

Figure 3.3   A case study that illustrates the benefits of applying whole life thinking to options appraisal (ICE, 2011).

3. Adopt a fixing regime which allows all components to be easily and safely removed and replaced through the use of simple fixings. Design connectors to enable components to be both independent and exchangeable.

4. Use only durable components which can be reused. Try to use mono-meric components and avoid the use of adhesives, resins and coatings which compromise the potential for reuse and recycling.

5. Pay particular attention to the differential weathering and wearing of surfaces and allow for those areas to be maintained or replaced separately from other areas.

6. Carefully plan services and service routes so that they can be easily identified, accessed and upgraded or maintained as necessary without disruption to surfaces and other parts of the building (SEDA, 2005).

As evidence of the complexity of sustainability, aspects of 'design for deconstruction' sometimes conflict with other means of achieving sustainability. Design for deconstruction needs to be balanced against:

- structural efficiency – structural continuity provides efficiency but makes dismantling into reusable elements difficult;
- integrated design – elements having multiple uses sometimes makes subsequent deconstruction layer by layer impossible (see section 3.2.3.5);
- prefabrication – 'For the sake of faster site construction, pre-fabricated elements are sometimes used where main structure, insulation, and finished skins are bonded together in a single piece. Unless they are demountable, such assemblies are subject to the weakest link in the chain – the least durable element – failing, whereupon the entire piece may need replacement, often at a higher cost than the simpler repair or maintenance of just the outer cladding, for example' (SEDA, 2005).

3.2.3.4 Orientation

The sustainability credentials, or otherwise, of the whole building can be strongly influenced by the orientation as it affects:

- positive (negative) solar heat gains in heating (cooling) seasons;
- heat losses through north facing windows (or southern windows in southern hemisphere);
- effectiveness of natural lighting and countering glare;
- effectiveness of natural ventilation (considering prevailing winds and external noise);
- effectiveness in blocking external noise.

For example: Orientation is important for concrete buildings in which the designer takes the opportunity to maximise Passive Solar Design (PSD) benefits in heating seasons. In PSD, the solar gains during the day are absorbed into the internal exposed thermal mass, in order that later re-radiation of heat can reduce the required heating energy. PSD relies on large sun facing glazed areas. The risk is that these result in overheating in the summer months, so solar shading is often required to minimise gains from sun at high angles.

3.2.3.5 Integrated design

Examples of integrated design associated with sustainable buildings are given below.

Exposed soffits
The absence of a ceiling, leaving the underside (soffit) of a slab and any supporting beams exposed, is a pragmatic economy for utility spaces.

Figure 3.4   Toyota Office, Surrey, UK; Exposed soffits for thermal mass. Reproduced by permission of The Concrete Centre.

However, because of thermal mass advantages and the potential for architectural expression, (e.g. 'honest architecture') exposed soffits became a regular feature in bespoke client led projects through the 1980s and 1990s. Examples include Powergen HQ, Inland Revenue, Phizer HQ, Portcullis House, and the Toyota office building (Figure 3.4). More recently speculative offices, education buildings and libraries are increasingly designed with exposed soffits, often with more utilitarian finishes.

The whole design team is involved:

- Architect for the aesthetics as well as acoustic and lighting performance.
- M&E (building physics) engineer for the thermal performance of the space.
- Structural engineer as the structural elements need to be specified to meet an architectural aesthetic. The slab may be a passive thermal element in which case there is no further work for the structural engineer, but if it is an active system with air or water passing through the slab, then there are design implications starting with space requirements within the structural zone.

To achieve visual concrete, that is, concrete that is designed to be visible throughout the lifetime of the building, architects, structural engineers and other members of the team must work together. It costs more to produce than basic finish concrete but this can be offset by a reduction in the cost of additional finishes and savings in ongoing maintenance (TCC, 2011).

The thermal mass benefits are explained in Appendix A.

Cladding as load bearing structure

Designers familiar with masonry structures take it for granted that load bearing structures will also be part of the cladding. However, for decades reinforced concrete and steel enabled skeletal structures to be separate elements from the cladding.

An integrated design has the perimeter vertical load bearing element also being part of the cladding. Rather than square columns or fin columns orthogonal to the façade, a fin column parallel with the façade can be the inner leaf of the cladding.

The whole design team is involved:

- architect for the visual impact of cladding from inside and out;
- M&E (building physics) engineer for the thermal performance of the cladding (insulation, solar gain);
- structural engineer for the structural efficiency of a component of the cladding which is structure.

(Also see section 3.2.7 Cladding)

Multi-functional internal walls

The clearest examples for multi-functional walls are in accommodation type buildings such as hotels, student accommodation, prisons and so on (Figure 3.5).

Figure 3.5   University of East London, UK; Multi-functional walls for student accommodation.

Walls are needed to provide fire separation, security/robustness and acoustic separation and in some cases, thermal mass is also utilised. Concrete or concrete masonry are the most effective materials to deliver these functions, so the architect may specify non-structural concrete walls between the structural engineer's discrete columns. If future use is unknown then this does allow for future flexibility. However, in most cases the demand for accommodation is almost guaranteed (e.g. accommodation blocks on university campuses). Therefore an integrated approach, where all the architectural functions and the structural load bearing functions are delivered by a concrete or masonry wall element, is a more efficient use of materials and hence more sustainable.

Structure and Services Integration

1. Integration between services and structure is common in many buildings to deliver efficiency and flexibility.

The horizontal distribution of services in ceiling voids may require integration with downstand beams. This is at both a strategic level – major ducts running parallel with deep primary beams – and at a detailed level – voids in webs for minor ducts. It can be argued that long term flexibility is better provided by a non integrated vertically separated solution, that is, a flat slab structure with services below.

The vertical distribution of major services is typically separated in vertical shafts (risers) usually located adjacent to lifts, stairs and toilets. It is the horizontal distribution out of these risers that often requires communication (integrated design team working) because it often requires penetration through structural shear walls.

The vertical distribution of small services through structural slabs also needs communication. For obvious architectural reasons they are often best placed adjacent to columns, but this is where beams are! Even for flat slabs (which do not have downstand beams) care must be taken because the highest shear values are adjacent to columns.

2. Integration of structure and services can also be in the form of structure being ductwork.

A vertical example is in a speculative office in London. On Tooley Street the design team utilised the fact that columns have a reducing load bearing requirement up the building and that air distribution from the top of the building to each floor requires reducing duct area down the building. Solution – hollow columns that act as structure and duct (Figure 3.6). The void in the column increases for each storey up the building meeting both structural and services needs.

A horizontal example is the product Termodeck (Figure 3.7). This product is a hollow core plank, which is manufactured in many locations and used widely. The hollow cores running the length of the unit can be connected at alternate ends to create a continuous long void. Air fed in at one end snakes

Figure 3.6 Tooley St Offices, London, UK; Hollow columns that act as structure and duct.
Reproduced by permission of The Concrete Centre.

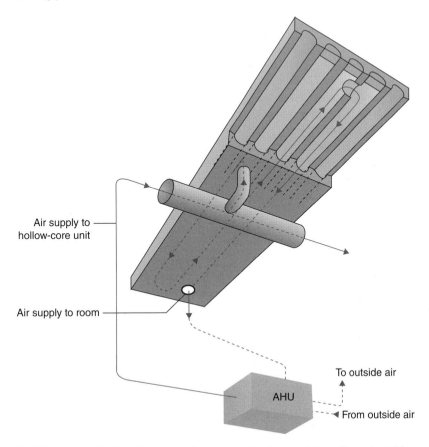

Air supply to
hollow-core unit

Air supply to room

To outside air

AHU

From outside air

Figure 3.7 Termodeck; Hollow floor slabs that act as structure and duct. Reproduced by
permission of Tarmac Building Products.

Case Study: Innovate Green Office, Leeds, UK

A commercial building in Leeds, the Innovate Green Office was awarded the highest ever BREEAM rating – 87.55%. At first glance it does not look particularly green (Figure 3.8). There are no windmills or solar panels and it is not naturally ventilated. Yet, the building emits 80% less CO_2 than a typical conventionally air-conditioned office, producing only 22kg of carbon dioxide per m^2 per year.

The concrete structure is externally insulated to substantially exceed the requirements of Part L at 0.15W/m^2°C and exposed internally allowing its high thermal mass to regulate the internal environment. The floor and roof planks are used as Termodeck to further increase the thermal mass. With the insulation levels achieved; the heat loss is reduced to a point where the internal gains provide the majority of useful heat. The building is mechanically ventilated and heat recovery AHUs (air handling units) collect the heat gains from people and computers and store the energy in the Termodeck for later beneficial re-use. Summer cooling is provided by a combination of passive night cooling and active cooling from the chiller using the Termodeck as a thermal store.

Figure 3.8   Innovate Green Office, Leeds, UK; An outstanding BREEAM rated speculative office comprises two parallel wings joined by a longitudinal atrium. Reproduced by permission of The Concrete Centre.

through the whole unit, transferring energy into or out of the concrete (active thermal mass). Typically the air flow is reversible, depending on whether it is heating or cooling, with one end open to the space below the slab and the other to the plant room for heat recovery, mixing with fresh air and so on.

3.2.3.6   Whole Building Design and BIM

Building Information Modelling (BIM) is 'the process of generating and managing digital building data during its life cycle'. BIM is a hot topic in the construction industry in the UK as the government announced that the use of

BIM will be compulsory for all centrally procured public projects from 2016. BIM will transform the way whole building design is carried out and make implementation of sustainability easier as BIM models could offer many advantages such as the following:

- Analysis of energy/carbon or thermal mass data of combined structural elements during design to help decision making
- 3D visualisations of structures to help identify potential problems on-site and lead to solutions, for example waste reduction during construction
- Detailed data on the longevity of structural components leading to decisions on end of life, recycling or reuse.

3.2.4 Substructures

Substructures are traditionally concrete and this remains the case in the vast majority of buildings because concrete is cost effective and has inherent durability, robustness and compressive strength.

3.2.4.1 Foundations

Foundations are responsible for a significant contribution to a building's environmental impact. For example, the ECO_2e of foundations in the ARUP/ The Concrete Centre buildings study (see section 3.2.11) is typically 11% for school and hospital medium rise buildings and 17% for medium rise office buildings. According to Brown (Reynolds et al., 2010), the foundations and ground floor represent 34% of the total environmental impact of a typical masonry building.

Options for designers to consider for reducing environmental impacts of foundations are:

1. Reduce embodied impacts through design:
   a. comprehensive site investigation;
   b. choosing foundation type that minimises impacts;
   c. influencing, if possible, superstructure, structural grid and stability system;
   d. avoidance of over design;
   e. trial pile load testing;
   f. presence of design engineer on site (resident geotechnical engineer).
2. Reduce embodied impacts through material specification:
   a. using Portland cement replacements;
   b. using recycled aggregates (appropriate caveats on use);
   c. using local responsibly sourced materials.
3. Reduce construction impacts:
   a. minimise waste/spoil;
   b. minimise transport impacts;

    c. minimise construction process plant impacts;

    d. ensure construction process is managed to minimise over-dig through appropriate equipment and accuracy of setting out. This will contribute to achieving the first three points made above.

4. Ensure foundations are fit for purpose, for if they are not, the environmental impacts can be disproportionately high because:

    a. excessive differential settlement results in damage to finishes or worse;

    b. repair or augmentation of foundations is a complex operation;

    c. total failure/catastrophic failure is not unheard of and self evidently has greater environmental impact than sufficient foundations in the initial construction.

The impacts of foundation failure are proportionately greater than for other elements of the building. This may be why there is more likelihood of and scope for over design – not an unreasonable response by designers and clients.

Each of the six considerations listed under '1. Design' above are expanded below. The considerations under '2. Material Specification' are covered in Chapter 4, and those in '3. Construction Impacts' and '4. Fit for Purpose' are self explanatory.

1a. A **comprehensive site investigation** enables the geotechnical engineer and foundations designer (the structural engineer and/or geotechnical engineer) to base decisions regarding foundation type and corresponding design parameters on the best possible information. This will result in a more cost effective and lower environmental impact foundation solution. For example, if the design decisions are based only on a desk study of available data (geological maps, and data from adjacent sites if available, historical maps etc.) then cautious assumptions must be made. The most likely consequence is more and/or larger piles, wider and/or deeper shallow footings than is necessary. However, it may be the case that the more comprehensive site investigation identifies poorer ground conditions than might have been otherwise assumed and the foundations chosen as a result will have greater initial environmental impact – but they will be fit for purpose and overall the solution will have less impact (noting item D above).

1b. A **choice of foundation type** generally starts with a choice between deep and shallow footings: piles or pads/strips/raft. In many cases the choice is dictated by ground conditions and the building (its size and arrangement of loads). In some cases, more than one foundation type is technically viable. Traditionally the decision between alternatives is based on cost and buildability but now sustainability is also a criterion. The choice of foundation type has a bearing on impacts at the material specification and construction stages as well as the most significant impact of volume of material required. The point of economic balance between piles and shallow footings is at a point where the volume of piles is significantly less than the equivalent shallow footings. Given that the environmental impact is largely dictated by the foundation volume: spoil removed, material required, transport impacts: application of environmental criteria increases the likelihood that piled foundations will be the more sustainable choice for a particular building.

1c.   The **structural grid and stability system** determines how the lateral and vertical loads are applied to the foundations and influence the relative settlement design criteria. It is not common for the economy of the foundations to heavily influence the structural grid and stability system because of the many other constraints and client requirements that the architect and engineering team must take into account. The foundation options available mean that the challenge is to get the best foundation choice for the loads applied. Hypothetical worst case layouts in terms of economy of foundations could be conceived, for example, permanent tension (uplift) loads on some piles and compressive loads on others, but constraints in the superstructure would rule out these structural grids in all but the most particular of cases (buildings comprising cantilevers over buried, surface or above surface infrastructure to maximise developed space would be such a particular case). As environmental considerations increase in importance, it may be that foundations are more often considered in determining the structural grid. An arrangement which results in equivalent loads in every column would permit an optimum solution whether it is piles, raft, strips or pads. This perfection would be unlikely to be achievable if the rest of the building solution is also optimised, but the weighting given to foundations will increase.

1d.   **Overdesign of foundations** is often expressed by theoreticians as a major problem, but practitioners are more pragmatic because the causes of overdesign on real projects are not simply overcome. The risk of over design can be reduced if:

- superstructure design is sufficiently resolved so that foundation design loads are accurate (not increased by a percentage design safety margin to allow for future design changes);
- rationalisation of foundations is not conducted and all pads, strips and piles are designed for actual design load rather than highest load applied to all. (Rationalisation has the advantage of making construction simpler reducing waste, reducing likelihood of error and minimising build time);
- thorough site investigation is conducted;
- resident engineer is available on site.

1e.   **Pile load testing** permits reduced safety factors in pile design. An example of this is given below.

> **Case Study: Wembley Stadium, London**
>
> 'The new Wembley Stadium in London, UK required the design and construction of about 4000 piles, of varying diameters between 0.45m and 1.5m, and varying lengths between 10m and 40m. All the piles were rotary bored, cast in situ straight shafted piles. Some of the piles were subject to complex combinations of vertical, horizontal, moment and torsional loads. Prior to and during the works a comprehensive pile test programme was undertaken including compression, tension and lateral load tests with some piles loaded to failure.... the interpretation of tests... and the application of the draft Eurocode 7 rules for deriving factor of safety resulted in significant cost and programme savings'. (Driscoll et al., 2008)

1f. A **site engineer** or resident engineer with responsibility for foundations can use observation and testing of soil conditions during the foundations work to influence the construction. Better information on soil conditions during construction may indicate poorer ground than expected and hence larger foundations (deeper or wider) will be necessary. However it is more likely that smaller foundations will be necessary because the design based on less data will have erred on the side of caution. Therefore, appointment of a site engineer is a means of achieving more efficient and more sustainable foundations.

3.2.4.2 Basements

Whereas building elements such as foundations, stability system, frame and floors, cladding and roof can be found in all buildings a basement is an option. Whether a building has a usable space below ground is generally not dictated by sustainability, but by the economic sense in maximising the usable space on high value land. Whilst it is usually cheaper to gain the extra space by going up, to design a new build project with an extra above ground storey or in retrospect with an extra storey on top, planning restrictions may limit overall building height and the extra usable space can only come from going down.

Other drivers for basements may be:

1. contaminated ground needing to be removed in any case makes provision of a basement cheaper;
2. poor ground necessitating a lower founding layer provides the opportunity for an earthworks sequence involving removal of overburden, installation of foundations from a lower working level, construction of basement boxes and replacement of overburden across the site with a higher average level or landscaped terraces.
3. a sloping site where balance of cut and fill to level site results in half basements.

Figure 3.9   Martin Grant Homes, Cambridge, UK; basement construction. Reproduced by permission of The Basement Information Centre.

Low rise residential

Basements, which are almost always of concrete construction, are more likely in the future in low rise residential developments because of their sustainable advantages (Figure 3.9).

1. energy efficiency results from the surrounding ground being at a nearly constant moderate temperature. The simple construction methods and minimal wall penetrations also minimise heat loss through cold bridging. BRE studies show a potential 10% saving in space heating for a two-storey house with a full ground basement compared with its three-storey equivalent above ground (TBIC, 2010). Better air tightness of basement construction compared with upper floors gives additional energy efficiency.
2. Greater stability and resilience to long-term changes in ground conditions is another advantage of basements on 'shallow' footings compared with a dwelling without a basement on shallow footings. An accepted consequence of climate change is an increased risk of building movement and settlement problems. Basements will have reduced risk of this hazard.

3. Increased usable space provided by a basement does enable higher density housing developments and all the sustainability advantages of reduced infrastructure per head of population. In sustainability assessment methods, credits can be claimed from provision of additional space for one or more of drying space, biomass fuel storage, waste recycling storage, bicycle storage or home office.

4. Flood risk houses benefit from a semi basement by raising the ground floor if the basement level is designed as a flood resilient 'sacrificial' space. This can score credits in the Code for Sustainable Homes (DCLG, 2010) under surface water run off.

5. A building footprint of 1/3 or less of the usable site is more easily achieved if there is a basement. This gives a credit under ecology in the Code for Sustainable Homes.

6. Basements provide additional ductility and strength to buildings in seismic zones.

Other buildings

The economic sense for basements in the commercial and high rise sectors means that many of the sustainability advantages are already being realised. The benefits itemised above for low rise housing are generally applicable to other buildings, though basement usage is generally car parking, mechanical plant or storage.

Sustainably designed and built basements

Options for designers to reduce the environmental impacts of foundations given in the previous section are applicable to basements.

3.2.5 Lateral stability

The lateral stability system must have the capacity to transfer the applied lateral forces with sufficient rigidity. Lateral forces result from wind, seismic and accidental loads and on sloping sites, from unbalanced earth pressures. These forces must be resisted with sufficient rigidity, which is generally expressed in terms of lateral deflection limits, inter storey drift or dynamic response in the case of slender buildings.

The lateral stability system comprises:

- cladding;
- floor slabs acting as diaphragms;
- some or all of vertical shear walls, cross bracing, beams and columns as part of a moment frame;
- foundations.

Only a few of these will be considered in this section, the others being addressed elsewhere. From hereon 'stability systems' describes shear walls or moment frames.

Designers can make the stability system more efficient and thereby reduce its environmental impacts by reducing the size of stability structures. This is achieved by:

- symmetrical arrangements of shear walls or moment frames which reduce torsional affects;
- locating shear walls towards or at the building perimeters because any torsional affects are efficiently resisted due to longer lever arms;
- locating orthogonal shear walls so they are joined to create efficient flanged sections in plan (c.f. – a channel, 'T' or 'I' section is more structurally efficient than a rectangular section for the same area of material and same length);
- for the same total length of shear wall, a few longer walls can be thinner than many shorter walls;
- placing voids for horizontal distribution of services (out of vertical risers) or door openings for lifts or stairs in the middle of walls.

These drivers need to be balanced with necessary and complex architectural constraints.

For minimisation of embodied impacts through specification see Chapter 4 – no particular issues apply for shear walls.

The decision for shear walls rather than moment frames is often dictated by either magnitude of lateral forces or stiffness requirements for which the moment frame columns would be prohibitively large or simply because the architectural requirement for lifts, stairs and services risers (shafts) and toilets provide the opportunity for shear walls. A benefit of moment frames is the long-term future adaptability they offer because there are no walls or bracing. In marginal cases this could be a reason for choosing moment frames over shear walls for medium rise buildings. In seismic zones, combined shear walls with moment frames is usually the most suitable solution for medium to high rise buildings.

Plan geometry and building height are the major influences on lateral wind loading. For tall buildings, minimisation of wind loadings is a critical design factor and plan shapes close to 1:1 are beneficial. Due to streamlining, curved corners and ultimately a circular cross section minimises horizontal wind loading. (Note that for slender buildings, cross-wind vibration effects should also be considered). The potential reduction in wind loading for medium rise and certainly low rise buildings is not significant enough to override other architectural constraints – primarily site utilisation (see Figure 3.10).

3.2.6   *Frame and flooring*

The frame and flooring design is heavily influenced by the column grid which in turn is heavily influenced by the architectural constraints. A long span solution requires more material in slabs and/or beams; it is more costly and has a bigger environmental impact. However, the long span may be necessary to deliver the required functionality or the agreed definition of future flexibility.

Figure 3.10   **The Shard in Central London stands 310m high making it the tallest building in Western Europe. The central core shear walls are designed to withstand lateral loads and provide strength, stiffness and robustness for the building. The tapered elevation reduces the 'sail' area at increasing height, where the wind loads are greatest.**

Efficient grid

Within the constraint of building performance being delivered, a repetitive grid is an efficient building grid. The construction process of the slab itself, as well as services and finishes will be quick and produce minimal waste. Also the structural design will be reasonably material-efficient.

There is a theoretical optimised minimum material for a constant thickness slab supported by a certain number of columns. This optimisation would balance the peak allowable deflections in each bay and along slab edges. The optimised layout would have cantilevers and several different column spacings. It is improbable that the cantilevers and spacings would be a standard multiple of the dimensions of ceiling tiles, floor finishes or cladding units. So whilst the structure may be efficient – nothing else would be!

Structural slab efficiency

The weight/cost of the floor slabs represents approximately 85% of the total weight/cost of the concrete frame of a multi-storey building. Choosing the right sustainable slab is therefore one of the critical decisions in the conceptual design of the frame. Once the column grid has been chosen, three ways of designing a structurally more efficient floor slab are given below:

1. For a given span the most material efficient slab solution is likely to utilise prestressing either in the form of pre-stressed precast planks or post tensioned in-situ slabs. Prestressing is efficient because the prestressing prevents the concrete going into tension for some or all in service loading conditions. (Concrete has low tensile resistance beyond which it cracks and the concrete beam or slab is subsequently less stiff). For short spans less than 7.5 or 8m, usually in residential projects, it may not be effective to pre-stress because the slab thickness is useful for acoustic performance and savings given by pre-tensioning are small.

2. Material efficiency can also be achieved by only having material where it is needed. The least efficient solution in this regard is the flat slab – a solid, constant thickness slab supported on columns. (Its advantages are noted later). Away from columns the concrete slab does not need to be solid – in fact the unneeded concrete adds to the dead loading. This can be overcome by using square or trough void frames to create waffle or ribbed slabs. Alternatively permanent spherical void formers cast into the slab have the same benefit. The precast equivalent of a ribbed slab is a hollow core plank – the cross section created by the hollow cores maximises the moment of inertia and hence structural bending efficiency. Flat solid slabs are very popular because they are quicker and simpler to build and they are much easier for follow-on trades. For example, the partitions in a hospital are significant in material volume and cost. A flat slab compared with a floor structure comprising steel beams and metal deck enables a 10% reduction in the cost of partitions. This saving equals to 4% of the cost of the structural frame. In-situ ribbed slabs and waffle slabs would also have adverse impacts on the partition package in terms of cost and wastage of material (TCC, 2006).

3. A third means of gaining structural efficiency is to utilise continuity. In-situ concrete or hybrid concrete (in-situ and precast) enables beams and slabs to be monolithic and if adequately reinforced hogging moments are developed at supports. The sagging moments at adjacent mid spans are reduced by the magnitude of the hogging moment. This reduction is not totally for free – the hogging does require additional reinforcement – but there is a significant saving in concrete. A particular case of this is that of the cantilever. If architectural constraints permit, the most efficient slab/column arrangement in in-situ concrete is for columns to be in board of the slab edge. The slab will cantilever beyond with no additional depth of slab or concrete, and only extra hogging (top) reinforcement (Figure 3.11).

For choosing slab/frame options see Appendix C. Choosing between different concrete slab/frame options for a multi-storey concrete framed building is made easy with Concept, a conceptual software design tool that will automatically choose the best cost-optimised structural solution from a list of options using different types of slabs/frames (TCC, 2012).

Figure 3.11 BDP Offices, Manchester UK; Cantilever slabs are efficiently provided, with minimum depth, due to the moment continuity of the post-tensioned slabs. Reproduced by permission of The Concrete Centre.

Building height

Reducing the total building height for a set number of storeys, reduces the materials required in the cladding and internal finishes and vertical structure. It reduces the size of stair cores if fewer steps are necessary. It also reduces heat loss and gain. The total building height is influenced by the thickness of the structural floor zone, the floor and ceiling finishes and any zones required for ventilation and lighting.

The minimum floor zone is often enabled by a post tensioned solid flat slab as it gives the thinnest structural zone achievable and total flexibility of services because there are no downstand beams that require penetrations or dictate the direction of major duct runs. It may be that integrated solutions can be developed for a particular project where the services (ventilation and/or lighting) zones overlap with the structural zone giving an even thinner overall depth. A warning, however, is that this will reduce long-term flexibility of the building.

Thermal mass of slabs

The energy performance of a building can be improved by utilising the thermal mass of the slabs. For more on thermal mass, see Appendix A, but the particular considerations for slabs are:

1. Exposing the soffit and investing in achieving the necessary/required/desired appearance delivers savings in both energy and ceiling finishes (both initial and regular ceiling replacement costs).

2. A profiled soffit has better heat transfer for two reasons – increased surface area and increased heat transfer per unit area (because the boundary layer is disrupted by turbulence).
3. Active systems where air or water is passed through the slab can deliver improved performance and ensure the building is future proofed against a warming climate.

For more on exposed concrete structures see section 3.2.3.5.

Column efficiency

Columns are either part of a lateral stability system (a moment sway frame) or only carry vertical load and are part of a braced frame. For moment sway frames refer to section 3.2.5.

In braced frames, columns are either tall and slender with their load carrying capacity limited by buckling, or stocky which makes them limited by concrete compressive strength. As was the case with optimising a structural slab and its support location to minimise material, column spacing and sizing optimisation is only of theoretical interest, because the architectural constraints on column spacing, derived usually from the intended building performance, are far more important. However, in principle, it is worth noting that many slender columns designed against buckling use more material than fewer broader columns, albeit with the allied consideration of how efficient the slab is for the different spans.

Another consideration is what concrete strength to specify for columns. The driver for this is typically an architect/client not being amused by large columns through entrance areas or through basement spaces planned for prestigious uses. The higher the strength of concrete, the bigger the environmental impact per unit volume because of higher cement content, but is the environmental impact per kN carried less? This needs to be assessed on a case by case basis and other secondary effects such as increase in net lettable space, should also be considered. Also see section 4.11.2.

3.2.7 Cladding

The cladding is typically the most significant part of the building fabric in influencing operational energy because it comprises the majority of the building envelope through which energy is lost or gained. Heat loss and gain is controlled by the insulation contained within solid elements, the insulation value of glazing, the thermal bridging (see Box 3.1), the air tightness of cladding elements and the air tightness at interfaces between these elements.

Cladding design specification is the responsibility of the architect, but with major input from the building physicist or services designer. The structural engineer has an increasing role as façades become more solid.

In the second half of the twentieth century, the engineering development of reinforced concrete and steel frames, together with the innovation of glass curtain walling, facilitated a new architectural vernacular of glass boxes, particularly

---

Box 3.1   Thermal bridging.

Thermal bridging is the term used to describe the thermal connection between external and internal elements across the insulation. For example, a typical masonry house comprises two masonry walls with an insulation filled cavity between. These walls are joined by 'wall ties' which are rods that are mortared into each wall. These wall ties, traditionally of steel, conduct heat across the cavity. Innovative wall ties reduce the thermal bridging because they are made from less conductive materials and are stronger and hence the cross sectional area is smaller. Another example of thermal bridging is a cantilever balcony formed from a portion of the concrete floor slab protruding from the edge of the building, through the insulation. There are many proprietary solutions available to overcome this thermal bridge (Figure 3.12).

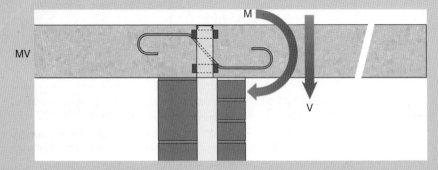

Figure 3.12   Overcoming thermal bridging in balconies; The Ancon Isolan MV system is one example which transfers moment (M) and shear forces (V) in cantilevered balconies, and minimises heat transfer. Note: tension and compression reinforcement, not shown, threads through circular voids which are shown dashed. Reproduced by permission of Ancon Building Products.

in the commercial office sector. However, building designers are responding to the environmental agenda with a new architecture which has more solidity in the façades. This reduces adverse solar gain but still permits sufficient day lighting thereby minimising energy for cooling and lighting. In addition the insulating performance and air tightness of cladding has had to increase. Increased solidity offers the option of the façade once again playing a major role in vertical load transfer, just as in traditional masonry and stone buildings; hence the increasing role of the building's structural engineer in cladding design.

More solid façades can be achieved by using:

- Opaque panels in curtain walling.
- Blockwork or concrete inner leaf with decorative external skin of glass, metal, brick, timber, render etc.
- Lightweight metal or timber studwork for inner leaf with decorative external skin as above.

Some of these options can be fabricated off site. Some can be designed such that the inner skin also provides vertical load bearing for floor slabs. Precast concrete cladding can deliver both.

Figure 3.13   Olympic Village, London, UK; Precast concrete cladding was chosen for its long service life. Reproduced by permission of The Concrete Centre.

Precast concrete cladding can be a sandwich comprising:

- inner skin of concrete;
- insulation;
- external skin of concrete with external decorative finish.

Typically the inner skin is fixed to the building frame and/or slabs. Alternatively the precast units can be stacked one upon the other with the building frame providing lateral restraint. A third option is that the inner skin of the precast units is the perimeter vertical load bearing structure for the building. This final option is a very efficient use of materials, particularly for low/medium rise buildings because the inner skin of concrete can perform multiple functions of:

- permanent vertical load bearing of floor slabs;
- temporary structural capacity for transport/installation;
- acoustic performance;
- fire performance;
- thermal mass performance.

The 2012 London Olympic village comprises over 60 mini towers typically 10 storeys tall and the vast majority are clad in precast concrete panels, supported from the in-situ concrete floors and frames (Figure 3.13). The advantages of precast concrete sandwich panels (inner leaf + insulation + decorative finish):

- speed of construction;
- minimum installation workforce increases health & safety credentials;
- range of decorative finishes;
- low maintenance;
- robust;
- long life – typically 60 years compared with lightweight cladding which is typically 20 or 30 years;
- factory construction ensures energy and resource efficient with low waste;
- excellent fire, acoustic and energy performance.

With respect to energy performance:

- the highest air tightness requirements can be met because the large panels mean few joints and the panels are stiff and dimensionally stable;
- the inner skin gives excellent thermal mass, unlike lightweight cladding solutions;
- the required levels of insulation can easily be incorporated between the inner and outer decorative skin.

3.2.8 Roofs

In addition to the obvious functions that the roof must perform as part of the building envelope – water barrier and thermal barrier – the roof may have additional functions and need to meet certain constraints. These are:

- compliance with planning with respect to aesthetics;
- support of services: equipment (plant), pipework and renewable energy system components;
- support of planting that in turn supports biodiversity;
- be adaptable for future alterations/ extensions.

Roofs for low rise housing, long span spaces and large scale developments are considered in turn below.

Low rise housing
The pitched roof remains the norm for UK housing. In recent decades the supporting structure is typically trusses of small section timber joined by gang nail plates (thin galvanised plates punched with holes in a manner to create multiple spikes orthogonal to the plate). The close spacing of these trusses (typically 600mm) limits the use of the roof space and prevents easy future loft conversion.

With respect to fire – research from Sweden identifies that fires in timber buildings are five times more likely to occur, and when they occur, are more serious. More critically in the context of roofs, many major fires spread through timber roof structures.

Precast concrete pitched roofs offer an alternative that has innate fire resistance and uninterrupted space throughout the loft to maximise its usability and future conversion potential.

The roof covering for pitched roofs can be natural slate or manufactured tiles of clay or concrete. When looking at manufactured tiles, a key differentiator between clay and concrete tiles is the ECO_2. Clay tiles must be fired at very high temperatures (around 1,000 °C) whereas concrete tiles are cured at less than 100 °C. The cement content (typically less than 20% by weight) in concrete tiles does not offset this energy difference. The embodied energy of concrete tiles is 91–146MJ/m^2 whilst for the equivalent clay tiles it is 240–478MJ/m^2 (Arup, 2007).

Long span roofs

Generally, long span roofs in excess of 25m are more suited to lightweight materials such as steel and glulam timber. There are exceptions which utilise concrete's compressive attributes in arch action and these were more prevalent in the middle of the last century for factories, airport halls, bus stations, grand stand roofs etc. There are also examples that utilise concrete's mass to resist wind uplift forces such as the Braga Football Stadium, Portugal and the Portuguese National Pavilion, Lisbon (Figure 3.14).

Figure 3.14   Portuguese National Pavilion, Lisbon Portugal; 200mm thick lightweight concrete (18kN/m^3) roof. Reproduced by permission of Arup.

Commercial and public buildings

Pitched roofs: Typically driven by planning requirements, some larger commercial and public buildings are required to have pitched roofs, or to at least appear to have pitched roofs. This is provided by a pitched roof around the perimeter of a flat roof. The issues noted above for low rise housing pitched roofs are generally also applicable here.

Flat roofs: Often a roof covering is supported by a lightweight structure because there is only a small live loading (dictated by snow or access only). However, this has been found to have disadvantages for the occupied space below because it has no ceiling thermal mass.

The environmental building at BRE (often referred to as the Energy Efficient Office of the Future or Building 16) has offices over three floors. The lower two enjoy the benefit of exposed concrete ceilings, whilst the top floor office accommodation has a lightweight structure above. Monitoring over three summer periods (Riain et al., in progress) showed higher temperatures and exceedance of comfort criteria on the top floor. The designers of the Wessex Water HQ building in Swindon UK, overcame the problem of a lightweight roof by placing heavyweight concrete panels in the roof to provide the necessary thermal mass to moderate peak summer temperatures. Therefore it can be seen that concrete roofs are beneficial, and if concrete is needed, it may as well also provide the structure as well as thermal mass.

Green roofs: roofs with some variety of plants installed on it are another reason for having a concrete structure to a roof. A 'living roof' is increasingly being encouraged by planning policies and in Germany, 10% of new buildings now feature a green roof (Green Futures, 2012).

Some advantages of green roofs are:

- promote bio-diversity;
- help building energy efficiency (winter and summer);
- good sound insulation and air filtration;
- help reduce urban heat island effects;
- absorb CO_2 and other pollutants;
- provide water storage capacity to 'slow the flow', reducing localised flooding from hard catchment areas after sudden downpours;
- increase points available from BREEAM rating system.

To support the heavy loading from green roofs – soil, water and increased live loading – concrete slabs are most commonly chosen.

3.2.9 *Innovations*

In this section, four innovations which may be considered by design teams to minimise the impacts of their buildings are briefly described. They are discussed with reference to the role concrete plays, if any, in how they are incorporated into designs.

Case Study: Strata SE1, London

The 43-storey Strata SE1 building in London is a concrete framed building with post tensioned slabs and has three 9m diameter 19kW wind turbines at the top of the building. It is noteworthy that it is surrounded by relatively small buildings. It was anticipated that the turbines would generate 50MWh of electricity per year equivalent to 8% of Strata's estimated total annual electricity consumption. Each turbine is sited on a five tonne inertia base and supported on anti-vibration mounts to prevent vibration being transferred to the building's structure. The use of five blades rather than the usual three is intended to reduce operational noise. However, there is evidence that they are rarely in operation. This in itself is an indication that implementation of this concept of turbines on a structure is innovative and carries risk (Figure 3.15).

Figure 3.15   Strata SE1, London, UK.

1. **Wind power generation on buildings**

    Micro-generation wind turbines on domestic scale buildings were popular for a very short period in the UK around 2008 and 2009 but quickly it was realised that in the suburban context there is too much turbulence and relatively low wind speeds at roof level. More significant wind speeds occur at height, and this is important because the power generated is proportional to the cube of the wind speed.

In addition to placing turbines at height, the massing of a building can be chosen to maximise wind speeds. For example, The Bahrain World Trade Centre has a turbine on each of three bridges between the two towers. The towers funnel the prevailing winds between them, maximising the energy generated.

In the context of wind power generation, concrete frames have the advantage of lower noise and vibration transmission characteristics compared with steel framed buildings.

2. **Solar energy**

Photo–voltaic systems remain the most common means of capturing solar energy. These are bolt on extras and have little impact on the structure or servicing of a building, apart from being a local renewable energy source. Embedding photo-voltaic cells in cladding elements such as roof tiles has also been implemented commercially. Less widespread are cladding products through which air or water is passed, so that heat absorbed from the sun is transferred away to heat exchangers.

3. **Thermal piles**

The ground offers a heat sink in summer and a heat source in winter and this can be accessed by utilising structural load bearing piles as thermal piles by casting in poly-butylene pipe or similar into the concrete piles. This pipework is typically in a closed loop and passes through a heat exchanger. In summer, the heat exchanger passes heat sourced from the building into the closed loop and this in turn is transferred to the ground. In winter relatively cold water is warmed in the thermal pile and this heat is removed in the heat exchanger and then transferred into the building. If higher temperature differentials are needed, a reversible heat pump can be used instead of the heat exchanger in both winter and summer. Many case studies exist where this has been successfully used.

Structurally, thermal gradients through thermal piles and change in pile average temperatures are small compared with other concrete elements or structures. If isolated piles are used as thermal piles, the differential thermal expansion can attract increased loading that is a function of the relative stiffness of piles (Laloui and Di Donna, 2011).

4. **Hypocausts**

A more traditional active method of accessing a ground heat source/sink is the Roman hypocaust. Air is passed through a subterranean labyrinth which maximises the surface area and hence heat transferred between air and ground. This is typically constructed from concrete. Recent examples of this include the Alpine House, Kew Gardens, London in which the labyrinth was formed of concrete blocks (Figure 3.16). A simpler example is to use long underground pipework to pre-warm or pre-cool fresh air into the building as at Butterfields Business Park, Luton, UK where concrete pipes were used.

Key to diagram

1. 'Labyrinth' formed by voids in the concrete floor structure acts as a damper to reduce temperature in the summer
2. Air supplied at floor level displaces warmer air upwards and produces a cool zone at
3. Supply air chamber within rockery construction distributes cool air to simple slot outlets at low level around planting beds
4. Concrete floor slab
5. Single glazed glasshouse facade
6. Automatic internal blind. Closes at night to reduce radiation losses
7. Heat gain from sun reflected and absorbed by blind. Heat gained through blind is vented by stream of air rising from below
8. Automated roof vents giving total operable area approx 20% of floor area
9. Perimeter air inlet
10. Incoming fresh air at low level
11. PV panels (optional) on south west elevation to power ventilation fan

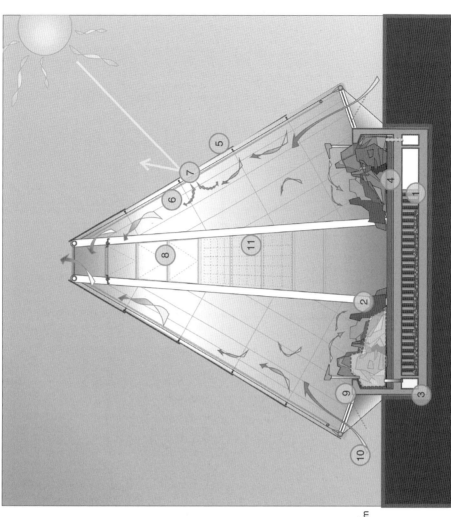

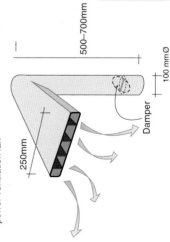

Figure 3.16 Alpine House, Kew Gardens, London, UK. Reproduced by permission of Atelier Ten.

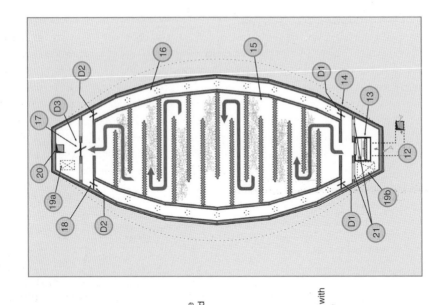

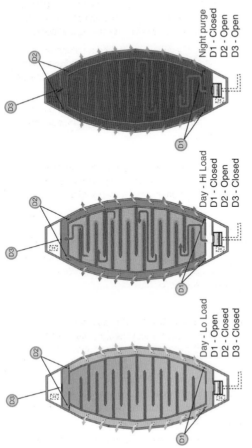

Day - Lo Load
D1 - Open
D2 - Closed
D3 - Closed

Day - Hi Load
D1 - Closed
D2 - Open
D3 - Closed

Night purge
D1 - Closed
D2 - Open
D3 - Open

Key to Diagram

12. Air intake through ground duct to +/− 20m from building
13. Air intake fan, filter and heater in 2m high accessible space
14. labyrinth by-pass control damper
15. Thermal storage labyrinth of concrete with rough rock base for additional storage
16. Supply air chamber beneath planter
17. Night cooling damper
18. Labyrinth shut off damper
19a. Man hole/access
19b. Man hole/access
20. Air exhaust
21. Access

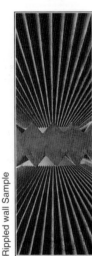

Rippled wall Sample

Figure 3.16 *(Continued)*

3.2.10　*Environmental Assessment Schemes*

In most developed countries there is an environmental assessment scheme that provides guidance to designers and is a tool for clients for directing their construction professionals. The schemes are also a means of marketing the sustainability credentials of a building to prospective owners or tenants.

Generally, the schemes assess a range of environmental impacts of a building over their life cycle, and in doing so, assess performance aspects such as energy performance. In addition some performance aspects which are not so directly associated with impacts, such as lighting and ventilation, are also assessed.

The assessed categories in the UK BREEAM (Building Research Establishment Environmental Assessment Method) and the Australian Greenstar Schemes are shown in Table 3.4 below as examples of what factors schemes take into account.

Table 3.4　Comparison of BREEAM and Greenstar sustainability assessment schemes

BREEAM (BRE, 2011)	Greenstar Australia (Green Building Council Australia, 2012)
Management: Good building management is essential for a building's performance as it impacts throughout the building's life.	Management: Credits address the adoption of sustainable development principles from project conception through design, construction, commissioning, tuning and operation.
Health and wellbeing: Our internal environment has a direct impact upon our health and quality of life.	IEQ: Credits target environmental impact along with occupant wellbeing and performance by addressing the HVAC system, lighting, occupant comfort and pollutants.
Energy: The operation of UK buildings accounts for over 50 per cent of CO_2 emissions. BREEAM looks at how the heating, air conditioning, lighting and use of white goods reduces energy requirements.	Energy: Credits target reduction of greenhouse emissions from building operation by addressing energy demand reduction, use efficiency, and generation from alternative sources.
Transport: Employee travel to site.	Transport: Credits reward the reduction of demand for individual cars by both discouraging car commuting and encouraging use of alternative transportation.
Water: Adoption of water efficient appliances and water metering.	Water: Credits address reduction of potable water through efficient design of building services, water reuse and substitution with other water sources (specifically rainwater).
Materials: Use of low-embodied, responsibly sourced and recycled construction materials.	Materials: Credits target resource consumption through material selection, reuse initiatives and efficient management practices.
Waste: Minimal site construction waste.	–
Land use and ecology: Minimal impact on land and ecology from manufacture of construction materials, use of green or brownfield site, ecological evaluation and conservation.	Land Use & Ecology: Credits address a project's impact on its immediate ecosystem, by discouraging degradation and encouraging restoration of flora and fauna.
Pollution: Minimising the building's potential air and water pollution over its lifetime.	Emissions: Credits address point source pollution from buildings & building services to the atmosphere, watercourse, and local ecosystems.
–	Innovation: Green Star seeks to reward marketplace innovation that fosters the industry's transition to sustainable building.

Credits are awarded for each category according to performance. A weighting for each category allows the credits to be added together to provide a single overall score. The simplification of sustainability to a single score is convenient. However, it does have drawbacks. The relative weightings should not necessarily be the same for different buildings, or for similar buildings in different geographical locations. Within the categories, there are typically step increases in credits for improved performance, which incentivises reaching a certain level and no more. For example, inclusion of a certain number of bike racks gives a credit, but if the architect cannot fit this number into the scheme and the credit threshold is not reached, there is no benefit from the assessment in providing any bike racks. To overcome such drawbacks would necessitate making assessments even more complex and yet the complexity of the scoring systems is already in itself seen as a drawback!

The assessment schemes are a means of encouraging and measuring performance that is better than required by, or outside the scope of, building regulations. There are indications in England (Code for Sustainable Homes has replaced the Ecohomes scheme and is part of regulatory requirements) and Scotland (where a seventh section, sustainability, is being added to the building regulations), that sustainability is moving from an optional extra to a regulatory requirement (Communities and Local Government, 2010).

3.2.11 Life cycle CO_2e studies

One metric of sustainability is CO_2e (often referred to in short hand simply as 'carbon equivalent' or even 'carbon'). Partly, in response to the complexity of sustainability and the difficulty in comparing one sustainability category with another, CO_2e is sometimes used as a proxy for sustainability. This should be resisted, and any CO_2e study should be a component part of a wider assessment.

Life cycle CO_2e studies encompass the extraction of materials required for the building all the way through to end of life, that is, materials, construction, operation and demolition (and subdivisions thereof). Embodied CO_2e (ECO_2e) may either be materials to factory gate, to site gate or to final part of structure and this should be considered when comparing ECO_2e values (see section 4.2).

Case Study: Housing

A housing life cycle CO_2 study (Hacker et al., 2008) considered a range of masonry houses with varying thermal mass and a lightweight timber house, from the perspective of embodied and operational. The study period was 100 years and took account of a warming climate. It demonstrated that the ECO_2 of heavyweight houses is about 4% more than lightweight timber houses. This is offset by a lower operational CO_2 because of thermal mass, making the medium-weight masonry house lower in CO_2 than the lightweight timber house after only 11 years (Figure 3.17).

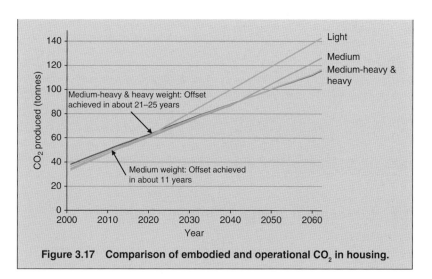

Figure 3.17 Comparison of embodied and operational CO_2 in housing.

Case Study: Non-residential

Research, carried out by Arup and commissioned by The Concrete Centre (Kaethner and Burridge, 2012) focused on the structures of three building types: office, hospital, school, and compared the ECO_2 impacts of different materials and structural frame solutions. Schemes were developed for flat slab, in-situ and precast, post-tensioned flat slab, composite, steel and precast composite and Slimdek. Arup also examined how the choice of structural frame can affect the impacts across the whole building for items such as construction, cladding, substructure and fit-out (mechanical and electrical services were excluded). All the buildings were medium-rise and were reasonably regular in layout. Twenty different structural solutions were evaluated across the three building types in order to determine typical values for 'cradle-to-site' ECO_2. Findings of the study showed that most construction methods have similar ECO_2. The variation between them is small compared with the variability arising from calculation method and the reductions possible through concrete material specification. Having chosen a design solution, the structural engineer can assist in reducing a typically-sized building's ECO_2 by as much as $100kgCO_2/m^2$ which, for a $10,000m^2$ building, equates to the personal ECO_2 of a lifetime of goods and services for a UK citizen.

The research did not consider operational or end-of-life impacts and in considering the ECO_2 results the operational energy savings potential of concrete solutions should be borne in mind. Construction, operational and end-of-life impacts can be added to the cradle-to-site approach of the research in order to obtain a whole life cycle comparison.

The ECO_2 of services (mechanical equipment and duct work, electrical systems and pipework) is difficult to estimate. Various studies presented in a confidential report for The Concrete Centre (Arup, 2010), estimated ECO_2 of services of up to 24% with an average of 12% contribution to total building embodied impact.

> The contribution of construction is similarly sparsely represented in the literature, and not surprisingly results vary widely for different building types and construction methods. Medium-rise commercial buildings have a construction impact of approximately 5% of the total building ECO_2 (Arup, 2010).
> A worked example of ECO_2 for a building slab is included in Appendix D.

3.3 Conceptual design of infrastructure

Infrastructure projects are normally civil engineering projects in the sectors of, transport, water or energy. Concrete is usually the local material of choice for sustainable infrastructure projects due to its inherent properties of durability, robustness, flood resilience, fire resistance, inertness, strength and versatility; a detailed account of the sustainability credentials of concrete is given in Chapter 4. Concrete is traditionally used in ground improvement, foundations, underground structures, retaining walls, pipes and culverts, water and sewage treatment plants, marine structures and coastal defences, tunnels, residential/industrial/port/airport pavements, roads, pipes, railway sleepers/platforms, bridges and nuclear related facilities.

This chapter covers a selection of sustainable solutions where modern concretes or cements, state-of-the art design methods and/or innovative construction techniques are part of the conceptual design of infrastructure projects.

At the end of the chapter a short description of a sustainability assessment scheme used for civil engineering projects called CEEQUAL is presented.

3.3.1 Ground remediation with stabilisation/solidification

Governments are concerned with the environmental impact of continuing development on greenfield sites and developers are increasingly forced to utilise previously developed or brownfield sites. Concentrating development on brownfield sites can help to make the best use of existing services such as transport and waste management. It can encourage more sustainable lifestyles by providing an opportunity to recycle land, clean up contaminated sites, and assist environmental, social and economic regeneration. It also reduces pressure to build on greenfield land and helps protect the countryside.

In the UK, brownfield land gained political significance after the government set a target in 1998 to ensure 60% of all developments were built on brownfield land. This target was reiterated by a Planning Policy Statement in 2006 and as a result, developments continued to be built on brownfield land on an annual basis; for example housing reclaimed approximately 17% of the total brownfield land reclaimed until 2010. A problem with developing previously occupied sites is the presence of contaminants in the soil.

Historically, the approach to dealing with contaminated land has been excavation of the contaminated material that sometimes is found in considerable depths and disposal to landfill, that is, 'dig and dump'. However, the EU Landfill Directive 1999/31/EC, as implemented in the UK by the Landfill (England and Wales) Regulations 2002, has forced substantial changes to landfill practice. Certain types of hazardous waste require pre-treatment prior to disposal increasing the cost and co-disposal of inert and hazardous waste is not permitted. As a result of the latter, the number of suitable landfill sites has reduced drastically increasing the transportation cost as well.

Stabilisation/Solidification (S/S) is a ground remediation technique that involves the controlled addition and mixing of hydraulic binders such as cement and lime with contaminated soil to generate a solid material in which contaminants are rendered immobile and virtually non-leachable, that is, unable to be washed out from the soil.

Stabilisation involves adding reagents to a contaminated soil to produce more chemically stable constituents and solidification involves adding reagents to a contaminated soil to contain contaminants in a solid product and reduce access by external agents such as air and water. The dual action means that the process is suitable not only for treating contaminated soil but also for enhancing the engineering properties of poor soil. As many derelict and brownfield sites are made up of both poor and contaminated soils S/S is an ideal remedy for them.

Therefore S/S helps strengthening of poor soils, treating of contaminated soils, eliminating the need to import fill and reducing vehicular movements to and from site. In doing so S/S is a cost effective and sustainable solution.

The principal binders used for S/S in the UK are:

- Cement, mainly Portland cement (CEM I) but including all other common cements (CEM II, CEM III, CEM IV, CEM V).
- Quicklime or hydrated lime.
- Fly ash, also called pulverised fuel ash.
- Ground granulated blastfurnace slag (GGBS).

Portland cement, or other common cements, and lime can be used on their own, in combination with each other or in combination with GGBS or fly ash which further reduce the embodied CO_2 content of the binder by replacing cement. Nevertheless, some cement or lime is required to initiate the cementitious reaction. Depending upon the nature of the contamination, minor additives or admixtures such as PH modifiers, wetting agents, flocculants, sorbents, fillers, and so on, may also be used with the main binder to improve the performance of the process. Their selection is based on experience and laboratory trials and is very specific to the particular material being treated and the remedial objectives.

S/S works well with many different types of contaminant, making it a versatile and flexible remedial technique. It is particularly effective for treating metals, but can also deal with other inorganic and organic contaminants.

Every site is different. It is therefore essential that a risk assessment is carried out to verify that the existence of contamination is a critical issue and determine what actions need to be taken to manage the risk. This is potentially a complex process for which specialist advice must always be obtained. The outcome is a site-specific conceptual risk model that involves obtaining readily available information by desk study from which an understanding can be gained of the likely contaminants present on the site, the characteristics of the ground conditions, the distribution of the contaminants and other conditions and features that will determine likely hazards and potential pathways (British Cement Association, 2004).

A conceptual risk model is used in the assessment of risk by a systematic evaluation of the potential hazards, the likelihood of their causing harm, the nature and degree of harm and the need to control adverse effects. Each application of S/S is designed to take into account the site conditions, contamination profile and remedial objectives with reference to the conceptual risk model and the requirements of the stakeholders such as the client and the regulator.

S/S is always designed on a project-specific basis through a series of laboratory and field studies. These trials are imperative and must not be circumvented: they are used to verify the composition of the binder, the dosage and the optimal application method. At this stage, interfering reactions and other constraints on the success of the process can be identified and testing protocols agreed by all parties. The treatability studies are also used to ensure that all stakeholder expectations and objectives are identified and addressed.

The implementation of S/S is flexible and can be tailored to meet site requirements. It can be carried out either as an in-situ or ex-situ process depending on the site conditions, the nature of contamination and other factors such as access, handling constraints and future needed use of treated materials. For both types of process, best practice and a high level of construction quality control should be followed in order to ensure the effectiveness of remediation.

In-situ S/S can be carried out in a number of ways and is broadly categorised by the depth of treatment as shown in Table 3.5.

Table 3.5   Methods for in-situ Stabilisation/Solidification (S/S).

<0.5m	Shallow treatment	The binder is spread over the surface of the ground to be treated at a predetermined dose rate and then mixed in using rotovating-type plant. The blended material is then compacted and the reaction between the binder and the moisture in the soil is allowed to take place.
0.5–5m	Intermediate treatment	The binder is mixed into the soil using modified plant. The plant is selected to suit the specific site conditions and application.
>5m	Deep treatment	The binder is introduced into the contaminated soil as a dry powder or slurry using vertical hollow stem augers. The binder is then mixed into the soil as the augers are advanced and/or withdrawn. Often the process uses a nest of augers which overlap to ensure greater efficacy of mixing and treatment.

Ex-situ S/S is usually undertaken at the contaminated site and can be carried out in a number of ways. In each case, the contaminated soil is excavated and possibly placed in a temporary stockpile. When the soil is required: the binder is introduced and mixed into the soil, before the blended material is taken to a final deposition area or the soil is taken to a final deposition area, where the binder is introduced and mixed to the soil.

Table 3.6   Methods for ex-situ Stabilisation/Solidification S/S.

Rotovator or other driven mobile plant	The excavated soil is transported to a final deposition area, where it is spread in layers, along with the binder and mixed using rotovating type plant. The blended material is then compacted and the reaction between the binder and the moisture in the soil is allowed to take place.
In-drum mixing	The excavated soil is placed in a drum, into which the binder is added and mixed. The reaction between the binder and the moisture in the soil is allowed to take place before the drum, mixing blades and contents are disposed.
Pugmill/Batchmixer	The excavated soil is mixed with the binder in a purpose-built plant (mobile or fixed) for a pre-determined time prior to transportation to a deposition area. The blended material is then compacted and the reaction between the binder and the moisture in the soil is allowed to take place.

Case Study: School Development, Leytonstone, London

Leyton School in Leytonstone was constructed on a former industrial site contaminated with elevated levels of the toxic metals arsenic, cadmium, lead and mercury and the phytotoxic metals boron, copper, nickel and zinc. Investigations carried out on the site identified risks of contamination to groundwater and so the site was remediated using S/S in order to mitigate against the migration of leachate. Over a 15 day period, 12,000m^3 of soil was treated by the addition of 5% cement by mass in an operation that ensured no off-site disposal of contamination and no importation of fill (Figure 3.18).

Figure 3.18   In-situ treatment of the site; The plant doses the soil with binder and then rotovates the soil immediately, thereby minimising dust levels. Courtesy of O'Keefe Soil Remediation.

The measured properties of the treated material included a CBR greater than 150% and water permeability in the order of 1×10^{-10}m/s.

> The S/S technique produced a material that was of sufficient strength to permit the reinforced concrete slab for the school to be constructed directly upon it, once the underlying strata had been vibrocompacted.
>
> It was estimated that the use of S/S techniques produced a cost saving of 75% compared with disposal to landfill, and reduced the project duration by over 10%.

Ex-situ S/S is ideal for addressing the problems of ground with buried foundations and situations where the treated materials are judged to be suitable for reuse as engineering fill and therefore a key contribution to sustainability (see Table 3.6).

3.3.2 Hydraulically Bound Mixtures (HBM) for pavements

Large quantities of imported natural aggregates are consumed for use as foundation materials on construction projects. In many cases cement stabilisation of the materials already in the ground or available nearby would render them suitable for use and avoid the need to bring in other material. Cement stabilisation can produce durable paving material that can be used for the foundation or base of road and airport pavements, parking and storage areas. Cement can be used to treat most soils. In addition, deteriorating or failed pavements and roads can also be reconstructed by stabilising (or recycling) the existing pavement using cement.

Materials treated by cement are described variously as soil cement, cement-treated materials or cement-stabilised materials. Where aggregate is being treated, the resultant mixture may, depending on strength or national terminology, be referred to as cement bound granular material, roller-compacted concrete (RCC), dry lean concrete, cement bound granular base (CBGB) and cement-treated base (CTB). Whatever the terminology, they are all part of that family of paving materials known generically as cement-bound materials (CBM).

CBM, however, are part of a larger family of paving materials known as hydraulically-bound mixtures (HBM) which all possess the advantages ascribed to CBM above. HBM describe soil or aggregate mixtures that use binders made from the following: cement, lime, gypsum, iron and steel slag, and fly ash. Such binders are known as hydraulic binders since they set and harden in the presence of water. HBM generally have water content compatible with compaction by rolling. After compaction, the water is free to hydrate the binder or hydraulic combination and commence the setting and hardening process.

Sustainability benefits of HBM include lower cost (can be over 30% cheaper than the conventional approach of importing granular or other treated materials), use of recycled materials or artificial materials and not primary aggregates, elimination of traffic between aggregate sources and site and

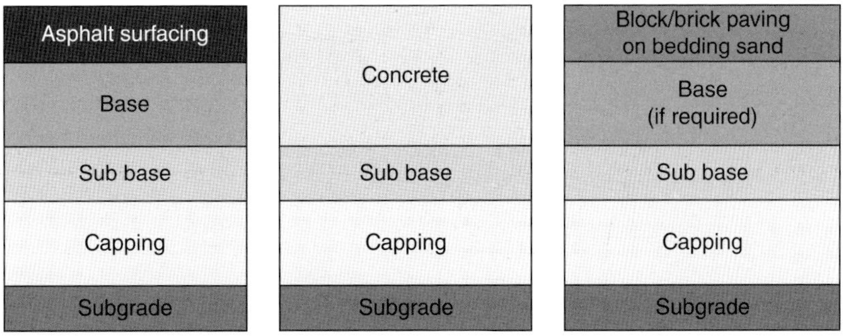

Figure 3.19   HBM are used for most construction layers (base, sub base and capping). Reproduced by permission of The Concrete Centre.

reduction of traffic needed to dispose site material. These combined with the improved performance compared with unbound granular materials make the use of HBM a sustainable choice (Figure 3.19).

The decision-making process starts with a site investigation and initial assessment to determine whether to proceed to the mixture design stage. An in-situ soil survey is carried out to locate, identify and sample the various types of soil so that it can be tested for suitability. During this part of the process, the economic viability of treatment also needs investigation so that the decision can be made whether to proceed with laboratory testing. This is done by estimating the binder requirement for the type of soil to produce HBM for capping, subbase and/or base (Kennedy, 2006). If this initial assessment indicates that stabilisation is economically viable, laboratory tests should be carried out on the material to determine its uniformity. Such tests should include classification tests for determination of particle size distribution for granular materials and determination of liquid and plastic limits for cohesive materials as well as chemical tests for organic or sulphate contamination. If the results are satisfactory, mixture design testing can be commenced.

For CBM, which traditionally have had a curing period of seven days before trafficking, the primary objectives of the mixture design procedure has been to find the correct water content for compaction of the material by rolling, and the cement content required at that water content to meet the required mechanical performance. Equally important objectives have included durability and volume stability.

However, with the advent of the lime/fly ash, lime/GGBS and ASS (Air-cooled Steel Slag)/GGBS binder combinations, where strength development is slower and curing periods not necessary, the ability of the mixture to support traffic immediately has also become one of the primary objectives of the mixture design procedure. This ability to support traffic is a function of the grading of the mixture.

The methods by which HBM layers can be constructed are similar to the S/S methods (see section 3.3.1), that is, the mix-in-place (or in-situ) method

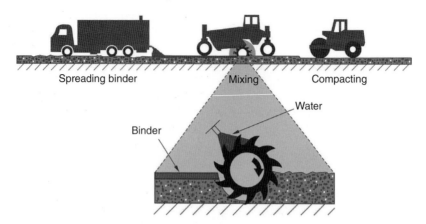

Figure 3.20   Mix-in-place stabilisation. Reproduced by permission of The Concrete Centre.

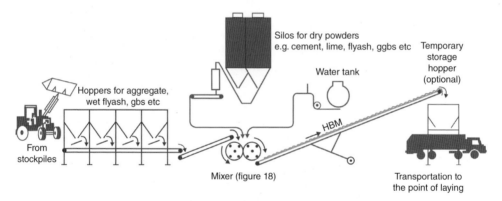

Figure 3.21   Mix-in-plant stabilisation. Reproduced by permission of The Concrete Centre.

and the mix-in-plant (or stationary plant or ex-situ) method (Figure 3.20 and Figure 3.21).

Both methods include compaction using vibrating or other types of rollers and curing by sealing the surface with sprayed bitumen emulsion to prevent loss of moisture, unless the material is to be covered immediately by another pavement layer.

3.3.3   Road construction

The UK trunk road and motorway network consists of almost 6,000 miles of pavement and with 20,000 to 60,000 tonnes of aggregate used to construct one mile of new motorway, it is understandable that the Highways Agency is keen to reduce the environmental impact of virgin materials going into new road construction. Subbase design using Continuously Reinforced Concrete Pavement (CRCP) produces a 20–30% reduction in the overall section of the road, which therefore requires less material to construct and in turn less excavation and reduced 'dig and dump' costs, whether the arising is used on site or elsewhere (Figure 3.22) (TCC, 2005a).

With regard to pavement maintenance, concrete pavements are easily repaired. Worn out sections of motorways are repaired when joints in the concrete paving have become noisy and offer poor ride quality. A new in-situ repair technique that capitalises on the durability of the existing concrete pavement is called 'crack and seat'. Having stripped the wearing course, the

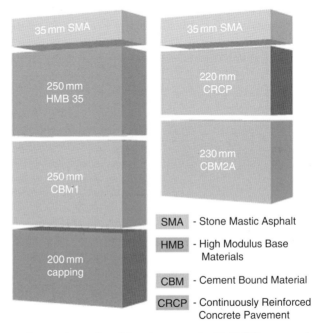

Figure 3.22   Comparison of traditional pavement with CRCP pavement. Reproduced by permission of The Concrete Centre.

Case Study: M6 Toll Motorway

CRCP and CBM were used on a major section of the M6 toll motorway which relieves congestion around Birmingham in the UK. The reinforced concrete pavement and cement bound material sub-base is stronger than a standard design solution and was slip-formed to accelerate the programme. The use of this and on-site concrete plants prevented some 400,000 lorry movements to and from site. In addition, a large quantity of aggregate was available along the path of the £485m motorway and the Highways Agency estimates that 3 million tonnes of sand and gravel were used for special fills and aggregates, half of which were processed for aggregates for the CRCP.

concrete sub-base is cracked by a guillotine, seated with a roller and has a new layer of concrete or asphalt put on top. 'Crack and seat' saves millions of pounds in delays and material costs because it is a strategic use of the existing concrete pavement – a smooth road also improves the fuel efficiency of vehicles. The benefit of using concrete pavement solutions for new construction is that compared with asphalt alternatives, they require less maintenance. With rising bitumen prices, concrete pavement solutions are competitive on initial costs.

In the UK, unlike most countries in the world, the majority of motorway barriers are steel resulting in the unfortunate statistic of 200 cross-over accidents per year with 40 fatalities at a cost of £1m each. The steel barrier also requires expensive annual maintenance and a significant number of repairs per month that cost millions of pounds to the tax payer.

The introduction of the Concrete Step Barrier (CSB) provides a fit-for-purpose, resource-and-carbon efficient, resilient and adaptable road safety solution that impacts positively on the whole life cycle sustainability of the infrastructure assets that it serves (The British In-situ Paving Association, 2008).

Following the development and testing of the CSB and since 2005 the Highways Agency has mandated that the CSB is the road restraint system of choice for motorway central reserves (Figure 3.23).

The CSB delivers the following sustainability benefits:

- locally produced cast-in-situ concrete;
- minimum material usage and waste (slipformed formwork);
- fully recyclable at end of life and recycled aggregates can be used;
- virtually maintenance-free over its 50-year design life;
- reduces traffic congestion and associated emissions;
- enhances road user and worker safety (through avoidance of repairs).

Detailed design, installation, performance, cost and maintenance information pertaining to the CSB is available from the relevant website (The British In-situ Paving Association, 2012).

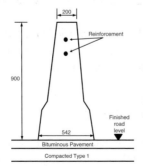

Figure 3.23   Concrete Step Barrier. Reproduced by permission of Britpave Barrier Systems Ltd.

Figure 3.24   Unsurpassed strength of concrete pipes demonstrated above. Reproduced by permission of Basal AS.

3.3.4 Pipes

With regard to pipeline systems, concrete provides substantial installed cost savings, faster installation and lower environmental impacts than other materials. Salient sustainability benefits delivered by concrete pipes include (BPCF, 2009):

- Reduced energy consumption and emissions in line with cement manufacturing. The use of lower carbon cements in the mix helps in reducing the overall carbon footprint of pipeline products by well over 30%.
- Resource efficiency in bedding. Concrete pipes can be installed using Bedding Class b, meaning that virgin aggregates are used to fill the lower part of the trench and the trench above can be filled with originally excavated material.
- Durability and service life of well over 100 years. In the USA, sections of a concrete sewerage pipe first installed in 1842 were exhumed, tested in 1982 and were found to be in good operational condition.

3.3.5 New modular precast concrete bridges

Concrete will be probably used somewhere in all bridges – in the foundations, abutments, piers, retaining walls and deck. For a bridge deck's main supporting members, there may be a choice between in-situ or precast concrete, structural steel beams or a combination of the two materials – known as

Table 3.7 Span ranges for various concrete bridges (TCC, 2008). Reproduced by permission of the Concrete Bridge Development Group.

CONSTRUCTION TYPE	DECK TYPE	SPAN RANGES (m)
IN SITU	RC solid slab	
	RC voided slab Prestressed voided slab (internal bonded)	
	Incremental launching	
	Span by span (Supported on launching truss)	
	Span by span (Supported on scaffolding)	
	Segmental balanced cantilever	
	Arches	
PRECAST	Inverted T beams cast into slab	
	M,U and Y beams with deck slab Segmental balanced cantilever (Erected by crane)	
	Segmental balanced cantilever (Erected by lifting gantry)	
	Cable stayed bridges by balanced cantilever	
		0 50 100 150 200 250 300 350 400

▬ Definite range   ▭ Possible range extension

composite construction. The ranges of spans that may be achieved using various types of concrete construction are shown in Table 3.7.

Concrete is the material of choice for the majority of short-span bridges (span< 15m). Precast concrete beams are appropriate for medium-span structures (15m < span < 50m) but their use has declined in the UK in recent years with composite construction controlling this portion of the market. It is considered that the new modular precast concrete bridge system has the potential to place concrete as the preferred option for medium-span bridges (Concrete Bridge Development Group, 2008).

The system benefits from relatively light, 2.5m long, precast concrete shell units that can be easily transported to site for assembly. Permanent prestressing cables are then placed and are covered by in-situ concrete to provide additional composite action as well as the required protection (Figure 3.25). The focus on precast concrete elements and off-site construction also ensures that a high-quality product is constructed within a safe environment. A further benefit is that the construction methodology can be varied to suit specific bridge sites and demands of the project programme. The flexibility of the system is such that it can enable the use of incremental launching, lifting using mobile cranes, lifting using transporters and erection using a temporary gantry. This allows the contractor scope to select the construction option that most suits the location and complexities of the project.

The modular system is suitable for a wide range of typical highway bridge layouts. Varying span lengths, carriageway widths, horizontal and vertical

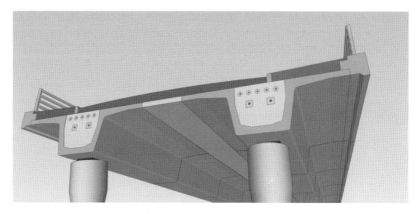

Figure 3.25   Modular precast concrete bridge. Reproduced by permission of the Concrete Bridge Development Group.

Table 3.8   Embodied energy during construction in GJ/m² for various bridge structural forms/materials.

Energy	Type	Steel	Concrete	Composite
Average	Viaduct	23.5	21.1/22.1	22.1
	Girder	39.3	30.6	37.0
	Arch	61.9	49.1	60.8
	Cable stay	50.6	43.9	47.7

curvatures, and skew can be readily accommodated by the match-cast shell units. The system provides an elegant solution with the benefit of being relatively maintenance-free.

Modular precast concrete bridges offer notable benefits over alternative solutions, namely safer (typically much less work at height and more factory-based work), higher quality (factory based and off-site construction), less maintenance (no exposed steel, joints or bearings) and more affordable.

A cost and programme comparative study for a three-span highway overbridge has shown that the modular precast system is more economical than the steel-composite solution by offering a saving between 8 and 10%. As expected the major cost savings are attributable to the reduced material costs for the superstructure. Substructure costs are only marginally higher for the concrete option. The modular system requires an initial capital investment of less than £250k (Concrete Bridge Design Group, 2008).

One metric for the sustainability credentials of concrete in bridge construction is the embodied carbon/energy. All projects are different, but indicative values are shown in Table 3.8 (Collings, 2006).

3.3.6   Sustainable urban drainage systems

Over two thirds of the 57,000 homes affected by the 2007 UK summer floods were flooded not by swollen rivers but by surface water runoff or overloaded drainage systems. The government's Foresight report estimated that 80,000 properties are at very high risk from surface water flooding causing, on average, £270 million of damage every year in the UK (Foresight, 2012). The continuing growth in urbanisation and ambitious government-driven housing programmes, combined with more extreme weather events linked to climate change, will only exacerbate the problem. Clearly, a sustainable approach to all surface drainage is needed to deal with existing overloaded systems and to accommodate future growth. It is now well recognised that Sustainable Urban Drainage Systems (SUDS) using Concrete Block Permeable Paving (CBPP) offers a solution (The Precast Concrete Paving and Kerb Association, 2008).

In conventional pavements, rainwater is allowed to run across the surface to gulleys that collect and direct it into pipes, removing it as quickly as possible. This means that water with the pollutants contained in it are rapidly conveyed into drains, streams and rivers, leading to floods in extreme conditions.

In contrast, CBPP addresses both flooding and pollution issues, unlike attenuation tanks which only deal with flooding. It also has a dual role, acting as the drainage system as well as supporting traffic loads. CBPP allows water to pass through the surface – between each block – and into the underlying permeable sub-base where it is stored and released slowly, either into the ground, to the next SUDS management stage or to a drainage system. Unlike conventional road constructions, the permeable sub-base aggregate is specifically designed to accommodate water. At the same time, many pollutants are substantially removed and treated within the CBPP itself, before water infiltrates to the subgrade (ground) or passes into the next stage of the management train.

One of the key criteria in selecting a CBPP system is the permeability of the existing subgrade (ground), which is established from tests on site. Other factors for consideration when choosing the most appropriate system for a site include ground water table level, pollution prevention, discharge consents and proximity to buildings.

There are three different CBPP systems, A, B and C (Figures 3.26, 3.27 and 3.28). There is no difference between the surface appearances of the different systems, but each has unique characteristics making it suitable for particular site conditions.

System A is suitable for existing subgrade (ground) with good permeability, as it allows all the water falling onto the pavement to infiltrate down through the constructed layers below and eventually into the subgrade (ground). Some retention of the water will occur temporarily in the permeable sub-base layer allowing for initial storage before it eventually passes through. No water is discharged into conventional drainage systems, completely eliminating the need for pipes and gulleys, and making it a particularly economic solution.

System B is used where the existing subgrade (ground) may not be capable of absorbing all the water. A fixed amount of water is allowed to infiltrate – which, in practice, often represents a large percentage of the rainfall. Outlet pipes are connected to the permeable sub-base and allow the excess water to be drained to other drainage devices, such as swales, ponds, watercourses or sewers. This

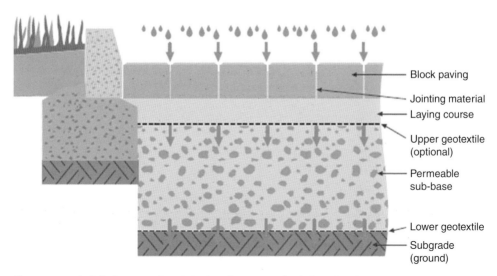

Figure 3.26   SUDS: Concrete Block Paving System A - full infiltration. Reproduced by permission of Interpave.

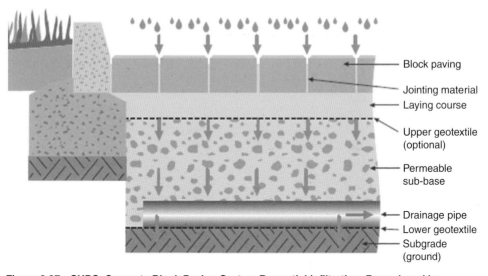

Figure 3.27   SUDS: Concrete Block Paving System B - partial infiltration. Reproduced by permission of Interpave.

is one way of achieving the requirement for reducing the volume and rate of runoff and will most likely remove the need for any long-term storage.

Where the existing subgrade (ground) permeability is poor or contains pollutants, System C allows for the complete capture of the water. It uses an impermeable, flexible membrane placed on top of the subgrade (ground) level and up the sides of the permeable sub-base to effectively form a storage tank. Outlet pipes are constructed through the impermeable membrane to transmit the water to other drainage devices, such as swales, ponds, watercourses

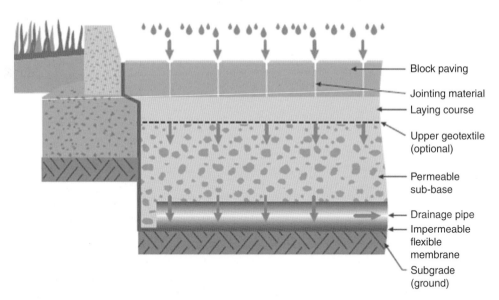

Figure 3.28   SUDS: Concrete Block Paving System C - no infiltration. Reproduced by permission of Interpave.

Figure 3.29   Example of System C (Hazeley School Milton Keynes, UK) – Clay subgrade; to protect rare newts all surface water is biologically treated before entering ponds. Reproduced by permission of Royal Haskoning.

or sewers. Importantly, the outlet pipes are designed to restrict flow so that water is temporarily stored within the pavement and discharge slowed. System C is particularly suitable for contaminated sites, as it prevents pollutants from being washed further down into the subgrade (ground) where they could reach groundwater (Figure 3.29).

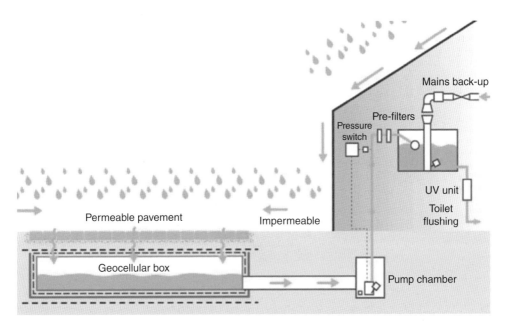

Figure 3.30   Rain water harvesting with CBPP. Reproduced by permission of Interpave.

Benefits of concrete block permeable paving

- providing a structural pavement while allowing rainwater to infiltrate into the pavement construction for temporary storage;
- contribution to removal of pollutants from water passing through;
- allowing treated water to infiltrate to the ground, be harvested for re-use or released to a water course, the next SUDS management stage or other drainage system;
- suitable for a wide variety of residential, commercial and industrial applications;
- optimising land use by combining two functions in one construction: structural paving combined with the storage and attenuation of surface water;
- handling rainwater from roof drainage and impervious pavements as well as the permeable paving itself (Figure 3.30).

3.3.7   Wind Energy Structures

Wind energy is one of the most commercially developed and rapidly growing renewable energy technologies worldwide. In the UK, the installation of onshore and offshore wind farms supports an industry that has been growing fast for the last eight years – from less than 1000MW in 2004 to 10 200MW in October 2013 (Renewable UK, 2013). The 2009 Renewable Energy Directive sets a target for the UK to achieve 15% of its energy consumption from renewable sources by 2020. The period to 2025 will see the implementation of a large programme of offshore and onshore wind farm developments nationwide, exploiting some of the best and most geographically diverse wind resources in Europe (TCC, 2005b).

One challenge to meet these renewable energy demands is purely physical. Towers must become taller, stronger and stiffer to accommodate both future site constraints and developments in turbine technology. Demands for increasingly higher power output, coupled with a decreasing number of prime sites with high wind availability and good access, means that there is a need to use higher towers to achieve optimal performance in less windy sites. The introduction of turbines with longer blades, together with the fact that wind speeds generally tend to increase with height, leads to increasingly taller wind towers.

Wind farm installations predominantly use 1.0 to 2.5MW turbines, which have 40m long blades and 60 to 70m tall towers. The new generation 4.5 to 5MW turbines have rotor lengths of up to 60m. Taller towers are needed to carry these more sophisticated turbine installations. The next generation of offshore wind farms will demand taller, stronger towers of up to and beyond 100m to support 8MW or 10MW turbines.

The wind industry's identified need for increased turbine sizes, rotor diameters and tower heights makes concrete a competitive option. Concrete can offer tall, strong, sophisticated wind farm structures for onshore or offshore deployment in aggressive marine or remote inland environments which require durable materials and details as a matter of course.

The benefits of using concrete solutions are summarised below:

- Low maintenance – concrete is an inherently durable material capable of maintaining its desired engineering properties under extreme conditions.
- Design and construction flexibility – concrete's versatility enables design solutions, with no restrictions on height or size, to meet any number of site and accessibility constraints.
- Material flexibility – concrete mix designs can be finely tuned to optimise key parameters such as strength, stiffness, density and environmental impact.
- Dynamic performance – concrete has inherently high damping properties and can deliver fatigue resistance solutions with less noise emissions.
- Whole life performance – concrete can deliver durable, large diameter pylons of unlimited height to providing higher levels of power generation.
- Environmental impact – concrete construction produces fully recyclable wind towers with significantly reduced levels of embodied energy and CO_2 in comparison to other methods.
- Upgradeable – concrete can provide long life wind tower solutions capable of accommodating multiple future-generation wind turbine retrofits.

Traditionally the foundations of onshore wind towers are concrete – typically 400–500m³ of concrete is used for each tower. For offshore wind towers in water up to 20m depth steel monopile foundations are normally used. Beyond this depth a steel monopile is too big and therefore a concrete

Case Study: Gravity base foundations for the Thornton Bank Offshore Wind Farm

A new design approach and offshore marine operation were developed for the construction of the foundations for the first phase of the Thornton Bank Offshore Wind Farm, located approximately 30km off the Belgian Coast. In contrast to the monopile foundations commonly applied to offshore wind farms, concrete gravity bases (CGB) were selected as the result of a risk assessment and technical evaluation (Figure 3.31).

Figure 3.31   Concrete Gravity Base solutions are being developed for water depths in excess of 20m to support turbines of 5MW and greater. These structures will be manufactured in serial production facilities, floated to site, and then sunk and ballasted. Reproduced by permission of Gravitas.

Innovative dredging technologies play a key role in the realisation of these foundations. Concrete caisson foundations for offshore wind turbines have traditionally been applied in near-shore wind farm projects, in relatively shallow and sheltered waters but licensed wind farm sites to be developed are in increasing water depths.

The Thornton Bank project used 5MW wind turbine generators (WTGs). This first offshore application at this exceptional scale represented a significant leap for the offshore wind industry and also required a different approach for the foundation structures. The water depths up to 28m, the harsh North Sea environment and complex soil conditions led to the monopile basic design requiring excessive diameters and wall thicknesses. The general increase in steel prices on world markets and the concerns raised with regard to the feasibility of pile driving gave advantage to the choice of the CGB.

The versatility of a CGB versus a monopile also resulted in less sensitivity of the design with regard to a particular type of WTG. The detailed design resulted in a slim concrete structure with a shape that can best be compared to an 'Erlenmeyer' or a champagne bottle.

The construction works offshore started with the dredging of foundation pits to create a foundation level that safely caters for the movements of the surrounding sand dunes. Afterwards, the installation of a two-layer gravel bed - a 50m diameter filter layer from the dredged level up to 0.55m below foundation level, followed by a 28.90m diameter gravel layer up to target foundation level - within very narrow vertical tolerances created the sub-foundation on which the CGB is installed. The latter installation and positioning works were performed by a twin shear leg crane heavy lift vessel, which loaded the CGB from the onshore construction yard for subsequent transport to the offshore site.

Following installation of the CGBs, the foundation pits were backfilled by means of a purpose-built backfill spreader barge fed by a trailing suction hopper dredger. The same multi-purpose barge is also fitted with dedicated installations for the ballast infill of the CGB and the installation of a two-layer scour protection system around the CGB.

The development of the offshore wind turbine support structure for the Thornton Bank Offshore Wind Farm demonstrates that the economic operating range of offshore wind farms can be significantly extended by innovative design and state of the art marine construction technologies, which build upon extensive experience gained in the dredging and marine construction industries (Peire et al., 2009).

gravity base is the preferred solution. These gravity foundations are based on well known techniques used in the offshore oil industry, and have been used in relatively shallow water. For deeper waters, the rate of innovation and development of these offshore gravity foundations during 2013 will continue in 2014 with prototypes designed for water depths of 30m to 50m (see Figure 3.31). These typically rely on self bouyancy to transport them from port side manufacturing facilities to their final location. For latest information see The Concrete Centre Wind Energy webpage.

3.3.8   *Environmental Assessment Schemes (CEEQUAL)*

CEEQUAL is an assessment and awards scheme for improving sustainability in civil engineering, landscaping and the public realm. Launched in 2003, more than 196 final and 75 interim awards have been achieved with a further 274 projects and contracts currently being assessed. CEEQUAL has assessed or is currently assessing civil engineering work costing over £23 billion (CEEQUAL, 2013).

CEEQUAL delivers improved project specification, design and construction to demonstrate the commitment of the civil engineering industry to environmental quality and social performance. CEEQUAL rewards project and contract teams in which clients, designers and constructors go beyond the legal and environmental minima to achieve distinctive environmental and social standards.

The questions in the scheme are arranged in 9 sections listed below. They have been weighted by CEEQUAL to reflect the contribution of the actions sought by each question to the overall performance of the project or contract. This has been done in two stages. The scheme sections have been weighted to reflect the contribution of performance in each section to overall performance, and the questions in each section have been weighted to reflect their relative importance within their section. These weightings are embedded in the scores awarded for each question.

The section weightings are based on consultation within the CEEQUAL Technical Advisory Group, assessors and verifiers, the Institution of Civil Engineers, and a range of other stakeholder groups and interested parties. Below are the sections of the latest version (V5) with example issues assessed:

1. Project Strategy: Sustainable development & pathway to sustainable living | Economic, social & environmental impact and benefits | Resource strategy | Construction management strategy
2. Project Management: Environmental management systems | Training |Environmental performance |Procurement
3. People and Communities: Effects on neighbours, users & the workforce| Relations with the local community & other stakeholders
4. Land use and Landscape: Contaminated land | Flood risk | Use of land & seabed | Landscape issues
5. Historic Environment: Baseline study of area | Planning guidance |Conservation & enhancement | Public information & access
6. Ecology and Biodiversity: Biodiversity conservation & enhancement | Habitat creation | Monitoring & maintenance
7. Water Environment (fresh & marine): Protection of ground & surface water | Marine environment | Enhancement
8. Physical Resources: Embodied impacts & life cycle analysis | Material choice & sourcing | Energy & carbon | Waste management & minimisation | Water resources | Recycling | Future de-construction
9. Transport: Operational transport | Construction transport | Minimising nuisance & disruption | Workforce travel.

3.4 Summary

The built environment – buildings and infrastructure – are fundamental for economic growth and social progress. In carrying out the conceptual design of building or infrastructure projects a balance must be found between the benefits to the environment and the potential impacts on the environment. This becomes a challenge especially when the concept of towns and cities is developed.

The most important part of the sustainable conceptual design of a building is the right brief, that is, ensuring that the right scope, purpose, size and location have been determined by the client. Strategic decisions at this earliest stage can arguably have the greatest influence on how sustainable the ultimate project is or is not.

Following the client brief, the design team can deliver a sustainable design by optimising the balance between minimising impacts and maximising the performance. The team moves from the whole (whole building design) to the parts (building components).

In whole building design the team considers design life and future flexibility, life time energy/CO_2, design for deconstruction, orientation and integrated design options that may contribute to a sustainable design. Examples of the latter include exposed soffits, cladding as load bearing structure, multifunctional internal walls and integration of structure with services.

In carrying out a sustainable design of building components the team looks at ways of reducing the environmental impact of substructures including foundations with optional basements and designs a robust and efficient stability system, a functional and economical frame/flooring, a durable and energy-efficient cladding and an appropriate roof. Due to the inherent properties of concrete and the versatility of how it can be used, concrete solutions are often the most sustainable.

In most developed countries there is an environmental assessment scheme that provides guidance to building designers. In the UK there is BREEAM that takes into account management, health and well-being, energy, transport, water, materials, waste, land use and ecology and pollution. Civil engineering projects are arguably even more reliant than building projects on the client's brief with respect to how sustainable they are. The decisions of where and what, and the ensuing operational impacts such as traffic volumes, distances travelled and efficiency (which are influenced by gradients) determine the scale of a projects environmental impacts. Nevertheless, within the imposed client constraints designers have choices that can be excercised to minimise impacts and maximise economic and social benefit.

The application of S/S using hydraulic binders such as cement provides a remediation treatment capable of dealing with contaminants in brownfield sites. S/S is a cost effective and sustainable alternative to 'dig and dump' as it avoids disposal of contaminated soils to landfill, drastically reduces the need to import fill and reduces vehicular movements to and from site.

Stabilisation of soil using Cement Bound Materials or Hydraulically Bound Materials can produce durable paving material that can be used for the foundation or base of road and airport pavements, parking and storage areas. Sustainability benefits of soil stabilisation include enhanced performance, lower cost, use of recycled materials or artificial materials and not primary aggregates, elimination of traffic between aggregate sources and site and reduction of traffic needed to dispose of site material.

In new road construction, Continuously Reinforced Concrete Pavement offers a substantial reduction in the overall section of the road, which therefore requires less virgin material to construct and in turn less excavation and reduced 'dig and dump' costs. The Concrete Step Barrier (CSB) provides a sustainable solution in motorways as it is produced locally with recycled aggregates and reinforcement; it is cost-effective and maintenance-free and enhances road user and worker safety.Concrete pipes are cost effective, fast to install, durable, reusable and unsurpassed in strength.

Modular precast concrete bridges offer notable benefits over alternative solutions, namely safer, faster, higher quality, less traffic disruption, less maintenance, more affordable, higher value and therefore more sustainable.

Concrete's inherent properties make it a natural choice for water projects such as Sustainable Urban Drainage Systems using Concrete Block Permeable Paving that provides a sustainable solution to flooding, removal of pollutants and water harvesting.

Durability is a key property of concrete that is mobilised to protect wind towers from onshore or offshore aggressive marine environments. Other sustainability credentials of concrete wind towers and foundations include low maintenance, material flexibility and dynamic performance.

CEEQUAL is an assessment and award scheme that rewards civil engineering project and contract teams in which clients, designers and constructors go beyond the legal and environmental minima to achieve distinctive environmental and social standards.

References

Arup (2010) *Embodied Carbon Study – Study of Commercial Office, Hospital and School Buildings*, Confidential report for The Concrete Centre, UK.

Arup (2007) *Report on Carbon Footprint of Monier Roof Tiles*, Ove Arup.

BCIS (2006) *Life Expectancy of Building Components*, Building Cost Information Service, UK.

BIS (2010) *Low Carbon Construction Innovation and Growth Team – Emerging Findings*, Department for Business, Innovation and Skills, Crown Copyright, UK.

BPCF (2009) *Concrete Drainage and Sewerage Products, Your Sustainable Option*, British Precast Concrete Federation (BPCF), UK.

BRE (2011) *BREEAM New Construction Technical Manual*, Building Research Establishment, UK.

British Cement Association (2004) *The Essential Guide to Stabilisation/Solidification for the Remediation of Brownfield Land Using Cement and Lime*, BCA, UK.

CEEQUAL (2013) Crane Environmental, UK http://www.ceequal.com/

Clark, D. (2013) *What colour is your building?*, RIBA, UK.

Collings, D. (2006) *An environmental comparison of bridge forms*, Proceedings of the Institution of Civil Engineers, Bridge Engineering, Volume 159, Issue BE4.

Communities and Local Government (2010) *Code for Sustainable Homes, Technical Guide.*

Concrete Bridge Development Group (2008) *Modular Precast Concrete Bridges, A State-of-the-Art Report*, Concrete Bridge Design Group, UK.

Driscoll, R., Scott, P. and Powell, J. (2008) *EC7 – implications for UK practice: Eurocode 7 Geotechnical design*, C641 CIRIA, UK.

EEF (2011) *Key Statistics*, UK Steel, UK.

Foresight (2012) *Mid-term Review, January 2011*, Foresight, Government Office for Science, UK.

Green Building Council Australia (2011) Greenstar Rating Overview, http://www.gbca.org.au/

Green Futures (2012) P11 No. 83, Forum for the Future, http://www.forumforthefuture.org/

Hacker, J., de Saulles, T., Holmes, M. and Minson, A. (2008) Embodied and operational carbon dioxide emissions from housing: A case study on the effects of thermal mass and climate change, *Energy and Buildings*, 40 (3), 375–84, Jan 2008.

ICE (2011) Building a Sustainable Future: ICE loa carbon infrastructure trajectory 2050, Institution of Civil Engineers (ICE), UK.

Kaethner, S. and Burridge, J. (2012) Embodied Carbon Comparison for Medium Rise Buildings, *The Structural Engineer*, due to be published, UK.

Kennedy, D. (2004) *Hydraulically-bound Mixtures for Pavements*, The Concrete Society for British Cement Association and The Concrete Centre, UK.

Laloui, L. and Di Donna, A. (2011) Understanding the Behaviour of Energy Geo-Structures, Proceedings of the Institution of Civil Engineers – *Civil Engineering* 164(4), 184–191, November 2011, UK.

MPA (2011) *Sustainable Development Report*, Mineral Products Association, UK.

Ni Riain, C., Fisher, J., MacKenzie, F. and Littler, J. (in progress) BRE's Environmental Building: Energy Performance in Use.

Peire, K., Nonneman, H. and Bosschem, E. (2009) Gravity Base Foundations for the Thornton Bank Offshore Wind Farm, *Terra et Aqua*, Number 115, June 2009.

Renewable UK (2013) UK Wind Energy Database (UKWED), www.renewableUK.com

Reynolds, T., Lowres, F. and Butcher, T. (2010) *Sustainability in Foundations: A Review*, Information Paper IP 11/10, IHS BRE Press, UK.

RIBA (2011) *Green Overlay to the RIBA Outline Plan of Work*, Royal Institute of British Architects, November 2011, UK.

SEDA (2005) *Design for Deconstruction*, SEDA Design Guides for Scotland, No. 1, Scottish Ecological Design Association, UK.

TBIC (2010) *Thermal Performance of Houses with Basements*, The Basement Information Centre, UK.

The British In-situ Concrete Paving Association (2008) *Sustainability Benefits of Concrete Step Barrier*, Britpave, UK.

The British In-situ Concrete Paving Association (2012) *Concrete Step Barrier*, Britpave, UK http://www.concretebarrier.org.uk/

TCC (2005a) *Civil Engineering: Sustainable Solutions Using Concrete*, The Concrete Centre (TCC), UK.

TCC (2005b) *Concrete Wind Towers, Concrete Solutions for Offshore and Onshore Wind Farms*, The Concrete Centre, UK.

TCC (2006) *Concrete Framed Buildings*, The Concrete Centre (TCC), UK.

TCC (2008) *Concrete Bridges The benefits of concrete in bridge design and construction*, The Concrete Centre (TCC), CBDG, UK.

TCC (2011) *How to Achieve Visual Concrete*, The Concrete Centre (TCC), UK.

TCC (2012) Concept Version 3, The Concrete Centre (TCC), UK http://www.concretecentre.com/online_services/design_tools/

The Precast Concrete Paving and Kerb Association (2008) *Understanding Permeable Paving, Guidance for Designers, Developers, Planners and Local Authorities*, Interpave, UK.

WRAP (2010) *Designing Out Waste: A design team guide for buildings*, Waste & Resources Action Programme, UK.

4 Material Specification

4.1 Introduction

The advent of sustainability has necessitated a better understanding of material specification and this extends to material constituents and their production. In this chapter the sustainability impacts and benefits of all constituents of concrete are discussed in sections 4.4 to 4.9. Production aspects of each are presented through these sections, as the overall concrete industry contribution to addressing the challenges of climate change, environmental protection, social progress and economic growth was presented in Chapter 2. To provide a common language for this topic, new terms and assessment methods have been developed and these are discussed in section 4.2. Responsible sourcing of materials is an increasingly important factor for specifiers and clients and this is covered in section 4.3. At the end of the chapter some special concretes (section 4.10) are explained, specification examples (section 4.11) are provided and key guidance to specify sustainable concrete is summarised (section 4.12).

4.2 Assessing environmental impacts of materials

Contrary to common perception, carbon dioxide emissions or 'carbon footprint' is not the only environmental impact when assessing the environmental impacts of a material. Furthermore, environmental impacts occur at many stages during the life cycle of a material and this makes the assessment process challenging. In this section the complete range of environmental impacts of materials are considered and current assessment methods are presented under the headings 'range of environmental impacts', 'life cycle of materials', 'life cycle

Sustainable Concrete Solutions, First Edition. Costas Georgopoulos and Andrew Minson.
© 2014 John Wiley & Sons, Ltd. Published 2014 by John Wiley & Sons, Ltd.

impact assessment' and 'international standards & concrete product category rules'. The section starts with the principles of 'project context and functional equivalence' which should be taken into account in assessment methods.

4.2.1   The project context and functional equivalence

The context of assessments should always be that materials are used in components, components in elements and these elements are brought together to deliver a project (Table 4.1).

The designer's ultimate purpose for assessing environmental impacts is to compare (and presumably minimise) impacts at the project level whilst meeting the client's brief (see Chapter 3). The summation of all the impacts of all the elements is not sufficient to achieve this. The interaction of the elements and project operational performance is also critical to obtain a true assessment. In the context of concrete construction the stand out example of this is the beneficial impact of thermal mass in reducing operational energy demands – comparison at the elemental level will overlook such an effect.

However, through the design process, different members of the design team in developing their options and solutions cannot, and indeed will not need to, wait for project level assessment. As long as they are cognisant of limitations of elemental, component or even material assessments, then these can still be sensibly done.

The key to this is being rigorous about comparing 'like with like'. When it comes to elements, a functional unit is defined by how it performs. In the case of a floor a functional unit has a prescribed load capacity, fire resistance, acoustic performance, service life, and so on. Thermal mass should also be included in the functional definition, but because of the interaction with ventilation, occupation and heating/cooling mechanisms, it may not be. Assessments of different floor options which meet the functional element specification can be compared by designers.

Table 4.1   Material, components, elements and a project.

Material (per tonne) Examples:	Component		Element (per m²) Examples:	Project
	Component Examples:	Associated components		
Aluminium	Façade framing	Glass panes, rubber seals, fixings etc	Façade	Through design and operation a project
Concrete	Floor Slab	Reinforcement, raised floor, carpet, suspended ceiling etc	Floor construction	is more than the sum of its elements
⋮	⋮	⋮	⋮	
⋮	⋮	⋮	⋮	
⋮		⋮	⋮	
Other materials		Other components	Other elements	

Sometimes functional equivalence in terms of the standards (BSI, 2009) may be satisfied but other details such as span, stiffness, service life and replacement rates need to be considered. For example, timber and precast concrete can both be used to produce cladding elements, and according to the standard these can be equivalent functional units, but they perform differently in terms of maintenance, durability and replacement rates. It could be argued that functional equivalence does not give the detail of 'like with like' comparison that may be expected or assumed.

The concept of 'like with like' also applies at the material level where it doesn't make sense to compare 1 tonne of each of steel, timber and concrete. This is most obviously because load carrying capacities are so different, but also because the impacts are different at the component, element and possibly project level (for example, fire resistance, acoustic etc.).

This difficulty is less significant but still remains when comparing different options for the same material. Different concrete specifications have different environmental impacts, but performance parameters can either be improved or reduced, and performance will influence environmental impacts in use.

In the remainder of this chapter, sections 4.4 to 4.10, the change in function as well as change in environment impacts will be highlighted for different constituents and specifications. But here, in the remainder of section 4.2, in the context of a project and functional equivalence, the other aspects of environmental impact assessment are presented.

4.2.2   Range of environmental impacts

As seen already in Chapter 2 there are many environmental challenges. The resources used and emissions released into the environment due to construction materials are many, but they can be classified into impact categories which might include:

Global warming
Petrochemical ozone creation (smog)
Acidification
Eutrophication
Ozone depletion
Human toxicity
Fresh water aquatic ecotoxicity
Terrestrial ecotoxicity
Petrochemical oxidation
Fossil fuel depletion
Solid waste
Radioactivity
Abiotic extraction (i.e. non living)
Water extraction

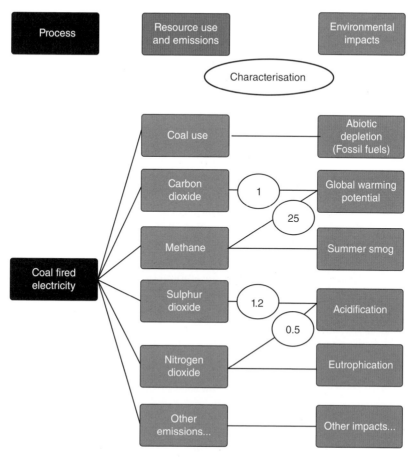

Figure 4.1   Classification of resource use and emissions into impact categories and characterisation. Reproduced by permission of Anderson and Thornback, 2012.

Classification into these impact categories is a useful step so that the sheer quantity of the resource and emission data, in the form of inventories, can be made manageable (see Figure 4.1). For example:

1. The extraction of different minerals and chemicals can be simplified as they will all contribute to the single abiotic impact category, as opposed to listing all the different minerals and chemicals separately. (The extraction, processing and use are also likely to have contributions to other categories, for example global warming and waste.)
2. A single emission such as nitrogen oxide contributes to both eutrophication and acidification impact categories.

Characterisation is the process of attributing a weighting to the different causes of an impact, in accordance with their relative impact per unit emitted (or per unit of resources used). For example methane and carbon dioxide both contribute to the climate change impact, but per unit weight methane has a weighting of 25 compared with the CO_2 weighting of one. One is typically attributed to CO_2 because it is the most common cause of global warming (Figure 4.1).

Classification and characterisation are important steps in life cycle assessment.

4.2.3 Life cycle of materials

The environmental impacts of construction materials occur at many stages (Figure 4.2).

Assessing the different impacts across all these different stages is not a straight-forward process. There are different entities responsible across the life cycle.

Whilst there are different entities involved up to the factory gate, a product supplier can (perhaps with some difficulty) have traceability and full environmental data from all their suppliers, through procurement policies and their implementation. From that point it can get more difficult. Different construction methods on site may cause different impacts (see worked example in Appendix D). For example, the amount of waste generated, not only has the direct impact of waste but if there is 10% waste then there was demand for 10% more product, and hence 10% more impact from that. Further through the life cycle the unknowns are greater. How the client treats and manages the assets will affect the operational life, maintenance and refurbishment. The

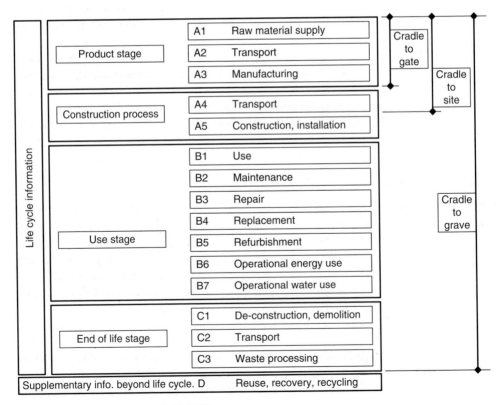

Figure 4.2   Life cycle stages (BSI, 2012).

treatment of the building at end of life is often down to another entity again, and they may or may not procure re-use and recycling.

It is for these reasons that life cycle assessments of construction products are often cradle to gate (the stages that the material/product producer can control). The project designer/client/assessor can then apply the best assumptions or knowledge (e.g. location of project compared to product manufacture to give transport impacts) that they have on their project to estimate impacts through later life cycle stages.

However, there is a desire for Life Cycle Assessment (LCA) data across all life cycle stages because cradle to gate alone is limited, may overlook significant impacts and doing the remaining stages for each project is time consuming and costly.

A middle ground is product or element life cycle assessments from cradle to grave, but how the products impact on the overall project is excluded from these life cycle assessments. An example of this is the Green Guide to Specification in the UK (BRE, 2009) which takes into account a study period of 60 years for elements. The study period is accounted for by using repair and/or replacement assumptions and end of life assumptions to summate impacts for the product or element over 60 years. Functional equivalence of elements is used to ensure comparability (section 4.2.1) between the products or elements. However, it must be recognised that such an LCA is limited because projects are more than a sum of their parts. For example air tightness and thermal mass benefits should be accounted for in cradle to grave assessment of a project. These and other project level aspects will be overlooked even if a product LCA is cradle to grave.

Particularly for the later stages of a product life cycle (from factory gate to grave), because of the unknowns and variations it is important there are rules about what assumptions are made and how calculations are done. This ensures that the impacts claimed by one manufacturer are comparable with that of another. For a product these rules are called product category rules and between different types of products the assumptions are set down in standards (section 4.2.5).

4.2.4   Life cycle impact assessment

Taking into account functional equivalence and like for like comparisons (section 4.2.1), and the process of assessing environmental impacts (section 4.2.2) across different life stages (section 4.2.3) is called Life Cycle Impact Assessment (LCIA).

The scope of an LCIA defines the product (material, component, element, building or process) to be assessed, the impacts of interest and the life cycle stages being assessed. It also gives details of the precise methodology, assumptions and boundary conditions of the assessment.

The required data for the assessment is:

- Quantities of inputs (materials, energy) and outputs (products, by-products, waste) from the system that defines the subject of the assessment
- Inventory of resource use and emissions associated with each of the inputs to the system.

Inventories of resource use and emissions for many products and energy sources are available, for example, the European Commission's Life Cycle Database (EU, 2012) or recognised commercial LCA databases. These can be used, together with quantities of inputs and waste outputs to compile an inventory of resource use and emissions for the subject being assessed.

Appropriate cut-off criteria need to be decided, below which insignificant contributions can be ignored. At European level it has been decided that the cut-off criteria shall be 1% of primary energy usage and 1% of the total mass input. Furthermore the items excluded cannot, when summated, represent more than 5% of energy usage or 5% of total mass input for any life cycle stage (see Figure 4.2) (BSI, 2012).

Allocation: If co-products are also produced the issue of allocation must be addressed. If the system outputs multiple products, how should the resource use and emissions be allocated between them? By value of products or by mass or other means? This has recently been codified:

Allocation shall be based on physical properties (e.g. mass, volume) when the difference in revenue from the co-products is low. In all other cases allocation shall be based on economic values.

Contributions to the overall revenue of the order of 1% or less is regarded as very low [and may be neglected] (BSI, 2012).

For concrete, an example of allocation pertains to GGBS – a co-product from iron production. In this case there is a strong argument that the only purpose of the process is iron production and that, whether a good use for GGBS could be found or not, the iron production process would still be continued. It can be argued that it is irrelevant if GGBS for environmental reasons has become a valuable product. It would be perverse if because of this environmental driver, GGBS was then allocated some of the burden (in the form of resource use and emissions) of the iron production process. Currently, this is generally recognised and the only resource use and emissions attributed to GGBS are those relating to the processes following its removal from the iron production furnace. An example of this view is:

There is already an agreement between the steel and cement industries regarding the allocation of impact to slag [GGBS] in Japan – in this instance no impact from steel production is transferred to the slag based on this agreement. Within Japan therefore, GGBS will have no impact from the steel production process, irrespective of its waste status or value (Product Category Rules for EPD of concrete, 2013).

System Expansion is a term describing the widening of the boundaries of an impact assessment to include more processes. The system for assessing the impact of aggregates may include all aggregates used in concrete (natural, recycled and secondary) or be expanded to include all aggregates irrespective of end use (fill, ballast, road base etc.). In the context of this book the former option was perhaps assumed at the start of the sentence. This serves as a reminder of the importance of clarity. The latter option is an example of system expansion. It is important because for the bigger system there is a far higher recycled/secondary aggregate percentage and, if the assessment is cradle to gate and ignores transport, the aggregates for this bigger system will have lower environmental impacts.

Abiotic Resource Depletion (ARD) or Total Mass Requirement (TMR): In the UK the Green Guide to Specification (BRE, 2009) is an element level impact assessment method through which ratings are determined. These ratings are an input into project level assessments for housing, The Code for Sustainable Homes (England and Wales) and buildings, BREEAM. The Green Guide to Specification gives a large reward for the use of recycled aggregates because the methodology doesn't acknowledge that aggregates are plentiful in the UK and available recycled aggregate stocks are being used in other non-concrete applications. It is based on the principle that extraction of a certain tonnage of material has the same impact whether it is abundant or scarce (BRE, 2007). This principle is called Total Mass requirement (TMR). This is now out of step with the latest thinking in European and international standards which provide common approaches to quantifying material environmental credentials. These approaches recognise that it is not the total mass but the ratio of depletion and reserves that is the important measure. This principal is called Abiotic Resource Depletion (ARD). In the European standard ARD is subdivided into fossil fuels (fossil resources) and elements (non fossil resources). The former is reported in Mega Joules (MJ) of net calorific value. The latter is reported in kg of antimony equivalent (BSI, 2012). To achieve this, the depletion of any element is converted to the equivalent depletion of the element antimony.

4.2.5 *International standards and concrete product category rules*

There are international standards, in particular, *ISO 14040, LCA – Principles and procedures* and *ISO 14044, LCA – Requirements and guidelines,* as well as the European standard *EN 15804, Sustainability of construction works — Environmental product declarations,* to provide a consistent framework and a set of rules for life cycle assessment. Within these there is still some scope for interpretation. To ensure that assessments can be compared with one another, there are also product category rules.

The issues discussed in section 4.2.4, and many more, are covered by these standards and product category rules. For further reading the WBCSD product category rules for concrete are useful because they provide reference to other standards and have guidance notes throughout.

Environmental Product Declarations, normalising and weighting

The output from a life cycle assessment can be communicated by an Environmental Product Declaration (EPD) which is defined by ISO 14025:2006. An EPD is a voluntary document that provides data in a predefined format, including information about the environmental impacts associated with the manufacturing of a product or system.

An EPD can be very detailed (Table 4.2) covering three stages (Figure 4.3). There is a demand amongst some, to communicate this more simply by weighting the different impacts and aggregating them into a single score or rating. The BRE Green Guide to Specification (BRE, 2009) is an example of this: each

Table 4.2   An example of a generic EPD based on CEN standard prEN 15804.

This information should only be used when comparing equivalent functional units over the full life cycle at the building level.	
Name and address of manufacturer(s)	Sustainable Concrete Forum Gillingham House, 38–44 Gillingham Street, London SW1V 1HU.
Declared unit ('The declared unit is used instead of the functional unit when the precise function of the product or scenarios at the building level is not stated or is unknown' (BSI, 2012).	1 tonne (m^3 assumed to be 2.38 tonnes)
Product Name and description	UK Generic Concrete without reinforcement.
Name of organisation that conducted the EPD	Data compiled from BRE Eco Profile 2007 (GEN 1 CEM1 No recycled aggregates) and average ready mix concrete data based on SCF 2009 annual reporting
Issue date & 5yr validity period	2009–2014
Scope of the EPD	Cradle to Grave
Product specific or generic EPD	Generic EPD
Content of substances of very high concern	None
Contact details	The Concrete Centre Gillingham House, 38–44 Gillingham Street, London SW1V 1HU.
Details of verification	This is an example of the data requirements for a generic EPD. The EPD is not verified and not all of the data in this EPD has been fully verified.
Reference Service Life (scenario based)	Not Applicable
LCA based indicators	
Global Warming Potential	100kg CO_2 eq. (100yr)

Table 4.2   (Cont'd).

This information should only be used when comparing equivalent functional units over the full life cycle at the building level.	
Depletion potential of stratospheric ozone layer	0.000046kg CFC11 eq.
Acidification Potential	0.45kg SO_2 eq.
Eutrophication Potential	0.06kg PO_4 eq.
Formation of troposheric ozone photochemical oxidants.	0.041kg ethane eq.
Abiotic Resource potential non fossil fuels	**No data available** – All LCA data on concrete currently available is based on the TMR impact assessment.
Abiotic Resource potential – fossil resources	393.55MJ
Resource Input Indicators	
Renewable primary energy, excluding renewable primary energy resources used as raw materials	0MJ
Renewable primary energy resources used as raw materials	Not determined
Total renewable primary energy resources (primary energy and primary energy resources used as raw materials)	0MJ
Non renewable primary energy excluding non renewable primary energy resources used as raw materials.	393.55MJ
Use of non renewable primary energy resources used as raw materials	0MJ
Total non renewable primary energy resources (primary energy and primary energy resources used as raw materials)	393.55MJ
Input of secondary materials	71.7kg
Input of renewable secondary fuels	0MJ
Input of non renewable secondary fuels	96.16MJ
Input of net fresh water	$0.075m^3$ – mains water
Responsible Sourcing – Certified to BES6001	Yes (check greenbooklive.com to confirm for specific manufacturer)
Waste Indicators	
Hazardous waste to disposal	None
Non hazardous waste to disposal	None
Radioactive waste to final disposal	None
Output Indicators	
Components for re-use	1000kg
Material recycling	800kg (WRAP)
Material for energy recovery	0kg
Exported energy	0kg
Third Party Verification of the declaration according to ISO 14025.	This EPD has not been verified either internally or externally
Third Party Verifier	Not Applicable

(Continued)

Table 4.2   (Cont'd).

Reference Service Life	
Reference Service Life	Minimum 100 years based on conformity of product specification and use to BS 8500-1/EN 206–1.
Quality of manufacture and installation	The product should be supplied by an organization operating to BS EN 45011 and meeting the requirements of BS EN ISO 9001, accredited by UKAS or equivalent accreditation body.
Maintenance	Minimum maintenance is expected providing the specification and environmental conditions conform to BS 8500-1/EN 206–1.

Additional Information	
Indoor air	Concrete is essentially an inert product when set and will not contribute to any air quality issues when used within buildings.
Soil and water impact	In hardened concrete the levels of leaching have been demonstrated to be very low and are not expected to present a risk to soil or water contamination.

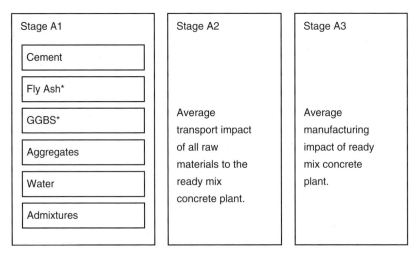

Figure 4.3   Diagram for stages (refer Figure 4.2) included in the EPD data in Table 4.2.

element (functional unit) is attributed a letter rating at the end of a process that includes 13 impact categories. The advantage is simplicity – just one letter. The disadvantage is that the weightings are subjective and are the same for all projects and all locations despite the fact that the significance of environmental impacts is often a function of location. The detailed useful data is hidden behind the single rating. Whilst communicating a single letter rating is convenient and simple, it arguably oversimplifies necessarily complex information.

4.3   Responsible sourcing of materials

Responsible sourcing is an increasingly important factor for specifiers and clients in the construction industry. The concept first emerged in fair trade of food products and fair employment conditions for manufacture of consumer goods. For example, the International Labour Organisation (ILO) was established to be responsible for drawing up and overseeing international labour standards. Responsible sourcing adds to this by including other environmental, social and economic aspects of sustainability. The UK government leads in this aspect of sustainability and in its published strategy for sustainable construction (BERR, 2008) established a target that 25% of products used in construction projects should be sourced from schemes recognised for responsible sourcing by 2012.

The development of the BRE responsible sourcing standard, BES 6001 (BRE, 2008) provides a benchmark to compare responsible sourcing performance for all construction products on an equal basis and provides a single criterion for responsible sourcing performance within assessment schemes such as BREEAM, CEEQUAL and Code for Sustainable Homes (England and Wales).

BES 6001 was launched in 2008 to integrate all of the activities associated with responsible sourcing, from the point at which a material is mined or harvested in its raw state through manufacture and processing; together with a delivery mechanism using certified management systems.

The responsible sourcing standard encompasses social, economic and environmental dimensions and addresses aspects such as stakeholder engagement, labour practices and the management of supply chains upstream of the manufacturer (Figure 4.4).

The UK concrete industry is supporting the BES 6001 responsible sourcing standard as it is the most comprehensive standard available and measures the whole infrastructure of the supply chain.

To gain accreditation to BES 6001 for a product, the organisation must have as a minimum:

- A responsible sourcing policy and comply with all relevant legislation.
- A quality management system that must follow the principles of ISO 9001.
- Have a greenhouse gas reduction policy and measures that comply with ISO 16064–1.
- Have policies that cover the efficient use of resources.
- Demonstrate that at least 60% of its constituent raw materials are fully traceable through its quality management system. This increases to 90% in order to achieve the highest performance in this area.
- Demonstrate that the supply chain has documented environmental management systems that comply with ISO 14001.
- Demonstrate that the supply chain has a documented health and safety system that is compliant with local legislation and record incidents.

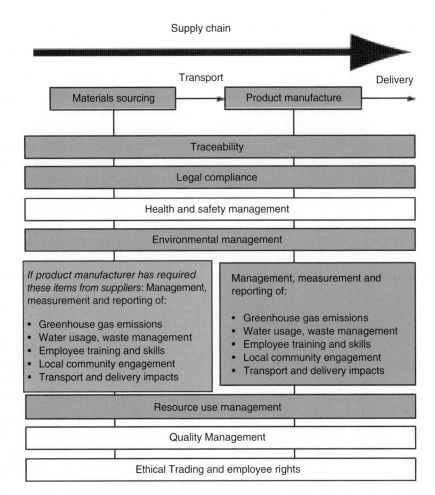

Figure 4.4 **The activities of the supply chain covered by the responsible sourcing standard BES 6001 (BRE, 2008). © Crown Copyright, reproduced under the terms of the Open Government Licence (http://www.nationalarchives.gov.uk/doc/open-government-licence/).**

The British Standards Institution has also published a framework standard for responsible sourcing, BS 8902:2009 (BSI, 2009a), which supports the development of sector based schemes. While it provides a similar scope to BES 6001, it does not contain specific performance requirements. Work has commenced on developing European standards for responsible sourcing.

Specification of responsibly sourced concrete

The concrete industry was the first in construction to issue a guidance document (MPA, 2008) supporting compliance with BES 6001, resulting in the widespread accreditation of concrete products in the UK. This is, in part, because the concrete industry is able to demonstrate the highest level of responsible sourcing, based on the local availability of materials, short supply chains and regulated management systems. The industry's high standards, achieved in areas such as employment rights, waste management and environmental management are also reflected.

The requirements of BES 6001 are consistent with commitments to the UK concrete industry's sustainable construction strategy. The strategy (launched in 2008) sets the vision that, by 2012, the UK concrete industry will be recognised as the leader in sustainable construction; taking a dynamic role in delivering a sustainable built environment in a manner that is profitable, socially responsible and functions within environmental limits. As a key part of the strategy, the concrete industry publishes annual sustainability reports – its sixth being published in October 2013 (TCC, 2013). This annual report is a vehicle for demonstrating active sustainable management across concrete manufacture and its supply chain.

Many concrete and reinforcement products have achieved accreditation to BES 6001, and the specification of accredited product enables designers to easily source certified materials and help gain maximum credits in sustainability assessment.

Case Study: White River Place, St Austell, UK 'Excellent' BREEAM rating.

This £75 million scheme, which involved the renovation of a brownfield site into a stimulating town centre for St Austell, features a mix of uses including retail, catering, cinema and a 550 space car park.

The cement addition, GGBS, was used to reduce the ECO_2 of the concrete. Local materials, including bricks from neighbouring Devon and concrete blocks sourced from St Austell were used. Slightly damaged blocks were used for areas of the building where finishes allowed, saving some 60 skips worth of construction waste.

Responsible sourcing was also important – sub-contractors and suppliers were required to provide the environmental credentials of materials used.

4.4   Cements and combinations

Cements are single powders supplied to concrete producers which are Portland cement or Portland cement blended with a cementitious addition, that is, a finely divided inorganic material used in concrete in order to improve certain properties or to achieve special properties (BSI, 2001a). There are two types of additions Type I: nearly inert additions and Type II: pozzolanic or latent hydraulic additions. Combinations are formed where concrete producers mix Portland cement with a cementitious addition in a concrete mixer.

Cements and combinations are often referred to as the cementitious component of concrete and they represent the majority of the ECO_2 of concrete. ECO_2 is the carbon emissions associated with the production and manufacture of a product (cradle to gate).

4.4.1 Portland cement

Portland cement is primarily produced from limestone or chalk (calcareous materials) with clay or shale that provide alumina and silica. These are abundant materials and available in most countries. The materials are ground, mixed and heated in a rotary kiln at approximately 1400 °C – a process that forms clinker (small balls of material). The clinker is ground to a fine powder and some gypsum added to form Portland cement.

The cement industry, through the implementation of a range of measures – including using dry plants, waste-derived fuels and incorporating cementitious additions – has made significant progress in reducing the ECO_2 of cement.

The grinding and mixing process prior to heating can be done with or without water. The old wet plant process requires significantly more heat to reach the necessary 1400 °C. Investment in new dry plants has delivered significant energy efficiencies and lower ECO_2. See also section 2.6.3 under Climate Change Levy.

The use of alternative fuels not only diverts waste from landfill and saves on the need for fossil fuels, but can reduce the need for raw materials; for example, the use of waste tyres provides a fuel and minimises the need to add iron-oxide to cement due to wire content. Waste-derived fuels used by the cement industry include solvents, meat and bone meal, sewage sludge, paper and plastics. Overall, 38.1% of the UK cement industry's fuel requirement in 2010 was met by alternative fuels (MPA Cement, 2011).

In the reminder of section 4.4, cementitious additions are described and their effect on performance and ECO_2 explained. But at this stage it is to be noted that ECO_2 of concrete should not be considered or specified in isolation of other sustainability factors such as strength gain (see section 4.4.5).

4.4.2 Cementitious additions

A number of by-products from other industries can be blended with Portland cement (CEM I) to improve performance, increase the recycled content and reduce the ECO_2 content of the concrete. The use of these secondary materials utilises material which might otherwise be disposed in landfill.

There is a long track record of using the following cementitious additions with CEM I. The UK average across all concretes is approximately 30% with the permitted percentage use of each given in Table 4.3 (TCC, 2013).

Ground granulated blastfurnace slag (GGBS)

GGBS is a by-product from the manufacture of iron. Molten slag is tapped off from the blast furnace during the production of molten iron. If it is cooled rapidly, the granulated material has latent hydraulic properties; that is, when water is added, it reacts very slowly but when placed in the alkaline environment created by CEM I, the reactions are accelerated. The most commonly used proportion of GGBS in UK-produced combinations is 50% by mass of total cementitious content. In addition to reducing cement

Table 4.3   Cement and combination types from British Standard for Concrete (BSI, 2006).

Broad designation a,b	Composition	Cement/combination types (BS 8500)
CEM I	Portland cement	CEM I
SRPC*	Sulfate-resisting Portland cement	SRPC
IIA	Portland cement with 6–20% fly ash, ground granulated blastfurnace slag, limestone, or 6–10% silica fume[c]	CEM II/A-L, CEM II/A-LL, CIIA-L, CIIA-LL,CEM II/A-S, CIIA-S, CEM II/A-V, CIIA-V, CEM II/A–D
IIB-S	Portland cement with 21–35% ground granulated blastfurnace slag	CEM II/B-S, CIIBS
IIB-V	Portland cement with 21–35% fly ash	CEM II/B-V, CIIBV
IIB+SR	Portland cement with 25–35% fly ash	CEM II/B-V+SR, CIIB-V+SR
IIIA[d,e]	Portland cement with 36–65% ground granulated blastfurnace slag	CEM III/A, CIIIA
IIIA+SR[e]	Portland cement with 36–65% ground granulated blastfurnace slag with additional requirements that enhance sulfate resistance	CEM III/A+SR[f], CIII/A+SR[f], CIIIA+SR
IIIB[e,g]	Portland cement with 66–80% ground granulated blastfurnace slag	CEM III/B, CIIIB
IIIB+SR[e]	Portland cement with 66–80% ground granulated blastfurnace slag with additional requirements that enhance sulfate resistance	CEM III/B+SR[f], CIIIB+SR[f]
IVB-V	Portland cement with 36–55% fly ash	CEM IV/B(V), CIVB

Key:
a) There are a number of cements and combinations not listed in this table that may be specified for certain specialist applications. See BRE Special Digest 1 for the sulphate-resisting characteristics of other cements and combinations.
b) The use of these broad designations is sufficient for most applications. Where a more limited range of cement or combinations types is required, select from the notations given in BS 8500–2: 2006, Table 1.
c) When IIA or IIA–D is specified, CEM I and silica fume may be combined in the concrete mixer using the k-value concept; see BS EN 206–1: 2000, Cl. 5.2.5.2.3.
d) Where IIIA is specified, IIIA+SR may be used.
e) Inclusive of low early strength option (see BS EN 197–4 and the 'L' classes in BS 8500–2: 2006, Table A.1).
f) '+SR' indicates additional restrictions related to sulphate resistance. See BS 8500–2: 2006, Table 1, footnote D.
g) Where IIIB is specified, IIIB+SR may be used.

* SRPC is no longer manufactured in the UK.

environmental impact benefits of GGBS include better workability, making placing and compaction easier; lower early-age temperature rise, reducing the risk of thermal cracking in large pours; high resistance to chloride ingress, reducing the risk of reinforcement corrosion and, high resistance to attack by sulphate and other chemicals.

Fly ash

The majority of fly ash used in the UK is a by-product from the burning of pulverised coal to generate electricity at power stations. When coal is burnt, the resulting fine ash is captured and classified. It has pozzolanic properties and therefore does not react when water is added but in the alkaline environment created by CEM I, the pozzolanic reactions are initiated. The most commonly used proportion of fly ash in UK-produced combinations is 30% by mass of total cementitious content. In addition to reducing cement environmental impact, benefits of fly ash include improved workability, pumpability and finishing; lower heat of hydration and drying shrinkage; improved long-term strength and durability; decreased permeability; improved resistance to Alkali Silica Reactivity and sulphate attack; low chloride ingress and good carbonation protection.

Silica fume

Silica fume is a by-product from the manufacture of silicon. It is an extremely fine powder (as fine as smoke) and therefore it is used in concrete production in either a densified or slurry form. Due to economic considerations, the use of silica fume is generally limited to high strength concretes or concretes in aggressive environmental conditions. The most commonly used proportion of silica fume in UK is 10% by mass of total cementitious content. In addition to reducing cement environmental impact, benefits of silica fume include reduced permeability, improved mechanical performance and improved sulphate resistance.

Limestone fines

Limestone fines are used as a constituent of cement to produce Portland limestone cement where the proportion is typically 15% by mass of the cement. BS 7979 (BSI, 2001b) provides additional information on the specification of limestone fines for use with Portland cement. The most commonly used proportions of limestone fines in UK-produced combinations is 6–10% by mass of total cementitious content.

Cement mainly consists of 60–67% Lime (CaO), 17–25% Silica (SiO_2) and 3–8% Alumina (Al_2O_3). The ternary diagram in Figure 4.5 shows the relative position of CEM I, GGBS, fly ash and silica fume in terms of lime, silica and alumina.

4.4.3   Designation of cements

For the UK, Table A.6 in BS 8500–1: 2006 (BSI, 2006) provides details of the cement and combination types recommended for UK structures. For most applications and construction scenarios, BS 8500 allows considerable specification flexibility in terms of cement or combination type used. However BS 8500 does not provide specific guidance on the relative merits of cements/combinations in terms of their associated performance and environmental impacts, apart from exposure classes.

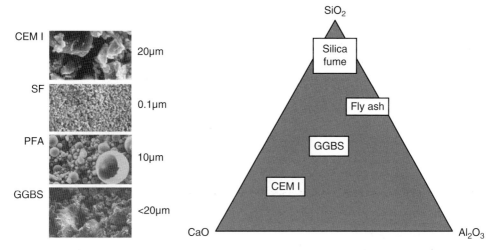

Figure 4.5   CEM I, GGBS, Fly ash (PFA) and Silica fume (SF) vs. lime (CaO), silica (SiO_2) and alumina (Al_2O_3).

The designation CEM refers to materials produced at a cement factory as a single powder (e.g., CEM III/A, a composite of GGBS and CEM I). Combinations (designated 'C') are recognised to have equivalent performance to factory-made composite cements.

Fly ash and GGBS are widely available in the UK, and transport distances from the point of production to the point of use are similar to that for Portland cement. At ready-mixed concrete plants, producers typically stock Portland cement and either GGBS or fly ash. Limestone fines and silica fume may be available in some ready-mixed concrete plants, or be made available given sufficient notice but may not be available at all locations.

When possible and appropriate, prepare specifications that allow flexibility and choice to enable the most appropriate and economic additions to be used.

4.4.4   Values of embodied CO_2 equivalent (ECO_2e)

In this sub-section values are able to be presented for all greenhouse gas emissions combined as ECO_2e rather than carbon dioxide emissions alone (i.e ECO_2). Non-CO_2 greenhouse gas emissions for concrete are negligible, and many calculations ignore them so ECO_2 is used elsewhere in the chapter. Indicative ECO_2e values for the main cementitious constituents of reinforced concrete are provided in Table 4.4. These figures are derived using data for the calendar year 2010 and represent 'cradle-to-factory-gate' values as they do not consider transport from place of manufacture to concrete plants. The figures also do not allow for carbonation, which on average in the UK equates to a re-absorption of 19% of ECO_2e of Portland cement (section 2.3.2.1).

Corresponding ECO_2e values for factory-made composite cements and combination types are presented in Table 4.5. The ranges presented are clearly

Table 4.4   Embodied CO_2e for main constituents of reinforced concrete. (MPA, 2013)

Material	Embodied CO_2e (kg/tonne)
Portland cement, CEM I	913
Ground granulated blastfurnace slag (GGBS)	67
Fly Ash	4
Limestone	75
Aggregate	4
Reinforcement (*figure is for ECO_2)	430*

Table 4.5   Embodied CO_2e of factory-made cements and combinations (developed from (MPA, 2013)). © British Standards Institution (BSI – www.bsigroup.com). Extract reproduced by permission of BS 8500–1:2006+A1:2012 Concrete. Complementary British Standard to BS EN 206–1. Method of specifying and guidance for the specifier.

Cement[a] (Factory made cement)	Combination[b] (CEM I and addition combined at concrete plant)	Secondary Main Constituent (SMC) or Addition (Low – High Content %)	Embodied CO_2e (SMC content Low – High, kg CO_2e/tonne)
CEM – Portland Cement			913
CEM II/A-LL or L	CIIA-LL OR L	6–20 Limestone	859–745
CEMII/A-V	CIIA-V	6–20 Fly ash	858–746
CEM II/B-V	CIIB-V	21–35 Fly ash	722–615
CEM II/B-S	CIB-S	21–35 GGBS	735–639
CEM III/A	CIIIA	36–65 GGBS	622–363
CEM III/B	CIIIB	66–80 GGBS	381–236
CEM IV/B-V	CIVB-V	36–55 Fly ash	598–413

Notes
a) For CEM I 1% minor additional constituent (MAC) and 5% gypsum is assumed. For CEM II, CEM III and CEM IV at the highest proportion of the SMC it is assumed that no MAC is incorporated and at the lowest proportion of SMC it is assumed that MAC is added at 1% with the appropriate proportions of limestone, fly ash and GGBS.
b) For combinations the ECO_2e figure for CEM I is used together with the figures for limestone, fly ash and GGBS in the appropriate proportions.
c) ECO_2e figures for CEM II, CEM III and CEM IV and their equivalent combinations are based on the range of SMC proportion, where the range is from the minimum to maximum proportion of SMC or addition. ECO_2e can be interpolated for proportions of SMC or addition between the minimum and maximum, noting that the minimum ECO_2e is associated with the highest proportion of SMC or addition. (see Figure 4.6).

a function of both the ECO_2e value of the individual materials and their permitted levels of use. The values range from 913kg per tonne (CEM I) to as low as 236kg per tonne (CEM III/B; 80% GGBS content).

The use of cement additions does affect the total amount of cementitious binder (section 4.4.6); yet any increases are typically small. Figure 4.6 shows qualitatively the effect on the embodied carbon of equivalent concrete mixes of using different cements. ECO_2e reductions for a range of typical concrete designation types are shown in Table 4.6.

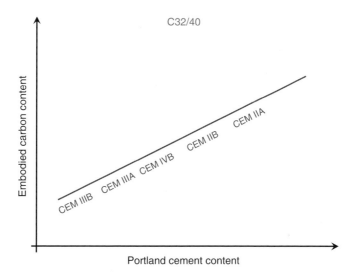

Figure 4.6   Indicative graph of embodied carbon content of concretes comprising different cements.

Table 4.6   Effect of cement type on ECO$_2$e content of designated concretes.

Concrete	Concrete Type	CEM I concrete (kg CO$_2$e/m^3)	30% fly ash concrete (kg CO$_2$e/m^3)	50% GGBS concrete (kg CO$_2$e/m^3)
Blinding mass fill, strip footing, mass foundations	GEN1 70mm	177	128	101
Reinforced foundations	RC25/30 70mm**	316	263	197
Ground floors	RC28/35 70mm*	316	261	186
Structural: in-situ, superstructure, walls, basements	RC40 70mm**	369	313	231
High strength concrete	RC50 70mm**	432	351	269

*includes 30kg/m^3 steel reinforcement.
**includes 100kg/m^3 steel reinforcement.
A worked example on ECO$_2$ for a building slab is in Appendix D.

4.4.5   Strength development

For a given value of 28-day strength, concrete containing additions such as fly ash and GGBS will exhibit lower relative early age strengths than those containing Portland cement only. This is because concrete's early strength is dependent, primarily, on its Portland cement content. The corollary of this is that following 28 days, concretes containing additions will have relatively

Table 4.7 Strength gain of concretes with different cement types.

Concrete	Strength* at 7 days	Strength* gain from 28 to 90 days
CEMI concrete	80%	5–10%
30% fly ash concrete 50% GGBS concrete	50–60%	10–20%
50% fly ash concrete 70% GGBS concrete	40–50%	15–30%

*strength as a percentage of 28 day strength.

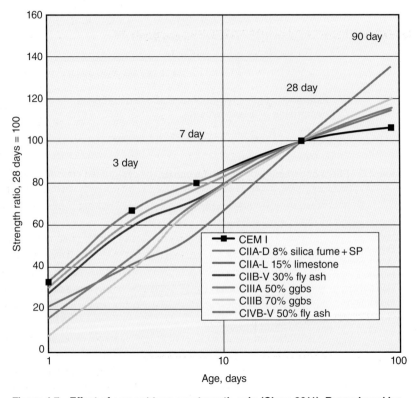

Figure 4.7 Effect of cement type on strength gain (Clear, 2011). Reproduced by permission of Chris Clear.

larger strength gains. Table 4.7 and Figure 4.7 provide information on strength gain of different concretes.

Water reducing and accelerating admixtures can be added to accelerate early strength gain (section 4.6).

The additional strength gain after 28 days for mixes with additions is not fully exploited because designers typically use 28-day strengths. This is because design codes have been established on this basis. The additional strength gain could potentially be exploited for elements that will be loaded over a longer time frame, for example foundations. Currently provisions for this are being considered for a future revision of Eurocode 2. Even without such code provisions, designers should consider using, say 56-day strengths for certain elements.

With respect to early strength, this relationship introduces a potential conflict between demands for achieving low concrete ECO_2 values (driven, most likely, by architects, consulting engineers or clients) and the achievement of adequate early strengths to satisfy programming requirements, such as timely formwork removal (driven, most likely, by contractors). Specifications should, therefore, be written to allow flexibility and compromise between conflicting concrete attributes. It may be beneficial to involve the contractor at the earliest stage of specification production to assist in optimising concrete specifications.

When early strength is important, some compromise on the level of cement replacement may be needed. In precast factories, rate of production and turnaround of mould may be important. For in-situ concrete, under normal circumstances, the striking times for concretes containing up to 50% GGBS do not increase sufficiently to significantly affect the construction programme. However, concretes with higher levels of GGBS will not always achieve sufficient strength after one day to allow removal of vertical formwork, particularly at lower temperatures, lower cementitious contents and in thinner sections. Generally, high (>50%) GGBS levels are not appropriate for soffit applications and thin sections; particularly during winter months unless the slower strength gain and prolonged striking times can be accommodated in the programme.

To limit any impact on programming, established methods for more accurately determining in-situ early age concrete strengths and/or formwork striking times are available (Reddy, 2007; Clear, 1994; Harrison, 1995). These include the use of maturity methods using site-specific or predicted input data; testing of site-cured or temperature-matched test cubes; and penetration, pull-out or break-off tests.

In terms of maturity methods, for example, it is understood that concrete strength is a function of time between casting and testing and the temperature at which concrete specimens are stored. For a particular concrete, therefore, it is possible to develop a time - temperature relationship to predict maturity and strength. On-site temperature history can be measured using thermocouples or predicted using established models which account for variables such as cement/combination type and content, section size, ambient conditions and formwork materials. Test cubes, match cured at the same temperature as the element poured, can add relevant data to decisions about striking and load transfer times.

Specialist contractors are able to erect in-situ concrete structures, such as framed buildings, conventionally (to programme and budget) using low ECO_2 concrete mixes. Indeed, using the established assessment techniques described above, innovative UK construction teams are presently erecting high rise structures year-round using average to high Portland cement replacement levels.

Case Study: The Shard, London

Figure 4.8   The Shard, London. Courtesy of AHMM/ Timothy Soar. Image © Edmund Sumner. Courtesy of VIEW Pictures.

The Shard in London is Europe's tallest building. An innovative approach was used on this project to allow construction above and below ground to start simultaneously. The core had already reached 21 storeys high by the time that 700 truckloads of concrete were poured into the basement to form the 3m deep raft foundation upon which the tower is supported. Carried out over 36 hours, the 5,500 m³ single concrete pour was one of the largest ever undertaken in the UK.

The C35/45 concrete contained a cement blend using 70% ground granulated blastfurnace slag (GGBS) to limit early heat gain. This high level of cement replacement has the potential disadvantage of low early strength gain. This was overcome by developing the concrete so that it would achieve sufficient strength gain to meet initial structural require-ments within 14 days with the full strength being achieved at 56 days. Levels 40 to 72 were constructed with post-tensioned concrete slabs on high strength (C65/80) concrete columns. Concrete was pumped to a height of 250m.

4.4.6   *Guidance for the specification of cements*

Portland cement or CEM I is the controlling constituent material in terms of the embodied carbon dioxide content of concrete. As such, if ECO_2 content is critical for a given structure, close consideration should be given to the concrete's CEM I content, but within the context of functional design requirements, construction practice and ultimate fitness for purpose. When specifying concrete to BS 8500–1: 2006 (BSI, 2006), there are several strength classes and cement/combination types permitted for selected minimum working lives, exposure classes and nominal covers to normal reinforcement. All of these strength classes and cement types should be considered by the designer.

Giving preference to options with low recommended minimum cement content, and permitted cement/combination types with the highest levels of Portland cement replacement, will directly reduce ECO_2 values of concrete. However, consideration also needs to be given to savings in concrete and reinforcement through the specification of higher strength concrete.

While meeting durability requirements, cement/combination contents and types may have a significant impact on associated structural and/or other concrete construction criteria and finishing processes.

As well as giving preference to specific cement/combination types at the specification stage, consideration may be given to attaching preferred minimum levels of addition. For cement/combination type IIIA, for example, a preferred minimum replacement of cement with GGBS of 50% could be stipulated, but should be discussed with the supplier.

Admixture use should be considered as an effective way of reducing cement/combination content. High range water-reducing admixtures (superplasticisers) typically give water reductions of 16% to 30% without loss of consistency or final properties, allowing corresponding ECO_2 reductions in cement/combination content (see section 4.6).

It is important to note that ECO_2 values for concrete should not be considered or specified in isolation. Adopting holistic approaches to sustainability-related decision making is always advisable, given the significant impact of cement/combination type and content on a range of key concrete properties and benefits.

Total cementitious content and the use of additions

The use of additions affects the total amount of cementitious binder. Although any increases are typically small, designers should be aware of these differences when assessing relative ECO_2 values for concrete.

Generally speaking, mass for mass replacement of cement with fly ash or GGBS may result in reduced 28-day strengths, particularly at higher replacement levels. As such, in order to achieve the specified characteristic strength, the total cement/combination type will tend to be higher for concrete containing additions.

For concrete containing 40% fly ash, the total cement/combination content may be around 15% higher than a reference concrete containing CEM I only. GGBS concretes typically require cement/combination content increases up to replacement levels of 50% of 5- 10kg/m³; at higher percentages the cementitious content may need to be increased further to achieve equivalent 28-day strength. Where practical, the characteristic strength can be specified to be achieved at a later age. Concrete producers can provide details for specific concrete specifications.

Concrete surface colour and the use of additions

The surface colour of concrete is dominated by its finest particles, which typically includes cement/combination and sand particles smaller than around 0.06mm. The colour of Portland cement varies according to the materials from which it is manufactured. The incorporation of additions such as fly ash, GGBS and silica fume also has a major influence. When aesthetics are critical, the cement/combination should be specified to ensure colour consistency.

GGBS is off-white in colour and substantially lighter than Portland cement. Concretes containing CEM III/B cements are often specified as a more sustainable and economic alternative to white Portland cement. Fly ash is dark grey in colour, resulting from a combination of iron compounds present and carbon residues left after the coal is burned as part of its manufacturing process; the shade depending on the source of coal and the process plant used.

Where aesthetics are critical, the impact of cement/combination type on concrete colour may dominate considerations of local availability and ECO_2 content.

Case Study: The Angel Building, London

Figure 4.9   The Angel Building, London. Reproduced by permission of The Concrete Centre.

Throughout the building the exposed concrete is of a very high quality finish. A self-compacting concrete containing 36% fly ash was specified in order to eliminate the need for traditional methods of compaction such as vibrating poker units. This reduced the potential for blemishes and honeycombing and improved the workability around difficult interfaces and cast-in elements. Fair faced concrete was used for the new core lobby areas, the entrance hall and atrium and the consistent quality finish is of an even light grey that features the tie-bolt holes and pour lines as aesthetic points of interest.

The retained concrete frame is wrapped with a highly-efficient glazed skin. The bespoke curtain walling works together with the exposed thermal mass of the concrete to passively control the internal environment and has contributed to the building's 'Excellent' BREEAM rating.

Sunlight glare and solar heat gain are reduced by fritting on the glass above eye level. The curtain wall includes opening windows that allow occupants direct control of natural ventilation.

There are many other sustainability benefits gained by using concrete as a finish. Although visual concrete may have a small cost premium compared with a standard concrete, considerable savings are made when comparing the cost including not requiring other materials that only provide the finish. Visual concrete also encourages the exposure of the concrete surface; lowering operational energy in buildings through the effect of thermal mass.

Precast visual concrete can be specified in collaboration with precast concrete manufacturers. Coloured concrete can also be produced by adding a colouring agent to the mix.

4.5 Aggregates

Aggregates are the major component of concrete by volume and, whilst a low carbon product, they make a big contribution to concrete's resource depletion impact because they constitute the majority of the mass of concrete. Most are naturally occurring materials requiring little processing and are usually locally sourced, with the associated benefit of low transport CO_2 emissions.

The European standard EN 12620: 2002 – Aggregates for concrete (BSI, 2002a) does not discriminate between different sources of material and permits aggregates from natural, recycled and manufactured sources. The focus is on fitness for purpose, rather than origin of the resource.

In addition to natural aggregates, suitable materials for use in concrete include recycled aggregate (RA), recycled concrete aggregate (RCA), blast furnace and zinc slag, foundry sand, slate aggregate and china clay sand or stent.

The UK leads Europe in recycling rates for hard demolition waste, and sources of secondary aggregates are utilised by the industry. Primary aggregates are needed and as a resource are abundant. Their extraction is tightly regulated and sites of mineral extraction are restored, often to an enhanced state, delivering significant biodiversity.

Depending on the type of recycled or secondary aggregates used, there may be increased water demand and a need to increase the cement content of the concrete to achieve the specified characteristic strength, with a consequential increase in ECO_2. When assessing the broader sustainability aspects rather than simply requiring recycled content, it will, in many cases, prove to be better if recycled aggregates are used in other applications such as fill or sub-base (in lieu of primary aggregate) in preference to their use in concrete.

4.5.1   Naturally occurring aggregates

In many countries, naturally occurring aggregates are abundant. They are predominantly locally sourced and in countries such as the UK, their extraction is tightly regulated and adverse environmental impacts – such as noise and dust are minimised.

In the UK, regulators such as the Environment Agency work closely with industry to ensure the life cycle of a quarry is environmentally positive. Over 700 sites of special scientific interest are current and former mineral extraction sites (Figure 4.10). The significant contribution to UK biodiversity from the minerals sector is increasingly recognised (see also section 2.3.4).

4.5.2   Recycled aggregates

Coarse RA and RCA in concrete is permitted in BS8500 (Tables 4.8 and 4.9), providing that certain quality and performance criteria are met. RA is aggregate resulting from the reprocessing of inorganic material previously used in construction, while RCA principally comprises crushed concrete (Figure 4.11).

Fine RCA and fine RA are not provided for in BS 8500 but this does not preclude their use when it is demonstrated that, due to the source of material, significant quantities of deleterious materials are not present and their use has been agreed.

Constraining factors for the use of RA and RCA include consistency of supply and original source. Due to their inherent variability, testing regimes for quality control of the aggregates may need to be more rigorous than for natural/primary aggregates.

Figure 4.10   An example of restoration of a former quarry: Marfield Quarry, near Masham in North Yorkshire, UK. Over 40.4 hectares of new wetland habitats for wintering wildfowl, like whooper swans, and summer wading birds like oystercatchers. Reproduced by permission of Lafarge Tarmac.

4.5.3   Secondary and manufactured aggregates

Secondary or manufactured aggregates may also be specified for use in structural concrete. These materials are typically industrial by-products not previously used in construction. These aggregate types are derived from a very wide range of materials; many having a strong regional character. UK examples include china clay waste in South West England and metallurgical slag in South Wales, Yorkshire and Humberside, and palletised and sintered pulverised fuel ash from coal fired power stations (traded as LYTAG).

Table 4.8 Designated concrete – allowable percentage of coarse RA or RCA (BSI, 2006).

Designated concrete	Example Applications	Allowable % of coarse RA or RCA
GEN 0 to GEN 3	Housing: floors, drainage and footings in relatively benign conditions (DC-1)	100%
RC20/25 to RC40/50	Lower strength reinforced concrete	20%*
RC40/50XF	Higher strength reinforced concrete	0%
PAV1 & PAV2	Domestic parking & Heavy-duty paving with rubber tyre vehicles	0%
FND2 to FND4	Foundations subject to chemical attack classes DC-2, DC-3, DC-4	0%

*Except where the specification allows higher proportions to be used.
RA and RCA are also permitted in designed concrete, although no direct guidance is given on limiting proportions. BS 8500 does, however, provide guidance on limiting concrete strength and exposure classes for RCA use, as shown in Table 4.9.

Figure 4.11 Separation of reinforcement and concrete following demolition and prior to RCA processing.

Table 4.9 Permitted use of RCA in designed concrete (BSI, 2006).

Exposure	Description of Exposure	Use of RCA permitted
XO	No risk of corrosion or attack	Yes
XC1, XC2 & XC3/4	Reinforcement corrosion induced by carbonation	Yes
XD1, XD2 & XD3	Reinforcement corrosion induced by chlorides (non-sea water)	Possibly**
XS1, XS2 & XS3	Reinforcement corrosion induced by chlorides- sea water	Possibly**
XF1	Freeze thaw attack (moderate water, no deicing agent)	Yes
XF2, XF3 & XF4	Freeze thaw attack (high water and/or de-icing agent)	Possibly**
DC1	Chemical attack (refer BSI 2006 for detail)	Yes
DC-2, DC-3 & DC-4	Chemical attack (refer BSI 2006 for detail)	Possibly**

**RCA may be used if it can be demonstrated that it is suitable for the exposure condition.
Note: The maximum strength class should be C40/50, unless the RCA comes from previously unused concrete of known composition, for example from a precast factory.

Materials such as china clay sand and stent have similar properties to primary aggregates. As such they conform to BS EN 12620: 2002 (BSI, 2002a) and their use is well established for fine and coarse aggregate substitution in concrete. However, it is important to ensure that the aggregates conform to all requirements of the specification and an appropriate mix design is used, while an enhanced level of testing may be required.

Case Study: One Coleman Street, London

Figure 4.12   One Coleman Street, London. Reproduced by permission of Arup.

The prestigious office development at One Coleman Street in the City of London is recognised as the first major use of china clay stent coarse aggregate in concrete outside the south west of the UK. The stent was used to completely replace the normal primary coarse aggregate in pile-caps, floor slabs and the structural frame. China clay sand was not used because of its high water demand and hence increased cement contents (Marsh, 2006).

Marsh also reported that: 'A conformity age of 56 days was permitted for the 40% fly ash pile cap concrete because of the elements being buried in wet ground and because of their large size giving enhanced strength development due to the heat development during hydration'. However, a section of one pile cap that was also the base for the construction crane, used CEM I to ensure faster strength gain (see section 4.4.5).

4.5.4 *Transportation impact from the utilisation of recycled/ secondary aggregates*

The UK construction industry is very efficient at recycling hard construction and demolition waste in non-concrete applications, and there is very little evidence that any material is being land-filled as waste (DCLG, 2007). In 2011, the Mineral Products Association reported the use of 56.5 million tonnes of recycled and secondary aggregates, representing 29% of the aggregate market. This level of performance is a real success story; the UK leads mainland Europe by a factor of three.

Given that recycling is already efficiently undertaken, primary aggregate extraction is unlikely to be reduced by further encouragement of use of recycled aggregates on particular concrete projects. Instead, overly prescriptive specifications will result in recycled aggregates being moved from one place to another, which is likely to be less environmentally-friendly than using primary aggregates. There will be no net reduction in primary aggregate use; just increased transportation of material.

The impact of this is illustrated in Table 4.10, which provides indicative ECO_2 for the extraction and production of virgin and recycled aggregates, as well as their delivery to site. Table 4.10 demonstrates that ECO_2 values for recycled aggregates may be higher than for virgin materials if delivery distances are longer than around 15km (10 miles). Furthermore, as recycling rates are so high, no benefits in terms of resource depletion will have been achieved.

4.5.5 *Aggregate size*

Aggregate size can have a significant impact on the cement content of concrete; larger aggregate sizes generally requiring lower cement contents.

As an example, the limiting mix design requirements for designated concretes are given in BS 8500–2: 2006 (Table 4.5). It should be noted that each designation

Table 4.10 Indicative embodied CO_2 for virgin and recycled aggregates.

Material and Delivery Distance	Cradle to gate kg CO_2/tonne	Transport kg CO_2/tonne	Total kg/tonne	+/– % CO_2
Virgin aggregates				
+ 58.5km (delivery and return distance by road)	6.6	2.7	9.3	–
Recycled C&D* aggregates compared to the use of virgin aggregates				
Used on-site 0km transport	7.9	0.0	7.9	−15%
+5km (delivery distance by road)	7.9	0.5	8.4	−10%
+10km (delivery distance by road)	7.9	0.9	8.8	−5%
+15km (delivery distance by road)	7.9	1.4	9.3	0%
+20km (delivery distance by road)	7.9	1.8	9.7	5%
+58.5km (delivery distance by road)	7.9	2.7	10.6	14%

*C&D – Construction and Demolition

class is assigned minimum cement contents (kg/m^3) for different maximum aggregate sizes. For an RC32/40 designation, for example, the minimum cement content concrete with maximum aggregate sizes of 10mm and 20mm is 340 and 300kg/m^3 respectively. Where possible, therefore, reduced ECO_2 levels will be achievable by specifying increasing maximum aggregate sizes. It should be noted that most plants and factories do not stock aggregate sizes greater than 20mm.

4.5.6 Guidance for the specification of aggregates

When specifying recycled and secondary aggregates, the factors to balance are resource depletion, transportation CO_2 impacts and implications on mix design. These are all impacted by availability, and concrete producers are well placed to ensure the most sustainable aggregates for each project are used. It is recommended to permit the use of recycled or secondary aggregates but to not over-specify. It is recommended not to specify aggregate sizes below 10mm unless necessary, because of the requirement for higher cement contents.

4.6 Water

Unlike CO_2 emissions which are a global problem, water scarcity is a local problem. It is generally accepted that water will become a more significant impact in many areas because shortages are becoming more common. These shortages may be due to increasing demand per capita and/or increasing population and/or decreasing availability because of depletion of underground reserves and/or reduced rainfall. It is also worth noting that water does also have a carbon footprint itself, although its contribution to the concrete ECO_2 is insignificant relative to that due to the cementitious constituent.

Due to the need to minimise water use, BS EN 1008: 2002 (BSI, 2002b) gives guidance on the use of water recovered from processes in the concrete industry. This includes water which was part of surplus concrete, used to clean the inside of stationary mixers, mixing drums of truck mixers or agitators and concrete pumps; process water from sawing, grinding and water blasting of hardened concrete; and water extracted from fresh concrete during concrete production. Limitations on use of recovered water include additional mass of solid material (which must be less than 1.0% by mass of the total mass of aggregates present in the concrete) and any impacts on chemical and physical concrete properties such as setting time and strength.

4.6.1 Water extraction and responsible sourcing

Water extraction is an important aspect of responsible sourcing certification to BES 6001 (BRE, 2008) (section 4.3). To achieve a primary level of performance the organisation must establish a policy and metrics for water extraction in terms of reducing mains water use and the efficient and effective use of 'controlled groundwater'. Controlled groundwater is defined as all water abstracted from boreholes and other surface water features which needs an abstraction license known as a 'Full License' in the UK Water Act 2003. To achieve a higher performance rating in BES 6001 (BRE, 2008) the organisation must demonstrate external verification of the reported data on water extraction.

4.6.2   Minimisation of water use

The concrete industry in the UK is monitoring both its mains and groundwater consumption, with the aim of achieving reductions in water use. An example of a water-saving industry initiative is wash-water admixtures.

Specialist admixtures are available that reduce the waste produced at a ready-mix concrete plant. At the end of a working day, ready-mix trucks need to be cleaned to prevent the build-up of hardened concrete in the mixer drum. Traditionally, large quantities of water have been added to the mixer, which has then been spun and the detritus dumped in a settlement pit. An alternative treatment involves incorporating a wash-water stabilising admixture into the drum overnight. The admixture stops the hydration of the main phase of the Portland cement even after initial hydration has started.

The following day, the wash-water residue is incorporated into the first delivery of the day. The addition of significant volumes of cementitious material activates the hydration reactions. Alternatively a special activator can be added to the wash-water.

4.6.3   Guidance for the specification of water

Recovered or combined (mixture of recovered and from other sources) water may be used for both un-reinforced and reinforced (including pre-stressed) concrete, and its use should be included at the specification stage.

If used, however, its influence should always be taken into account if there are special requirements for the production of concrete; for example, air-entrained concrete or concrete exposed to aggressive environments. Also recovered water generally contains varying concentrations of very fine particles (typically less than 0.25mm), so its use in visual or architectural concrete should also be assessed.

4.7 Admixtures

Admixtures are defined in BS EN 934–2 (BSI, 2009b) as 'material added during the mixing process of concrete in a quantity not more than 5% by mass of the cement content of the concrete, to modify the properties of the mix in the fresh and/or hardened state'. In the hardened state admixtures can significantly improve the durability of the concrete to a range of aggressive environments, extending the maintenance free service life. However, as well as modifying the physical properties of the concrete, admixtures can be used to enhance sustainability credentials and reduce the ECO_2 content of concrete.

Figure 4.13   Admixtures. Reproduced by permission of Lafarge Tarmac.

Table 4.11   Typical UK admixture use and dosage (Minson and Berrie, 2013).

Admixture Type to BS EN 934-2	Proportion of total admixture sales %	Average dosage % by weight of cement
Superplasticisers	45	0.70*
Normal Plasticisers	34	0.45
Accelerating	2	1.65
Retarding	2	0.45
Air Entraining Agents (AEA)	4	0.20
All other concrete admixtures	13	–

*Dosage based on 40% solution, some superplasticisers will be sold at greater dilution with a correspondingly higher dose.

Admixtures can reduce ECO_2 of concrete, despite having relatively high ECO_2 themselves. This is because the dosages are so small, they contribute less than 1% to the total ECO_2 of concrete while allowing other high ECO_2 constituents to be reduced. (Under BS EN ISO 14001 (BSI, 2004) components, constituents contributing less than 1% of the impacts can be ignored, and this would apply to most cases of admixture usage). Admixtures can reduce the ECO_2 of concrete while maintaining and even enhancing the properties of the concrete.

Current admixture use in the UK is reported as saving about 600,000 tonnes of ECO_2 per annum and this could be significantly increased by further mix optimisation (CAA, 2012). Typical dosage rates for admixtures are shown in Table 4.11. In certain specialist applications such as very high strength concrete, these dosages may be exceeded.

4.7.1 Concrete for different exposure conditions

When specifying concrete consideration needs to be given to the environmental conditions the concrete will be exposed to. The five main exposures classes defined in BS 8500 (BSI, 2006) are listed below. Each class has a number of sub-categories depending upon the severity of exposure.

- XC Exposure class for risk of corrosion induced by carbonation.
- XD Exposure class for risk of corrosion induced by chlorides other than from the sea water.
- XS Exposure class for risk of corrosion induced by chlorides from sea water.
- XF Exposure classes for freeze/thaw attack.
- XA Exposure classes for chemical attack.

Depending upon the exposure condition and the cover, BS 8500 defines a minimum cement content, maximum water cement ratio and possibly required strength to give desired design life.

The use of water-reducing or superplasticising admixtures enables a given strength and/or water cement ratio to be achieved with lower cement content (subject to achieving the minimum cement content). The correct use of admixtures can reduce the ECO_2 of the concrete while maintaining or enhancing its long-term durability performance.

Example: Resistance to freeze thaw

The specification of concrete exposed to significant freeze thaw cycles should be carried out in accordance with the guidance set out in BS 8500–1 Table A.8 to resist XF exposure. To achieve this, either a minimum quality of air is entrained using an air-entraining admixture or a minimum strength class is specified.

The most severe form of freeze thaw exposure is when there is also the possibility of high water saturation; typically horizontal surfaces. Under these conditions, freeze thaw resisting aggregates are required and there are limitations on the type of cement which should be used. Cement with more than 35% fly ash should not be used and, when de-icing is used, no more than 55% GGBS should be added to minimise surface scaling.

XF3 exposure is when concrete is exposed to significant freeze thaw cycles and high water saturation, but where de-icing agents are unlikely to be used. For a maximum aggregate size of 20mm, the requirements are shown in Table 4.12.

From Table 4.12, it is evidently easier to call up the designated concretes PAV1 or RC40/50XF rather than set out the limiting values of a designed concrete.

A freeze thaw resisting aggregate will be a reasonably strong aggregate and coupled with a minimum cement content of $280kg/m^3$, plus addition of

Table 4.12   Designated concrete for freeze thaw exposure XF3.

Exposure class	Min. Strength class	Max. w/c ratio	Min cement content kg/m³	Min. air content	Alternative designated concrete
XF3	C25/30	0.60	280	3.5	PAV1
XF3	C40/50	0.45	340	–	RC40/50XF

a water-reducing agent, could give a concrete that achieves around 45MPa at 28 days, in the absence of an air-entraining admixture. However, introduction of entrained air affects strength and each 1% entrained air reduces 28-day strength by about 5% (Neville, 2011) and to ensure a minimum air content of 3.5%, as required for a PAV1 concrete, the average air content will be about 5%. At 5% air, 280kg/m³ may only achieve 35MPa (approximately 25% [c.f. 5% air/1% air *5% strength] reduction of 45MPa); to safely achieve the required C25/30 strength class, the cement content may need to be 300–320kg/m³.

Even with a reasonable quality aggregate and a water reducing admixture or high range water reducing admixture, it is likely that the cement content required to achieve C40/50 concrete will be in excess of 340kg/m³ and may be as much as 380kg/m³.

Thus, air-entrained concrete will normally have lower cement content than a non-entrained concrete to meet the recommendations for freeze thaw resistance, and therefore a lower ECO_2 content. However, if C40/50 is required anyway to meet structural requirements, then all the cement is usefully employed.

4.7.2   Extending design life through use of admixtures

Concrete structures designed to BS 8500 are generally specified to have a 50- or 100-year (BSI, 2002c) design life. The Design Manual for Roads and Bridges (Department for Transport, 2011) calls for 60- or 120-year design life. This is achieved through a combination of specifying cover (where corrosion of steel reinforcement is a risk) and concrete quality (specified through maximum water cement ratio and minimum cement content and possibly strength). Admixtures can be used to achieve these durability requirements in a more sustainable way.

When the concrete is exposed to a particularly aggressive environment or guaranteed long-term performance is critical, specialist admixtures can be utilised. Admixtures falling within this category include corrosion inhibitors, waterproofers and shrinkage reducers. The small increase in ECO_2 using these products will easily be offset if significant repairs to a structure are prevented.

4.7.3   *Guidance for the specification of admixtures*

It is recommended, as a minimum, that the use of admixtures by the concrete producer should be permitted in specifications. Minimisation of cement through use of admixtures is often commercially astute for the producer and delivers ECO_2 savings to the specifier/client. Discussion with admixture producers to optimise use of admixtures with respect to function, performance and ECO_2, particularly for large and/or unusual projects is also suggested.

Examples (Minson and Berrie, 2013)

Example 1   Strength requirement: C32/40, Exposure: XC3/4, Cover: 35mm + deviation

From BS8500-1 Table A.4 the minimum cement content is 260kg/m³ with a maximum water/cement ratio of 0.65.

For a range of cement types, that is with or without limestone, fly ash or GGBS:

(a)   The benefit of incorporating a normal water-reducing admixture (WRA) is to enable a reduction in cement content by about 30kg/m³ giving a 5–8% saving in ECO_2 for reinforced concrete.

(b)   The benefit of incorporating a high-range water-reducing admixture (HRWRA) is a potential further reduction of around 30kg/m³. This total reduction cannot be realised for all cement types as the cement content cannot be reduced below the 260kg/m³ minimum. A saving in ECO_2 for reinforced concrete of 10–15% can be achieved.

Example 2   Exposure: XS1, Cover: 35mm + deviation.

Normally a resistance to chloride ingress requirement will mean there is sufficient strength to meet the engineer's structural requirement. For normal or high quality aggregates, strength of C40/50 will be readily achieved by a concrete meeting the BS8500-1 Table A.4 XS1 exposure requirement, where the minimum cement content is 360kg/m³ with a maximum water/cement ratio of 0.45.

For a range of cements (as in Example 1):

(a)   The use of a WRA gives a potential cement reduction of around 40kg/m³, but this is not achievable for all cements because it would reduce the cement content below the 360kg/m³ minimum. A saving in ECO_2 for reinforced concrete of 1–8% can be achieved.

(b)   Using a HRWRA will not give any further savings because the minimum cement content can be achieved with WRA. In this example, as the specified maximum water/cement ratio is 0.45, there are occasions where the water/cement ratio is higher than specified due to the available aggregates, or where a higher level of consistence is required, in these cases a HRWRA may be usefully incorporated to further reduce the cement content, and therefore the ECO_2, as long as all the other criteria such as minimum cement content and/or maximum water cement ratio are still complied with.

4.8 Novel constituents

Whilst production and specification of conventional constituents has been improved with respect to sustainability, novel constituents are the subject of much research and investment. As environmental impacts are being considered in monetary terms, there is potential financial gain from successful development and commercialisation of novel constituents.

4.8.1 Novel cements

'Novel' for our purpose is applied to any alternative to the cements and combinations currently in standards and covered in section 4.4. As Portland cement is the biggest contributor to the carbon footprint of concrete the primary aim of novel cements is to address this. Any novel cement that meets this carbon reduction ambition will also need to meet the following challenges if it is to succeed commercially:

- cost parity;
- scalability of production process to produce necessary volumes;
- availability of raw materials;
- ease of use;
- suitable physical/chemical properties;
- durability performance;
- mechanical strength performance;
- no issue with products/leachates;
- robustness with respect to temperature/humidity/admixtures (Chana, 2011).

Initial uses of novel cements are likely to be in non-structural applications. Through these uses, certification of product quality, validation of performance and wider acceptance will be sought. During this period the requisite research and testing for strength and serviceability performance across the spectrum of anticipated uses will need to be conducted. Ultimately design standards will need to include the constituent as a permitted material if the novel cement is to become an alternative to CEM I/ordinary Portland cement.

Some examples of novel cements are introduced below, starting with those that have been known for decades.

Alkali-activated cements and geopolymer cements use alumina-rich materials sourced from waste streams such as incinerator ash, fly ash and slag. These pozzolans/latent binders are activated by an alkali silicate solution or a sodium hydroxide solution (also an alkali). These types of cements were first developed in the 1950s and have been commercialised at a small scale but they have not been used in large scale applications where strength is critical (Chana, 2011).

CSA – belite cements are manufactured and commercially used in China in a range of compositions. Structural grades comprise 35%–70% CSA (calcium sulphoaluminate) 10%–30% ferrite (calcium ferroaluminate) and a belite (dicalcium silicate) content of less than 30%. They use industrial wastes (e.g. fly ash), gypsum and limestone in rotary kilns at 1200 °C–1250 °C. With such a high temperature process it is not surprising that the savings compared with Portland cement are not large: 25% energy and 20% CO_2. It must be noted that such savings are already achievable with Portland cement by using GGBS and fly ash (see section 4.4.2). There is a significant saving in limestone of 60% relative to Portland cement, so if access to limestone is problematic then CSA-belite cements may have a role (Chana, 2011).

Magnesium oxide cements from magnesium carbonates, sometimes called 'eco-cements', are produced by heating the mineral magnesite to 650 °C where it dissociates producing a large quantity of CO_2 and reactive magnesium oxide. This is either combined with industrial waste streams (fly ash, GGBS), or, to form a composite, can be blended with Portland cement. When hydrated, it is claimed that the CO_2 liberated at manufacture is absorbed (re-carbonated). However, this requires high humidity and the claim is not verified (Chana, 2011). Readers should note the re-carbonation of Portland cement explained in section 2.3.2.1.

Magnesium oxide cements from magnesium silicate are being developed as 'novacem' and are produced in a low temperature, low carbon process. The raw material, magnesium silicate, has large global reserves, but is not uniformly distributed and requires pre-processing. To accelerate strength development and CO_2 absorption, mineral additives are blended with the magnesium oxide. It is considered one of the most promising technologies and has potential to reduce carbon emissions from cement manufacture by 80%–95% (CAN, 2010).

C-Fix cement is an organic carbon based binder as opposed to the inorganic cements described above. It is produced as a waste from crude oil. Historically it was burnt as a waste thereby emitting CO_2. A process developed by Shell and the University of Delft requires heating the waste to 200 °C and addition of fillers and aggregates to make a 'carbon concrete'. The carbon in the name does not refer to its CO_2 emission claims but its organic basis. The developer claims a carbon footprint of 30% of that of Portland cement – the claim assumes no allocation of CO_2 from oil production. C-Fix cement is temperature and pressure sensitive and has a very large creep factor, so it is not technically suitable for many applications (Chana, 2011).

Fine recycled glass as an addition

When finely ground, recycled glass may exhibit pozzolanic properties depending on fineness and reactivity and, in this form may have properties similar to a Type II addition. That is, it may theoretically be used as a material that contributes to strength when used in combination with Portland cement. Depending on its properties the material may perform similarly to fly ash, but unlike fly ash, finely ground glass is not a material with established suitability for use in concrete. Fly ash is widely and economically available, does not have a closed loop recycling alternative (i.e. recycled glass into glass manufacture) and has an established track record of use. Adding finely ground recycled glass to material supply for the concrete sector would not have a significant beneficial environmental impact and due to the high energy cost for grinding glass it is not generally considered economically viable.

4.8.2   Novel aggregates

Often prompted by the idea of finding a use for what would otherwise be waste, many novel aggregates have been investigated. However, as was seen in section 4.5 the cradle to gate CO_2 impact is small for natural aggregates and they are typically both commonly and locally available, therefore, the resource depletion environmental impact, if based on scarcity is not significant. Furthermore, because they are locally available there is only a small transport CO_2 impact. And finally natural aggregates – even with environmental taxes like the UK extraction tax 'aggregate levy' (section 2.6.3) – are still cheap.

Therefore there is a high barrier to novel aggregates becoming more widely adopted. There is often higher value and better uses for the waste streams. A few examples are:

- tyre rubber which is restricted in concrete to low strength applications such as foamed concrete for use as trench reinstatement, but waste tyres are used in many other non-concrete applications.
- waste plastic which theoretically, in lightweight blocks and in normal strength concrete, can replace 50% and 15% respectively of aggregates;
- recycled glass, on which more detail is provided below.

Recycled glass aggregate, as a coarse aggregate in concrete, risks an expansive and therefore damaging alkali-silica reaction (ASR). The measures required to mitigate this risk, in terms of quality control of the recycled glass are onerous. This is particularly the case because the supply of recycled glass has not been found to be reliable or consistent.

The annual available recycled glass in the UK is potentially of the order of 1 million tonnes. There is total glass production of 4 million tonnes per year, with 2.3 million tonnes being container glass and 1.3 million tonnes being flat glass for the automotive and construction sectors. There are 1.6 million tonnes of glass recycled annually with 0.66 million tonnes of recycled cullet being used for container glass manufacture. In Great Britain there are reports of 30% glass recycling. In Europe some reports quote figures greater than 50%.

Therefore the available recycled glass is a very small tonnage in the context that 29% of the 208 million tonnes of aggregate used annually is from non-glass recycled sources. Also, the drive to increase use of recycled glass in glass manufacture will further reduce the 'available' tonnage. Hence recycled glass aggregate in concrete is neither desirable nor likely.

The best environmental practicable option for recycled glass is as feedstock in glass manufacturing where it reduces energy consumption, CO_2 emissions (from energy used and chemical reactions) and quantity of virgin materials per tonne of manufactured glass. For these reasons, pressure is likely to be brought to bear via European Directives to increase the recycled content in manufactured glass.

4.9   Reinforcement

Concrete on its own performs well in compression but not in tension. Steel reinforcement is used to deliver tensile capacity where it is needed. Hence reinforced concrete uses the two materials very efficiently. This minimisation of material use is often taken for granted but is a major contributor to sustainability.

About half of all concrete cast in Britain is reinforced. Steel reinforcement should comply with BS 4449: 2005 (BSI, 2005a) or BS 4483: 2005 (BSI, 2005b) and be cut and bent in accordance with BS 8666: 2005 (BSI, 2005c). Efficient use of reinforcing steel is dependent on good structural design and on the material's chemical composition, mechanical properties and rib geometry, as well as accurate cutting, bending and fixing.

The embodied energy values of reinforcing steel are based on the energy used to melt scrap metal and reform it. Although all steel manufacture is an energy-intensive process, the energy needed to produce one tonne of reinforcing steel is as low as one third of that needed to make one tonne of structural steel from iron ore. Equally, reinforcing steel itself can be recovered, recycled and re-used at the end of a building or structure's service life.

4.9.1   Manufacturing of reinforcement steel

There are two common steelmaking processes used for steel in the UK market. These are Basic Oxygen Steelmaking (BOS) and Electric Arc Furnace (EAF) steelmaking (Figure 4.14). The BOS route is the most widely-used steelmaking process worldwide and involves the smelting of iron ore, coal and other raw materials in a two-stage process. The EAF production process involves passing an electric charge through scrap metal, melting it; thus enabling recycling into new products.

The EAF process normally uses approximately 98% scrap metal as the raw material. An EAF furnace generally produces 0.5 to 1.0 million tonnes per annum, making it ideally suited to smaller-scale steelmaking operations typically used for the manufacture of reinforcing steel. EAF production sites typically include specialised rolling mills producing long products such as reinforcing bar.

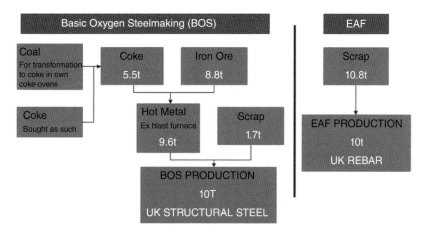

Figure 4.14   Comparison of basic oxygen steelmaking and electric arc furnace production methods. Adapted from reference (UK Steel, 2012).

The majority of reinforcing steel used in the UK is produced by the EAF process.

4.9.2   *Sustainability accreditation of reinforcement steel*

The UK is leading in the concept of responsible sourcing (section 4.3). The schemes developed in the UK are likely to be replicated elsewhere. Sustainability credentials can be demonstrated by specifying reinforcement accredited to the Eco-Reinforcement or the CARES (Certification Authority for Reinforcing Steel) sustainability certification scheme.

Eco-Reinforcement is a third-party certification scheme developed by the UK reinforcing steel industry to comply with BES 6001 (BRE, 2008) (section 4.3).

Eco-Reinforcement provides a means for construction clients, specifiers and contractors to purchase reinforcing steel from a supply chain which is pro-actively addressing issues of sustainability. The Eco-Reinforcement scheme assesses against a number of different organisational, supply chain, environmental and social criteria; with some defined as compulsory and others voluntary or 'tradable'. Certificates are awarded on a 'Pass', 'Good', 'Very Good' and 'Excellent' scale, based on the number of points awarded for different performance levels. All Eco-Reinforcement companies manufacture through the EAF process, from recycled scrap metal. They are required to print information such as transport-related CO_2 emissions from scrap-yard to site on their delivery notes.

CARES is an independent, not-for-profit product certification body, based in the UK but now with an international reach. CARES has developed The CARES Sustainable Reinforcing Steel scheme that quantifies the environmental impact of the reinforcing steel supply chain. The CARES scheme has been established to comply with BS 8902 (BSI, 2009a), which provides a framework

Table 4.13   Indicative ECO$_2$ for C28/35 concrete; unreinforced and reinforced.

UK Concrete products	Cementitious content (kg/m³)	Water (kg/m³)	Aggregate (kg/m³)	Rebar (kg/m³)	(kg CO$_2$/m³)	(kg CO$_2$/t)
	Constituents of products				**Embodied CO$_2$ for the product**	
C28/35 Unreinforced	300	165	1915	0	225	95
C28/35 Reinforced	300	165	1915	110	275	110

for the management, development, content and operation of sector certification schemes for responsible sourcing and supply of construction products. It will enable the CARES approved reinforcing steel supply chain to demonstrate the responsible sourcing of construction products and its commitment to sustainable development.

4.9.3   Guidance for specification of reinforcement steel

The ECO$_2$ of reinforcing steel is shown in Table 4.4 (section 4.4.4). Steel contents of reinforced concrete will vary and this will influence the ECO$_2$. At a value of 110kg of reinforcement per cubic metre of concrete (considered typical for the UK), the reinforcement will add 15kg of ECO$_2$ per tonne of concrete as illustrated in Table 4.13.

The ECO$_2$ for the cementitious content in this example is based on the UK weighted average value of 720kg CO$_2$/t plus an allowance for transport. If a cement/combination utilising fly ash or GGBS at a normal UK addition rate of 30% or 50% respectively was used, a lower ECO$_2$ would be achieved for both examples, but the differential due to reinforcement would stay the same.

In order to guarantee that the material is produced in conformity with relevant standards, it is recommended that all steel reinforcement should be obtained from companies holding a valid third party conformity certification of product approval. It is also recommended to specify reinforcement is certified as responsibly sourced.

4.10   Special concretes

Concrete describes a range of materials and this is evidenced by the variation in the constituents in 'normal' concretes discussed in sections 4.4 to 4.7. The term 'special concrete' might be applied to those with a particular functional performance such as pumpability, low shrinkage, high insulating properties or high early strength gain. Three further examples are considered in more detail in sections 4.10.1, 4.10.2 and 4.10.3 below.

The sustainability credentials of these special concretes will become easier to assess as environmental product declarations (section 4.2.5) of proprietary products are made public. Given the functional benefits delivered by special concretes, comparisons with 'normal' concretes should take into account environmental benefits ensuing from their functional benefits and any additional burdens. For example low shrinkage concrete will require less anti-crack reinforcement so comparisons should be made on the basis of a functional unit such as per m² of floor slab and not per m³ concrete.

4.10.1 *Fibre reinforced concrete*

Polypropylene and steel fibres are now commonly used in concrete with or without conventional reinforcement. Class 1 polypropylene fibres (6-20mm long, tens of microns in diameter, dosages approximately 0.9kg/m³) are primarily used to modify properties of fresh concrete, such as control of plastic shrinkage or bleeding rate, and/or control of spalling in the event of fire in applications such as tunnels. Class 2 polypropylene fibres (10-60mm long, 0.4-1.4mm in diameter, maximum dosages of 12kg/m³) provide the concrete with some post cracking and load bearing capacity. Steel fibres (10-60mm long, 0.4-1.4mm in diameter, dosages of 20 to 80kg/m³) are used as anti crack reinforcement with conventional bar or on steel metal decking, or on their own in ground bearing slabs to reduce shrinkage cracks and increase bay sizes (i.e. joint spacing). Steel fibres are also used in precast tunnel linings. Despite claims and on-going research, doubts remain as to whether structural concrete elements such as suspended slabs and beams can solely have fibres to provide tensile capacity for moment resistance and stiffness (Concrete Society, 2007a; 2007b).

When fibres are used in lieu of steel reinforcement, it is argued that fibre reinforced concrete is more sustainable as it saves processes on site (e.g. deliveries, steel reinforcement bar fixing) with consequential benefits such as health and safety. Use of fibres with conventional reinforcement can improve functionality with associated environmental benefits. On the other hand, fibres are supposedly homogeneous through the structural element meaning that if their purpose is to deliver tensile capacity, they do this even in areas where tensile capacity is not required. This is not an efficient use of materials.

4.10.2 *Self compacting concrete/flowing concretes*

These special concretes can be produced with careful mix design, including grading of aggregates, together with addition of admixtures (Figure 4.15).

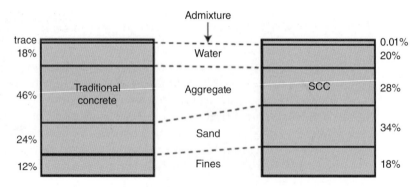

Figure 4.15   Traditional concrete vs. Self Compacting Concrete (SCC).

They do not segregate when they flow through a form and congested reinforcement. They overcome the need for vibration during placing. They can be used in exceptional cases when 'normal' concretes won't do the task, or in 'normal' cases to reduce environmental noise, reduce manpower to place the concrete or reduce time to place concrete. Typically they have higher cement contents and hence the environmental burden of the mix will be higher than normal, so on environmental grounds there needs to be significant savings accruing from the concrete's performance to justify their use in 'normal cases'. In addition to the conventional slump test or 'flowability test' (Figure 4.16) Self Compacting Concrete requires tests to verify its viscosity, segregation stability and passing ability and these tests increase the cost, making it less sustainable.

4.10.3   *Ultra High Strength Fibre Reinforced Concrete (UHSFRC)*

Concrete with compressive strength of over 200MPa, bending strength exceeding 50MPa and high ductility is an exciting material for engineers and has enabled the construction of some landmark structures. In general this high performance is achieved by high cement content – double that of a normal mix – high dosage of steel fibres and grading of aggregates that is closer to a mortar than 'normal' concrete. More particularly, a huge investment in product development has led to a highly sophisticated product and detailed understanding of how to reliably achieve the desired performance. Because of the higher density of UHSFRC it is highly durable and resistant to chemical attacks and abrasion. In cases where conventional steel reinforcement is used, in addition to the steel fibres, the cover required for durability is small, allowing the choice of stunningly thin sections, where fire is not the governing design criterion (Figure 4.17).

Examples of UHSFRC are CRC (Compact Reinforced Composite) and Ductal by Lafarge. For normal applications, the reduced cross section, and

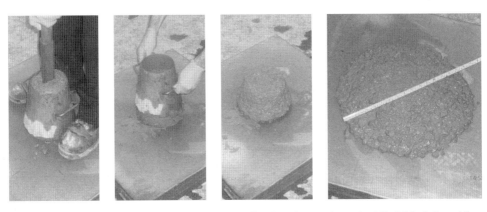

Figure 4.16   A flowability test (diameter of spread) rather than a slump test (height of slump) is used for Self Compacting Concrete. Reproduced by permission of BASF Plc.

Figure 4.17   UHSFRC makes stunningly thin structures possible. Reproduced by permission of The Concrete Centre.

hence reduced volume is not sufficient to offset the greater environmental impacts per m³ of product. For special applications, perhaps the project is unrealisable without the special concrete, and on a project scale environmental assessment, it may deliver environmental benefits.

4.11   Specification examples

4.11.1   Designed concrete

For a building with external reinforced vertical elements exposed to rain (exposure class XC3/4 to BS 8500 (BSI, 2006)) with an intended working life of at least 50 years, a range of designed concretes are appropriate depending on the minimum cover to the reinforcement. These are shown in Table 4.14.

In practice, for reasonable quality aggregate, RC30/37, RC28/35 and RC25/30 should be achievable at the minimum cement content with the use of water reducing or high range water reducing admixtures. This applies to all cements incorporating not more than 20% silica fume or limestone, 35% fly ash or 65% GGBS. At higher levels, an extra cementitious content above the minimum should be expected.

Even with reasonable quality aggregates and high performing admixtures, an extra cementitious content is likely to be required for RC40/50 concrete. This grade is generally restricted to precast concrete elements when the minimum cover can be consistently achieved at minimum tolerance, and extra cement content is useful to minimise formwork striking and reinforcement stressing times.

4.11.2   Optimising strength class

A reduction in concrete strength class will typically offer immediate savings in terms of ECO_2 (reduced cement/combination content) unless limited by minimum cement content specifications. As an example, a reduction in strength class from C70/85 to C32/40 may reduce concrete's cement/combination content by around 150kg per m³ of concrete, with corresponding ECO_2 reductions of around 185kg of CO_2.

For a typical concrete column scenario (applied load of 24000kN and moment of 500kNm), however, the higher strength class would afford element size reductions of around 30% (from around 900 × 900mm to 750 × 750mm) and corresponding reinforcement content reductions of about a third. In addition, there may be potential reductions in foundation size. Clearly, in this simple example, any increases in ECO_2 for the higher strength class would have to be offset against a more slender structural solution offering potential

Table 4.14   Designed concretes for exposure class XC3/4 and minimum 50 years.

Minimum cover (mm)	Strength class	Min cement content (kg/m3)	Max w/c ratio	Designed concrete
20	C40/50	340	0.45	RC40/50
25	C30/37	300	0.55	RC30/37
30	C28/35	280	0.60	RC28/35
≥35	C25/30	260	0.65	RC25/30

Table 4.15   Comparison of concrete structure embodied CO_2 for different concrete strength classes.

	Base Option	Option 1	Option 2	Option 3
Concrete class for slab	C32/40	C32/40	C50/60	C50/60
Concrete class for vertical elements	C32/40	C50/60	C50/60	C60/75
Volume of concrete in slab m³	2,110	2,110	1,841	1,841
Volume of concrete in verticals	1,112	956	956	885
Change in net lettable area	0%	1.22%	1.22%	1.78%
Tonnes ECO_2	1,369	1,346	1,492	1,477
Percentage of base option	100%	98%	109%	108%

Note: Eurocode 2 requires the slab strength to be no less than two-thirds the column strength.

economic, environmental and social benefits to the design team, contractor and client alike.

In Table 4.15, three options compared with a base case are presented to investigate the effect of changing concrete strength class on ECO_2. The effect of increasing concrete strength and reducing section size on the floor area available to let and the total ECO_2 of a structure is considered in more detail in Concrete Structures 9 (TCC, 2009).

4.12   Key guidance to specify sustainable concrete

Guidance that balances the desire to specify concrete with low environmental impact, whilst ensuring other performance parameters are optimised can be summarised as follows:

- Specify responsibly sourced concrete and reinforcement.
- Permit the use of recycled and secondary aggregates but do not over specify as they may not be the most sustainable option.
- Specify that concrete should always contain CEM II/CEM III or an addition.
- ECO_2 of concrete should not be considered or specified in isolation of other factors such as strength gain.
- Permit the use of admixtures.
- Do not specify aggregate sizes below 10mm unless necessary.
- Do not over specify strength.
- Consider the possibility of strength conformity at 56 days rather than the conventional 28 days.
- When aesthetics are critical, specify the type and % of additions to ensure colour.

4.13 Summary

The advent of sustainability has necessitated an increased understanding of material specification and this extends to material constituents and their production. A thorough assessment of the sustainability impacts and benefits of all constituents of concrete should be an integral part of material specification.

Assessing environmental impacts of materials is introduced with the concepts of 'project context' and 'functional equivalence' which should be taken into account in assessment methods. The context should always be that materials are used in components, components in elements and elements in systems to deliver a project. Key to functional equivalence is about comparing 'like with like'. The complete range of environmental impacts is considered and classified into impact categories. The process of assessing environmental impacts across different life stages is called Life Cycle Impact Assessment. The output from a Life Cycle Assessment can be communicated by an Environmental Product Declaration which is defined by ISO 14025: 2006.

Responsible sourcing is an increasingly important factor for specifiers and clients in the construction industry. The concrete industry was the first in construction to issue a guidance document supporting compliance with BES 6001 (BRE, 2008), resulting in the widespread accreditation of concrete products in the UK.

Cements and combinations represent the majority of ECO_2 of concrete. Cementitious additions such as GGBS, fly ash and silica fume are used as cement replacements to lower the ECO_2 of concrete, but they also improve concrete's properties such as workability, durability and sulphate resistance. With regard to strength, concretes with GGBS and fly ash additions exhibit lower early age strengths than those containing Portland cement only. They have relatively higher strengths after 28 days.

Aggregates are the major component of concrete by volume, and whilst a low carbon product, they make a big contribution to concrete's resource depletion impact. Recycled aggregates, recycled concrete aggregates and, secondary & manufactured aggregates may be specified to replace naturally occurring aggregates. However, the resource depletion impact should be balanced against transportation CO_2 impacts and implications on mix design. In the UK, the ECO_2 impact of recycled aggregates may be higher than virgin aggregates if the delivery distance is further than 15km.

Unlike ECO_2 emissions which are a global problem, water scarcity is a local problem. The concrete industry in the UK is monitoring both its mains and groundwater consumption, with the aim to achieving reductions in water use. Particular admixtures are also used that reduce the waste produced at ready mix concrete plants.

Admixtures such as superplasticisers and accelerating, retarding or air entraining agents can reduce ECO_2 of concrete, despite having relatively high ECO_2 themselves, while maintaining and even enhancing properties of concrete such as resistance to freeze thaw.

Novel constituents of concrete include novel cements such as alkali-activated cements and geopolymer cements, CSA – belite cements, magnesium oxide cements from magnesium carbonates, magnesium oxide cements from magnesium silicate and C-Fix cement and, novel aggregates such as recycled glass aggregates.

The embodied energy values of reinforcing steel are based on the energy used to melt scrap metal and reform it. Although all steel manufacture is an energy-intensive process, the energy needed to produce one tonne of reinforcing steel is as low as one third of that needed to make one tonne of structural steel from iron ore. Equally, reinforcing steel itself can be recovered, recycled and re-used at the end of a building or structure's service life. The UK is leading in the concept of responsible sourcing of reinforcement.

Special concretes have a particular functional performance such as pumpability, low shrinkage, high insulating properties or high early strength gain and at the same time provide sustainability benefits. Examples of special concretes include fibre-reinforced concrete, self-compacting concrete and ultra high strength fibre-reinforced concrete.

Acknowledgements

Sections 4.3, 4.4, 4.5, 4.6, 4.7, 4.9 and 4.11 contain extracts reproduced with permission from 'Specifying Sustainable Concrete' edited by Andrew Minson and published by The Concrete Centre in 2011, or from its intended reprint in 2014. The authors acknowledge the work of colleagues at The Concrete Centre, Chris Clear of BRMCA and Mike Taylor of MPA Cement with thanks.

References

Anderson, J. & Thornback, J. (2012) *A Guide to Understanding the Embodied impacts of Construction Products*, Construction Products Association, UK.

BERR (2008) *Strategy for Sustainable Construction* BERR (Department for Business Enterprise & Regulatory Reform), UK, http://www.berr.gov.uk/files/file46535.pdf

BRE (2007) *Methodology for environmental profiles of construction products, section 7.2.1*, Building Research Establishment (BRE), UK.

BRE (2008) *BES 6001, BRE Environmental & Sustainability Standard Framework Standard for the Responsible Sourcing of Construction Products – Issue 1*, Building Research Establishment (BRE), UK.

BRE (2009) *The Green Guide to Specification*, 4th Edition, Building Research Establishment (BRE), UK.

BSI (2001a) *BS EN 206–1 Concrete: Specification, performance, production and conformity*, British Standard Institution (BSI), UK.

BSI (2001b) *BS 7979, Specification for limestone fines for use with Portland cement*, British Standard Institution (BSI), UK.

BSI (2002a) *BS EN 12620: 2002+A1:2008, Aggregates for concrete*, British Standard Institution (BSI), UK.

BSI (2002b) *BS EN 1008: 2002, Mixing water for concrete - Specification for sampling, testing and assessing the suitability of water, including water recovered from processes in the concrete industry, as mixing water for concrete*, British Standard Institution (BSI), UK.

BSI (2002c) *EN 1990, Eurocode. Basis of structural design*, British Standard Institution (BSI), UK.

BSI (2004) *BS EN ISO 14001: 2004, Environmental Management Systems*, British Standard Institution (BSI), UK.

BSI (2005a) *BS 4449: 2005 Steel for the reinforcement of concrete - Weldable reinforcing steel - Bar, coil and decoiled product specification*, British Standard Institution (BSI), UK.

BSI (2005b) *BS 4483: 2005, Steel fabric for the reinforcement of concrete - Specification*, British Standard Institution (BSI), UK.

BSI (2005c) *BS 8666: 2005, Scheduling, dimensioning, bending and cutting of steel reinforcement for concrete - Specification*, British Standard Institution (BSI), UK.

BSI (2006) BS 8500–1: 2006 *Concrete - Complementary British Standard to BS EN 206–1 - Part 1: Method of specifying and guidance for the specifier*, British Standard Institution (BSI), UK.

BSI (2009a) *BS 8902: 2009 Responsible sourcing sector certification schemes for construction products - Specification*, British Standard Institution (BSI), UK.

BSI (2009b) *BS EN 934-2 Admixtures for Concrete Mortar and Grout - Part 2: Concrete admixtures - Definitions, requirements, conformity, marking and labelling*, British Standard Institution (BSI), UK.

BSI (2012) BS EN 15804: 2012 *Sustainability of construction works — Environmental product declarations — Core rules for the product category of construction products*, British Standard Institution (BSI), UK.

CAA (2012) Cement Admixtures Association (CAA), UK, www.admixtures.org.uk

CAN (2010) *A Long Term View of CO_2 Efficient Manufacturing in the European Region*, Climate Action Network Europe (CAN), CE Delft, Netherlands.

Chana, P. (2011) *Low Carbon Cements: The Challenges and Opportunities*, First Global Future Cements Conference, London, UK.

Clear, C.A. (1994) *Formwork striking times of ground granulated blastfurnace slag concrete: test and site results*, Proceedings, Institution of Civil Engineers, *Structures & Buildings*, 104, Nov. 441–448.

Clear, C.A. (2011) *Cement type/early age properties, Concrete Today*, The Magazine of the British Ready-Mixed Concrete Industry, EMap, UK.

Concrete Society (2007a) *Technical Report 63 Guidance for the Design of Steel-Fibre-Reinforced Concrete*, Concrete Society, UK.

Concrete Society (2007b) *Technical Report 65 Guidance on the use of Macro-synthetic-fibre-reinforced concrete*, Concrete Society, UK.

DCLG (2007) *Survey of Arisings and Use of Alternatives to Primary Aggregates in England 2005*, Construction and Waste, Department of Communities and Local Government (DCLG), UK.

Department for Transport (2011) *The Design Manual for Roads and Bridges*, Department for Transport, UK.

EU (2012) LCA Tools, Services, Data and Studies, Joint Research Centre, European Commission (EU) http://lca.jrc.ec.europa.eu/lcainfohub/datasetArea.vm

Harrison, T.A. (1995) *Formwork striking times – criteria, prediction and methods of assessment*, CIRIA Report 136, UK.

Marsh, B. (2006) *One Coleman Street – A Case Study In The Use Of Secondary Materials In Concrete*; The Institute of Concrete Technology; Annual Technical Symposium; UK.

Minson, A. and Berrie, I. (2013) *Admixtures and Sustainable Concrete*, The Institution of Structural Engineers, *The Structural Engineer*, UK.

MPA (2008) *Guideline to BES 6001, Concrete Industry Guidance Document to support BES 6001, Issue 1*, Mineral Products Association (MPA) on behalf of the Sustainable Concrete Forum, UK. Download from www.sustainableconcrete.org.uk.

MPA (2008) *Sheet C1 – Embodied CO2 of concrete and reinforced concrete*, Mineral Products Association (MPA) on behalf of the Sustainable Concrete Forum, UK. www.sustainableconcrete.org.uk

MPA Cement (2011) *Performance 2010 – A Sector Plan Report from the UK Cement Industry*, Mineral Products Association (MPA) - Cement, UK.

MPA (2013) *Fact Sheet 18 Embodied CO_2e of UK cement, additions and cementitious material*, Mineral Products Association with CSMA and UKQAA, UK.

Neville, A.M. (2011) *Properties of Concrete*, Fifth Edition, UK.

Product Category Rules for EPD of concrete (2013) *Product Category Rules for Environmental Product Declaration (EPD) of concrete*, UN CPC 375, International.

Reddy, J. (2007) *A Decision Making Tool for the Striking of Formwork to GGBS Concretes* (a project report submitted for the award of diploma in Advanced Concrete Technology), The Institute of Concrete Technology, UK.

TCC (2009) *Concrete Structures 9*, The Concrete Centre (TCC), UK.

TCC (2013) *Concrete Industry Sustainability Performance Report, 6th report: 2012 performance data*, MPA - The Concrete Centre (TCC), UK.

UK Steel (2012) *Key Statistics 2012*, UK Steel.

5 Construction, Operation and End of Life

5.1 Construction

The method of construction is mostly determined at the conceptual or scheme design stage of a building project where decisions on the structural form are taken, for example, on-site for post tensioned slabs or off-site for precast slabs. Both on-site and off-site solutions offer sustainability benefits. For example in-situ concrete is more flexible, more economical and supports local employment although precast concrete offers better finish, reduction in waste materials and less noise, dust and local disruption. A modern method of construction that combines and maximises the benefits of in-situ and precast concrete is hybrid concrete construction. Precast concrete is used where there are many repetitions and in-situ can be used for the remainder of the build. Precast can be used where longer lead times can be accommodated and in-situ is ideal for basement and/or lower levels. Precast may be preferred for exposed surfaces due to higher quality finish and the opportunity to check quality before incorporating the element into the works. In-situ is ideal for providing stitching together of precast elements on-site in a manner that gives structural continuity and hence efficiency from hogging moments over supports. The result is a more economic and faster construction system.

Construction affects the natural environment and therefore all stakeholders involved such as contractors, suppliers, and so on, must take responsibility for the environmental impact of their activity. Environmental Management Systems (EMS) provide contractors with a structured framework for managing, evaluating and improving their environmental performance. An EMS can help a company reduce emissions, comply with environmental regulations, improve resource efficiency and reduce costs. Implementation of an EMS is usually carried out in accordance with a recognised standard and

Sustainable Concrete Solutions, First Edition. Costas Georgopoulos and Andrew Minson.
© 2014 John Wiley & Sons, Ltd. Published 2014 by John Wiley & Sons, Ltd.

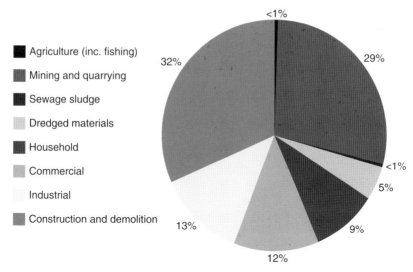

<1%

■ Agriculture (inc. fishing)   32%   29%

▦ Mining and quarrying

■ Sewage sludge

▒ Dredged materials

▦ Household   <1%

▒ Commercial   5%

░ Industrial

▦ Construction and demolition   13%   9%

12%

Total = 335 million tonnes
Source: Defra, ODPM, Environment Agency, Water UK

Figure 5.1   Estimated total annual waste arising by sector. © Crown Copyright, reproduced under the terms of the Open Government Licence (http://www.nationalarchives.gov.uk/doc/open-government-licence/).

companies aim to achieve certification that is an independent recognition of their performance. For example in the UK, all cement plants and 95% of ready-mix concrete suppliers are certified to the international standard BS EN ISO 14001 (BSI, 2009).

Construction also uses a large quantity of resources and produces a large amount of waste. The UK construction industry produces a third of all waste generated in the UK (Figure 5.1).

Reduction in site waste is an important part of sustainable construction because it helps optimise the use of energy, water and materials. Furthermore waste reduction reduces transportation and processing of the waste itself and the land area required. For example, with the UK running out of space to store and dispose of waste, the government set a target to reduce waste to landfill that includes a reduction of construction, demolition and excavation (CDE) waste volumes by 50% by 2012 (from a 2008 benchmark) and to zero by 2020 (TCC, 2010).

A mechanism to achieve these reductions is the Site Waste Management Plans (SWMP) which are required for all projects in England and Wales in excess of £300,000 with increased requirements for those in excess of £500,000. The SWMPs require planning, monitoring and reviewing of levels of waste generated on site and they are also mandatory in BREEAM and Code for Sustainable Homes for projects of £300,000 or more.

Concrete, in its various forms, can support achieving the waste target as well as resulting in programme and cost benefits, as follows:

Figure 5.2   SKYDECK aluminium panel slab formwork. Reproduced by permission of PERI.

- Concrete waste is simply segregated and recycled: For new build projects concrete waste can be returned to the batching plant or recycled on site.
- Careful ordering and storage on site: As with all building materials waste can be reduced by careful estimations of materials required, an organised site layout and just in time deliveries.
- Re-use formwork and falsework: System falsework and formwork is designed to be used hundreds of times and can be recycled.

From 2008 to 2012, the UK concrete industry has reduced the total tonnage of waste it sends to landfill by 72% (TCC, 2013).

Innovations in formwork have also improved health and safety on site. For example, with PERI's SKYDECK (Figure 5.2) all components are made of aluminium weighing not more than 15kg. This enables easy and safe erection and striking from below.

5.2   Operation

The energy used for space heating accounts for 20–50% of a building's energy consumption depending on type, and around a third of the carbon emissions from all UK buildings (TCC, 2012). There is also concern that buildings in London will consume more energy for air conditioning in the future in order to cope with increased temperatures due to climate change. Exposed concrete can contribute in saving energy for both heating and cooling of buildings with its inherent property of thermal mass. For more information see Annex D.

Concrete offers low maintenance and robust structures, cladding and separating walls – not damaged by moisture ingress, flood waters or internal water leaks/flooding. Concrete structures do not need corrosion and fire protection such as steel structures and concrete cladding does not need treatment such as some timber cladding. Concrete's long life and low maintenance operation arises from its unsurpassed durability – this means that embodied impacts are, in effect, spread over a longer period.

5.3 End of life

The optimum sustainable solution for an existing structure at the end of its life is reusing it as the energy required for refurbishment and the amount of waste produced would be typically less than demolishing and rebuilding. Concrete structures are durable and robust; concrete framed buildings are more likely to come to the end of their life because no further use can be found for them, rather than the concrete having failed due to age. Concrete structures are also flexible and adaptable; seemingly redundant structures can often be stripped back to their core and rebuilt to new, contemporary specifications. It is therefore quite common these days to refurbish and extend the life of old concrete structures rather than demolish them. An example is Elizabeth II Court, one of Hampshire County Council's office buildings.

Instead of demolishing the old concrete framed building it was decided to reuse it and take advantage of exposed concrete in meeting the challenge of providing a more sustainable building whilst maintaining its required functionality. The existing concrete frame was retained, significantly reducing the demolition waste, and the concrete cladding was removed and reused as aggregate in other materials. At the same time thermal mass from exposed concrete was fully exploited to improve the energy efficiency of the building (TCC, 2010).

If a concrete framed building has to be demolished then its concrete is 100% recyclable. Concrete and reinforcement can be separated out for recycling. The rubble from a demolished structure can be segregated and crushed. If concrete is mixed with other inert materials such as brick then the demolition waste can be used for recycled aggregates for hard core in highways or fill in landscaping. Pure concrete rubble can be used for recycled concrete aggregates in structural concrete. Furthermore demolition and crushing of concrete increases the amount of carbonation – see also 2.3.2.1 – (recarbonation) significantly and therefore reduces the net CO_2 impact. Existing models for calculating recarbonation in Nordic countries do not take into account what takes place after concrete has been demolished

(Pade & Guimaraes, 2007). In the UK, when averaged across the key UK cement markets/applications, recarbonation provides around a 20% reduction in whole life CO_2 emissions (Clear & De Saulles, 2007). Consequently, the contribution of the cement and concrete industry to net CO_2 emissions is significantly overestimated.

The majority of secondary and recycled aggregates end up as sub-base and fill, including use in road building and airfield pavements. The wide taxiways at Terminal 5, Heathrow Airport, built to accommodate the coming generation of 'super jumbo' aircraft use recycled concrete aggregates. Approximately, 100,000 tonnes of recycled concrete aggregates was used at Heathrow in the 12 months to August 2004.

Although Construction and Demolition Waste (C&DW) is the UK's largest single source of recycled material, only a small percentage of C&DW is used in the manufacture of new concrete. Barriers are usually the locations of supply and demand, the availability and consistency of recycled concrete aggregates and historically adverse perception of its quality, however, this latter barrier has been largely overcome. To help reduce and remove these barriers, the Waste Resources and Action Programme (WRAP) was set up in 2002 to promote the greater use of recycled and secondary aggregates, including recycled concrete aggregates (WRAP, 2012).

London Remade's construction and demolition waste site in Greenwich tackles some of the 14 million tonnes of C&DW produced by London every year and primarily reprocesses the debris for reuse in concrete production rather than as low-value bulk fill – making it the first of its kind in the UK. The facility is capable of processing 200,000 tonnes of C&DW per year or approximately 1,500 tonnes every day. The site is built on brownfield land, and its location alongside the River Thames gives the potential for more transportation of waste and recycled concrete aggregate by river rather than road (London Remade, 2012). However, as seen in Chapter 4, transportation carbon impacts are relatively significant for aggregates which are otherwise a low carbon product. Given that use of recycled aggregates always replaces use of virgin aggregates, it is largely irrelevant to what purpose they are put, but more critical that they are recovered and used. And this is the case in the UK with 29% of all aggregates being either recycled or secondary.

5.4 Summary

Construction affects the natural environment and therefore all stakeholders involved such as contractors, suppliers, designers and clients must take responsibility for the environmental impact of their activity. Environmental Management Systems (EMS) provide stakeholders with a structured framework for managing, evaluating and improving their environmental performance. In the UK, all cement plants and 95% of ready-mix concrete suppliers are certified to the international standard ISO 14001.

Construction uses a large quantity of resources and produces a large amount of waste. The UK construction industry produces a third of all waste generated in the UK. Concrete, in its various forms, can support reducing construction waste by recycling waste and returning it to the batching plant, careful ordering and storage of materials on site and reusing formwork and falsework.

The energy used for space heating accounts for 20–50% of a building's energy consumption depending on type, and around a third of the carbon emissions from all UK buildings. Exposed concrete can contribute in saving energy for both heating and cooling of buildings with its inherent property of thermal mass.

The optimum sustainable solution for an existing structure at the end of its life is reusing it.

Concrete structures are durable, robust, flexible and adaptable; seemingly redundant structures can often be stripped back to their core and rebuilt to new, contemporary specifications. It is therefore quite common these days to refurbish and extend the life of old concrete structures rather than demolish them. If a concrete framed building has to be demolished then its concrete is 100% recyclable. Furthermore demolition and crushing of concrete increases the amount of carbonation (recarbonation) significantly and therefore reduces the net CO_2 impact of the cement and concrete industry.

References

BSI (2009) *Environmental management systems – Requirements with guidance for use* (2004 incorporating corrigendum July 2009), British Standard Institution (BSI), UK.

Clear, C. and De Saulles, T. (2007) *BCA Recarbonation Study*, British Cement Association, UK.

London Remade (2012) Construction and Demolition Waste Site at www.london remade.com

Pade, C. and Guimaraes, M. (2007) *The CO_2 Uptake of Concrete in a 100 year Perspective*, Cement and Concrete Research, Science Direct, Elsevier.

TCC (2010) *Material Efficiency: Optimising performance with low waste design solutions in concrete*, MPA – The Concrete Centre (TCC), UK.

TCC (2012) *Thermal Mass Explained*, MPA – The Concrete Centre (TCC), UK.

TCC (2013) *Concrete Industry Sustainability Performance Report*, Sixth report: 2012 performance data, MPA – The Concrete Centre (TCC), UK.

WRAP (2012) Waste and Resources Action Programme (WRAP) UK www.wrap.org.uk

Appendix A: Thermal Mass

A.1 Introduction

Until recently, the use of thermal mass in heating and/or cooling a building was ignored in favour of energy consuming alternatives. With the advent of climate change and the need to reduce carbon emissions, thermal mass is increasingly utilised to help provide energy efficient solutions for new and existing buildings. In the UK, the benefits of thermal mass have now been incorporated into the Building Regulations Part L1 on Energy. Designers can demonstrate and justify compliance with the regulations taking into account thermal mass if they choose to do so. The benefits of thermal mass can be exploited in the winter to help reduce the heating load when used with greater levels of insulation and airtightness – as required by building regulations – and, in the summer to help reduce the cooling load when used in combination with good ventilation and shading. The following sections comprise a definition of thermal mass, how thermal mass works, how to take thermal mass into account in design, measuring thermal mass, the difference between thermal mass and insulation and, a case study of a code level 6 home – that is, using the potential of thermal mass to achieve a zero carbon home in accordance with the Code for Sustainable Homes.

A.2 Definition of thermal mass

The term thermal mass describes the ability of a material to absorb and release heat. With respect to buildings, thermal mass can be used to help stabilise the internal temperature and provide a largely self-regulating environment with a more constant temperature irrespective of variable external temperatures. When used appropriately, this stabilising effect (Figure A.1) helps prevent overheating problems during the summer and reduces the need for mechanical cooling and, helps reduce fuel usage during the winter by capturing and later releasing solar gains and heat from internal appliances.

For a material to provide a useful level of thermal mass, the following combination of three basic properties is required (TCC, 2012):

1. A high specific heat capacity; so the heat absorbed into every kg is maximised.

Sustainable Concrete Solutions, First Edition. Costas Georgopoulos and Andrew Minson.
© 2014 John Wiley & Sons, Ltd. Published 2014 by John Wiley & Sons, Ltd.

2. A high density; the heavier the material, the more heat it can store.
3. Moderate thermal conductivity – so the rate heat flows in and out of the material is roughly in step with the daily heating and cooling cycle of the building.

Heavyweight construction materials such as brick, stone and concrete all have these properties. They combine a high storage capacity with moderate thermal conductivity, a combination of all the points above (Table A.1). This means that heat moves between the material's surface and its interior at a rate that matches the daily heating and cooling cycle of buildings. Some materials,

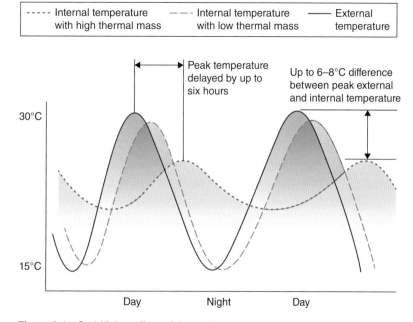

Figure A.1   Stabilising effect of thermal mass on internal temperature. Reproduced by permission of The Concrete Centre.

Table A.1   Thermal properties of common construction materials (CIBSE, 2006).

Building material	Density (kg/m3)	Specific heat capacity (J/kgK)	Thermal conductivity (W/mK)	Effective thermal mass
Brick	1700	800	0.73	High
Concrete: precast and in-situ	2300	1000	1.63	High
Concrete block: Medium weight aggregate	1400	1000	0.51	Medium-High
Concrete block: Light weight aggregate	1000	600	0.19	Medium
Steel	7800	480	50.0	Low
Timber	650	1200	0.14	Low

like timber, have a high heat capacity, but their thermal conductivity is relatively low, limiting the rate at which heat is absorbed during the day and released at night, although this can be useful in other ways. Steel can also store heat, but in contrast to timber, it possesses a very high rate of thermal conductivity, which means that heat is absorbed and released too rapidly to be synchronised with a building's natural heat flow.

Maximum solar altitude in summer 40°–64°

South

Summer day

- During very hot weather, windows are kept shut to keep out the warm air.
- Overhangs on the south elevation keep out the high angle sun during the hottest part of the day. Alternative forms of shading can also be used.
- Radiant and convective cooling is provided by thermal mass in the floor and walls, which absorb heat and help stabilise the internal temperature.

Summer night

- Windows are opened at night to ventilate the building and cool the fabric.
- If another hot day is expected, the windows are closed again in the morning and the cycle is repeated.

Figure A.2   Thermal mass in summer (UK type climate). Reproduced by permission of The Concrete Centre.

Maximum solar altitude during the heating season 17°–40°

South

Winter day

- During the heating season, the low angle sun can shine through south facing windows, and the heat is absorbed by thermal mass in the floor and walls.
- In the evening when the sun goes down and the temperature drops, the heat flow is reversed and passes back into the room.

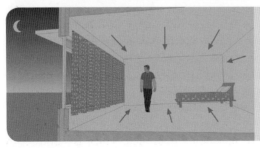

Winter night

- At night, curtains are drawn and windows kept shut to minimise heat loss.
- Heat continues to be released by the thermal mass and supplementary heating is adjusted so only the minimal amount is used.
- By morning the thermal mass will have given up most of its heat and the occupants will typically have to rely on supplementary heating until later in the day.

Figure A.3   Thermal mass in winter (UK type climate). Reproduced by permission of The Concrete Centre.

A.3   How thermal mass works

Figures A.2 and A.3 show how thermal mass works in the summer and in the winter respectively.

In the UK, the daily heating and cooling cycle in the summer works well as the air temperature at night is typically 10 degrees less than the peak daytime temperature. In warmer parts of the world such as northern Australia the temperature difference between night and day is small, thermal mass offers little or no benefit at all and lightweight materials are more appropriate in vernacular architecture.

A.4   How to take thermal mass into account in design

Making the most of thermal mass on a year-round basis requires a holistic approach to design in which issues such as location/orientation/glazing/internal layout, and internal surfaces/insulation are considered together with thermal mass in order to provide comfortable, low energy solutions. In the UK climate, Passive Solar Design (PSD) describes this holistic design method with respect to minimising winter heating.

A.4.1   Location/orientation/glazing/internal layout

PSD optimises a building's form, fabric and orientation to maximise solar gain from autumn to spring, whilst minimising it during the warmest part of the summer. At the same time, day-lighting is maximised at all times, adding to the overall well-being and comfort of the occupants. PSD may cost very little to implement and can make a useful contribution to the energy efficiency of new build and, to some extent, refurbishment projects.

The basic requirements of PSD are:

- A sufficiently clear view of the sky from the south avoiding over shadowing (Figure A.4).
- A high standard of insulation and airtightness that meets or exceeds modern requirements such as Fabric Energy Efficiency Standard.
- Adequate south facing windows (or within 30° of south) to maximise solar gains during the heating season. The optimal area of glazing will be determined by various design issues including cost, ventilation rate and level of thermal mass, but as a very rough guide it should be at least twice that of any north facing windows, but no more than around 40–50% of the façade to avoid overheating problems. Low iron glass (clearer than normal glass) can be used to optimise solar gain (Figure A.5).
- Minimal north facing windows to avoid excessive heat loss. Over the course of the year north facing windows have a net heat loss and should be limited to around 15% of the room's floor area, which is sufficient to provide adequate day-lighting.

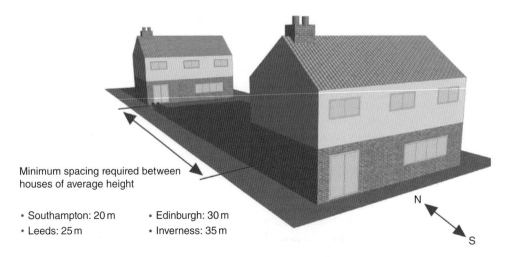

Minimum spacing required between
houses of average height

- Southampton: 20 m
- Leeds: 25 m
- Edinburgh: 30 m
- Inverness: 35 m

N

S

Figure A.4   House spacing to avoid over shadowing. Reproduced by permission of The Concrete Centre.

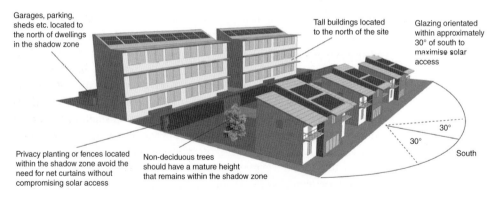

Garages, parking, sheds etc. located to the north of dwellings in the shadow zone

Tall buildings located to the north of the site

Glazing orientated within approximately 30° of south to maximise solar access

30°

30°

South

Privacy planting or fences located within the shadow zone avoid the need for net curtains without compromising solar access

Non-deciduous trees should have a mature height that remains within the shadow zone

Figure A.5   To maximise solar gain during the heating season, most of a building's glazing should face south or within 30° of south, with minimal overshadowing from around 9am to 3pm. Reproduced by permission of The Concrete Centre.

- A medium to high level of thermal mass. The Thermal Mass Parameter (TMP) – see definition in A5 – should ideally exceed 200kJ/m²K and include a solid ground floor with a finish that partially or fully exposes the floor's thermal mass.
- An ability to adequately ventilate the building during the summer, taking account of any site specific security and/or noise issues.
- Adequate shading. Overhangs, balconies and brise soleils are particularly effective on south facing windows (Figure A.5), but other forms of shading can be used. Although not popular in the UK, shutters are highly effective, with the added benefit of offering a means of secure ventilation and reduced heat loss in winter.

Where practicable, the most frequently used rooms should be on the south side of the dwelling, so that they enjoy the greatest benefit to be had from solar gain during the heating season. Bathrooms, utility rooms, hallways, stores and so on, should be located on the north side of accommodation. The cooling benefits from thermal mass tend to be slightly lower in bedrooms than for the general living spaces. So, in southern England where summer temperatures are highest, there may be some benefit in locating bedrooms on the north side. Another option that can help is to specify a concrete upper floor. Providing the mass remains reasonably accessible, this can improve year-round thermal performance. A further option is to locate south facing bedrooms on the ground floor, so they get the full benefit of stack ventilation at night. The stack effect uses the difference in air temperature at high and low level to draw cool night air into ground floor rooms, where it then travels upwards through the building and exits from windows on the upper floor(s), having absorbed heat from the building fabric on route. A house designed to take advantage of stack ventilation will benefit from more consistent air flow, particularly on still nights.

A.4.2   Insulation/internal surfaces

Thermal mass is not a substitute for insulation, and a combination of the two is needed to optimise fabric energy efficiency. The position of the insulation relative to the thermal mass is of particular importance. The simple rule is that the thermal mass should be located inside the insulated building envelope. In practical terms, a cavity wall already satisfies the basic rule, as the insulation is located in the cavity, allowing the inner leaf of block work to be exposed to the room. For solid masonry walls, the insulation should be located on the outer surface, which is usual practice (Figure A.6). The insulation for solid ground floors should ideally be located under the slab, although screed placed on top of insulation will also provide some useful thermal mass.

Typically, thermal mass is provided by concrete/masonry walls and floors, but other heavyweight materials can be equally effective. It is not essential for the sun to shine directly on all internal surfaces for heat to be absorbed, as convection

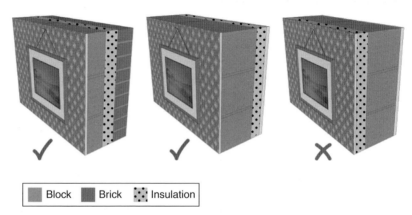

Block   Brick   Insulation

Figure A.6   Locating insulation in external walls to maximise thermal mass. Reproduced by permission of The Concrete Centre.

and radiation between surfaces will help distribute warmth throughout the space. Surfaces do not have to be a dark colour, as any small benefit in heat absorption may impact on day-lighting. However, it is important that the surface of heavyweight walls and floors remain as thermally exposed as practicable.

For walls, this is best achieved with a wet plaster finish, as this will conduct heat relatively freely and offers the added benefit of providing a robust air barrier that will help minimise air leakage. Dry lining such as plasterboard will reduce heat flow, but its impact will depend on the thermal mass potentially available in the wall. For an aircrete block inner leaf (which has a relatively low thermal conductivity), plasterboard is less of a thermal bottle-neck than for heavier weight aggregate blockwork, which has higher thermal conductivity and is more sensitive to the choice of finish. Therefore, to fully exploit the high level of thermal mass available in aggregate blocks, the use of dry lining is best avoided.

With some forms of concrete wall and floor construction, it is possible to achieve a high quality, fair-faced finish which requires little more than a coat of paint. From a thermal mass perspective, this is particularly beneficial as heat can pass directly between the room and the concrete. Although not often used in residential buildings, a fair-faced finish is more common in low energy commercial offices or schools where an exposed concrete soffit is often used to provide thermal mass.

Wherever practicable, floors should be tiled, and the use of carpet avoided, as placing carpet on a concrete floor can reduce its ability to admit heat by half (Nelson, 1995). A shiny or glossy floor finish will absorb less heat than a dull finish however this must be evaluated alongside day-lighting requirements and the tendency of such a surface to absorb light. A tiled floor also works well with under floor heating (Figure A.7).

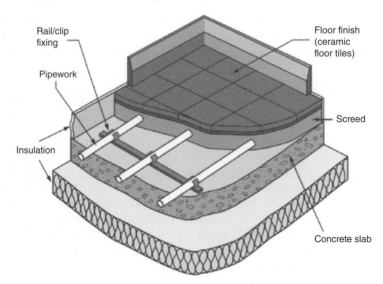

Figure A.7   A tiled floor will allow a concrete floor slab's thermal mass to be fully exploited and is also suited to under-floor heating. Reproduced by permission of The Concrete Centre.

A.5   Measuring thermal mass

In accordance with Part L of the Building Regulations and Standard Assessment Procedure (SAP) – (BRE, 2009) – thermal mass is accounted using k-values (kJ/m²K) which represent the heat capacity per square meter of floor or wall measured from the inside surface stopping at which ever of the following conditions occur first:

- halfway through the construction element;
- an insulating layer (thermal conductivity less than 0.08W/m.K);
- a depth of 100mm.

Typical k-values for different construction elements can be found in SAP 2009 Table 1e and also in The Concrete Centre publication: Thermal Performance: Part L1A. SAP calculates a dwelling's overall thermal mass by multiplying the surface area for each construction element by its k-value and adding the results. The total is then divided by the floor area of the dwelling to give the Thermal Mass Parameter (TMP) measured in kJ/m²K, where 'm²' refers to the dwelling's floor area.

Describing a material as having high, medium or low thermal mass gives a useful indication of its ability to store heat, as does its k-value, but in order to know how effective a chosen material will be in practice, there are a couple of other important factors that need to be taken into account. These are, firstly, the length of time available to get heat in and out of the material, which is typically assumed to be 24 hours (i.e. heating during the day and cooling at night), and secondly, the resistance to heat flow at the surface of the material, which can be significant. These factors are both accounted for in admittance values, along with thermal capacity, conductivity and density. Admittance values provide a practical means of assessing the approximate in-use heat absorption performance of walls and floors and so on.

From a technical perspective, admittance can be defined as the ability of a material or construction element to exchange heat with a space when it is subject to cyclic variations in temperature. Admittance is measured in W/m²K, as U-values. However the 'K' represents something different, that is, the difference between the mean internal temperature and the actual temperature at a specific time of day. It is this dynamic temperature difference that drives heat in and out of the fabric. In contrast, the 'K' in U-values is the difference between internal and external temperature, which is assumed to be constant, which is why U-values are the steady state. Another difference is that high admittance values are desirable from a thermal mass perspective, whilst low U-values will minimise heat loss.

Bespoke k-values and other thermal mass related information can be calculated using a free Dynamic Thermal Properties Calculator developed by Arup, which can be downloaded at The Concrete Centre website.

A.6   Difference between thermal mass and insulation

The difference between insulation and thermal mass is widely misunderstood. Insulation is to do with heat transfer through the wall (Figure A.8) whereas thermal mass is transfer of heat in and out of the all from the internal space (Figure A.9).

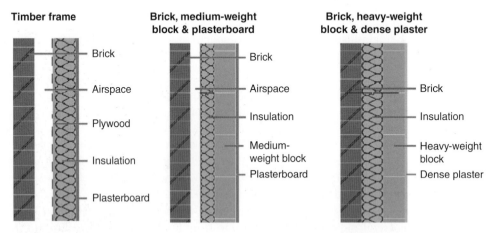

Figure A.8   Insulation reduces the energy transferred THROUGH the wall. The U value (in W/m²K) is the same for all three wall constructions. Reproduced by permission of The Concrete Centre.

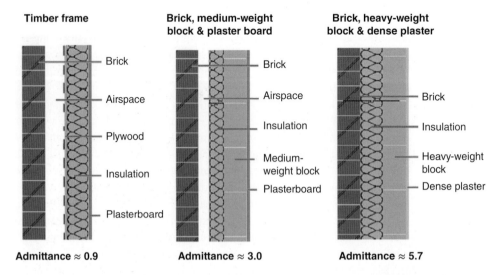

Figure A.9   Thermal mass is different for the three cross sections as indicated by the admittance (in W/m²K) value for each. Energy is stored IN the wall on the internal side (right) of the insulation. Reproduced by permission of The Concrete Centre.

A.7 Case study of a code level 6 home

The Tarmac Homes project, a test-bed initiative led by Tarmac, affordable housing developer Lovell and The University of Nottingham's Department of the Built Environment (Lovell, 2012), built two prototype semi-detached homes – one to level 4 and the other to the highest level 6 of the Code for Sustainable Homes (Figure A.10).

Figure A.10a   Tarmac homes project (front). Reproduced by permission of Tarmac Building Products.

Figure A.10b   Tarmac homes project (back). Reproduced by permission of Tarmac Building Products.

Both properties are traditional, semi-detached homes built using concrete and masonry to maximise their thermal efficiency. The houses were constructed of regular brick and concrete masonry with internal walls coated with lightweight plaster in order to achieve a high airtightness standard. This, together with external insulation, minimises heat loss and reduces energy demand. The masonry fabric, with its high thermal mass, helps achieve passive heating and cooling, integral to achieving the targeted carbon saving in this design.

A mix of heat recovery and micro-generation technologies incorporating a biomass boiler, a solar thermal hot water system, photovoltaic roof panels and a passive wind cowl, deliver the heat, power and ventilation for the house.

The project, which also tested the commercial viability of building zero-carbon homes, provided the housing industry with an indication of the costs to meet the government's residential carbon reduction targets. The code level 6 home, designed to achieve a CO_2 reduction target of 150% compared to 2006 Part L levels, cost £38,000 more than a typical house of the same size.

Unlike some other showcase sustainable homes, the houses will be fully occupied by students and/or university staff and monitored for up to 20 years to provide feedback to designers on zero carbon performance over time.

Acknowledgments

The authors acknowledge with thanks the work of Tom de Saulles, Building Physicist at The Concrete Centre, whose authorship of all The Concrete Centre publications on Thermal Mass was the basis for this appendix and who developed the images contained herein.

References

BRE (2009) *The Government's Standard Assessment Procedure for Energy Rating of Dwellings*, Building Research Establishment (BRE), UK.

CIBSE (2006) *Guide A: Environmental Design*, Chartered Institute of Building Services Engineers (CIBSE), UK.

Lovell (2012) Tarmac Homes, http://www.lovell.co.uk/Eastern/Tarmac-Homes/, Lovell, UK.

Nelson, G. (1995) *The Architecture of Building Services*, Batsford, London, UK.

TCC (2012) *Thermal Mass Explained*, MPA – The Concrete Centre (TCC), UK.

Appendix B: Biomass Substitution

Elsewhere in this book the credentials of concrete have been presented and guidance provided on how to design using concrete and specify the material so as to deliver sustainable solutions. It is often argued that concrete can be substituted by biomass alternatives. Examples of biomass substitution for construction include structural timber, laminated timber (e.g. glulam beams) or hempcrete which is a cladding material using the fibres from the fast growing hemp plant with a binder typically made of lime. In this appendix the biomass substitution argument is debated.

B.1   Background

Biomass substitution in the construction sector is part of a wider agenda to maximise use of biomass. Other uses that are encouraged by government initiatives include the use of biomass for the production of heat, electricity and bio-fuels. The demand for the latter could come into conflict with the demand for food crops. Whereas concrete and its constituents could only be used for construction, biomass (or its land take) could be used for construction, energy or food. Resource strategies must not be constrained to separate sectors such as food, energy or construction. This is an obvious statement but often overlooked due to government departmental structures which then leads to invalid conclusions.

Furthermore, the local and sufficient availability of aggregates and cement strikingly contrasts with that of construction grade biomass in the UK and many other countries.

Finally, the strategies often do not draw on the expertise of construction professionals to correctly assess where materials can be used appropriately. The rest of this appendix provides information to aid this assessment.

B.2   Product performance

Durability
It is evident to most readers that the lifetime of bio-based products is likely to be inferior to the more moisture and rot resistant concrete products. An example is the case of cladding for which the UK Timber Research and Development Association (TRADA) give service life values for timber of between 20 and 60

Sustainable Concrete Solutions, First Edition. Costas Georgopoulos and Andrew Minson.
© 2014 John Wiley & Sons, Ltd. Published 2014 by John Wiley & Sons, Ltd.

Table B.1   Evidence from timber industry on service life for timber cladding (Mayer, 2006). Reproduced by permission of Building Magazine.

The Timber Research and Development Association and BRE provide detailed good practice guidance.	
Specification options	**Service life years**
Timbers not requiring treatment, heart wood only	
Western red cedar Thuja plicanta finished size 18mm thick and 125mm exposed face	40–60
European Larch Larix decidua finished size 21mm thick and 135mm exposed face	30–40
Douglas fir Pseudotsuga menziesii finished size 19mm thick and 125mm exposed face	25–35
European oak Quercus robur finished size 19mm thick and 125mm exposed face, screw fixed.	40–60
Treated timbers	
European redwood Pinus sylvestris heat treated finished size 25mm thick and 125mm exposed face.	25–35
Lodgepole pine Pinus contorta finished size 16mm thick and 125mm exposed face. Preservative treated and pre-coated high performance paint system	25–35
European whitewood Picea and Abies species finished size 19mm thick and 120mm exposed face. Preservative treated. Paint or stain finish.	20–30
Table notes All finished naturally and fixed using stainless steel nails, unless otherwise stated.	

years (see Table B.1). A range of 20 to 40 years is perhaps more reasonable as the species with up to 60 years' service life (European oak and Western red cedar) are in low volumes and hence have high cost. Masonry cladding has a service life of at least three times the timber service life values. Also it is noteworthy that timber cladding needs repainting every two to five years, according to TRADA – a very poor comparison with the maintenance-free masonry cladding.

Fire

It is worth noticing the increased frequency and damage severity of fire incidences in timber dwellings in the UK and USA (FPA, 2011). The UK government published data also highlights the increased extent and severity of fire in timber framed buildings (DCLG, 2010).

Furthermore, it is taking an unnecessary risk to rely on the fire protection of timber structures for 60, 80 or 100 years during which alterations and refurbishment will take place and the fire protection may be compromised, when compared with concrete and masonry that do not burn or melt.

Flood resilience

Several factors are leading to the increased need to design and construct flood resilient buildings. These include pressure on land available for construction and increased building in areas of flood risk, increased incidences of flooding due to man-made changes in river catchments and climate change leading to coastal flooding, river catchment flooding and intense localised flooding even in areas that are not low lying.

The UK government guidance on flood resilience is clear:

> 'Suspended timber floors, particularly when including timber engineered joists, are not generally recommended in flood prone areas because most wooden materials tend to deform significantly when in contact with water and therefore may require replacement. Rapid drying can also cause deformation and cracking.'

And with respect to framed walls:

> 'Timber framed walls are generally not recommended, unless a sacrificial approach is adopted whereby some materials will be stripped to allow drying.'

For flood resilient design

> 'materials that retain their integrity and properties when subjected to flood water (such as concrete)'

are recommended (DCLG, 2007).

Whole life carbon

Discussions regarding whole life carbon and materials are often in the context of whole life of the material or product alone, and ignore the material's or product's impact on the whole life carbon of the project. This happens because it is simpler. The high thermal mass of masonry and concrete solutions compared with biomass alternatives has been shown to save ECO_2 over even a short lifetime of a building. In housing the period to offset any additional ECO_2 is 11 years (Hacker, 2008). This means that after 11 years the heavyweight/high thermal mass solution is the low carbon solution (see also Chapter 3).

B.3 Product Credentials

Cost

Sustainability does not only encompass environmental matters but also economics. The experience in the UK housing market is that masonry solutions cost less than timber alternatives. Concrete masonry is a more cost effective form of construction, in addition to delivering better performance.

Embodied Carbon

The process of plants absorbing carbon dioxide during growth is called carbon sequestration. In the case of timber and other crops used for construction, if the end of life part of the life cycle is ignored then these construction products can be falsely attributed an embodied carbon value which is negative. However at end of life, biomass is either burned and fully releases all the sequestered carbon, or it is composted in which case methane is released and this is an even more onerous greenhouse gas (see section 4.2.2). The University of Bath Inventory of Carbon and Energy database (ICE database) consciously excludes sequestration (IStructE, 2011). Therefore accordingly, timber has an embodied carbon burden. The Bath inventory will remain a frequently used source of data until Environmental Product Declarations become available (see section 4.2.5).

Responsible sourcing

The timber stewardship schemes are not as comprehensive as recently developed construction industry responsible sourcing schemes which to date the timber industry has not adopted. (See also section 4.3).

References

DCLG (2007) *Improving the Flood Performance of New Buildings: Flood Resilient Construction*, Department for Communities and Local Government (DCLG), UK.

DCLG (2010) *Fire statistics monitor, April 2009 to March 2010. Issue No. 03/10*. London. Department for Communities and Local Government (DCLG), UK.

FPA (2011) *Fire in timber frame buildings: A review of fire statistics from the UK and the USA*; BDM14, The Fire Protection Association (FPA) on behalf of RISC Authority, UK.

Hacker, J. et al. (2008) *Embodied and operational carbon dioxide emissions from housing: a case study on the effects of thermal mass and climate change*, Energy and Building 40, 375–84.

IStructE (2011) *A short guide to embodied carbon in building structures*, The Institution of Structural Engineers (IStructE), UK.

Mayer, P. (2006) First published in Building 2006, Extract from www.greenspec.co.uk, peter.mayer@buildinglifeplans.com .

Appendix C: Choice of Concrete Slab Options

C.1 Introduction

Concrete's versatility gives designers many options of how to form floor slabs (Figure C.1). The most commonly used options are described in this appendix together with summary data of spans and depths. This information will help the reader to make the best choice of slab at the conceptual design stage. If sustainability criteria are part of this choice then the best and most sustainable slab will hopefully be chosen. This appendix is based on updated extracts from the publication Concrete Framed Buildings (TCC, 2007). For rapid sizing and selection of reinforced concrete frame elements in multi-storey buildings refer to the publication Economic Concrete Frame Elements to Eurocode 2 (TCC, 2009).

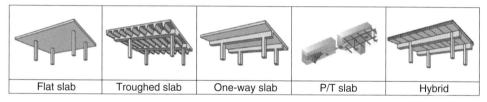

Figure C.1 Examples of different types of concrete floors. Reproduced by permission of The Concrete Centre.

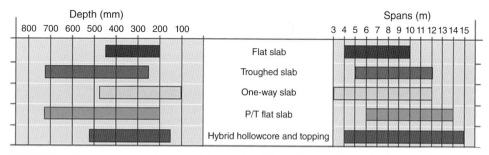

Figure C.2 Spans and typical range of depths for different types of floor. Reproduced by permission of The Concrete Centre.

Sustainable Concrete Solutions, First Edition. Costas Georgopoulos and Andrew Minson.
© 2014 John Wiley & Sons, Ltd. Published 2014 by John Wiley & Sons, Ltd.

Typical depths are required for different spans for a selection of slab forms (Figure C.2). The slabs have been designed using a superimposed dead load of 1.5kN/m², a range of imposed loads between 2.5 and 10kN/m² and grade C28/35 concrete.

The graphs assume that multiple, square bays are considered except for the hybrid hollowcore and topping which is assumed to be a single span (Figure C.3). For loads not shown interpolation between graphs is acceptable.

C.2   Flat slabs

Flat slabs are highly versatile elements providing minimum depth, fast construction and allowing flexible column grids.

Design

Flat slabs may be designed using the strip method set out in BS 8110 Part 1, finite element analysis (FEA) programmes or yield line analysis (TCC, 2004). Use FEA (TCC, 2006b) or yield line analysis for irregular grids.

Punching shear around the column heads can be the limiting factor on either depth of slab or column size. Shear reinforcement can be provided by links, shear rails, beam strips (to the relevant American code) or steel cruciform sections, which are formed from steel 'I' sections to make a cross in plan centred on the column below and cast within the depth of the slab.

Deflection can be a limiting factor on depth. In tests, corner bay deflections have been shown to be greater than in other bays, as the membrane action in the slab plate is less at the corners. It is therefore sensible to consider the corner bay for reinforcement design as it will be the worst case, or shortening the end grid to make reinforcement similar across all spans. There is a limit to the slab moment that can be transferred into the edge columns. If the moment from the design method used is greater than allowable the moment should either be redistributed to allow the moment to be within the limit, or column width or slab depth should be modified.

Construction

Construction of flat slabs is one of the quickest methods available. Table forms can be used; these are lightweight and permit large areas to be constructed on one table form. Table forms are lifted by the tower crane and are used as repetitively as possible to take most advantage of the construction method. However, to avoid the need to crane large table forms between concrete pours, with the associate risks from over sailing adjacent properties or roads, new proprietary system formwork which comprises smaller elements is becoming popular in the UK. These systems can be erected from below, reducing working from heights, and the smaller elements make movement around the site safer (Figure C.4). Down stand beams should be avoided wherever possible as forming beams significantly slows construction.

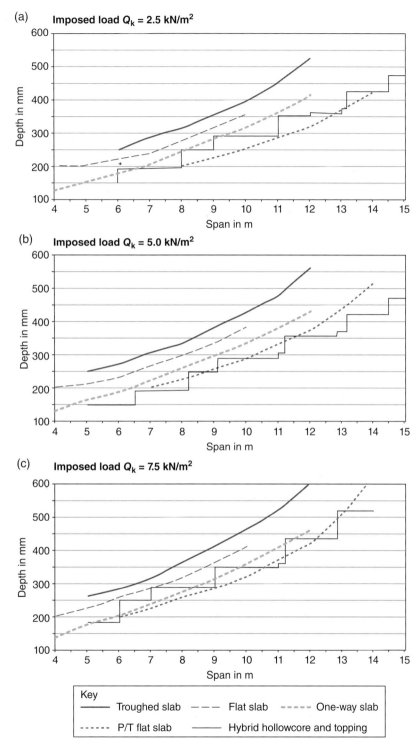

Figure C.3   Graphs showing span and depth information. Reproduced by permission of The Concrete Centre.

Figure C.4   Table forms (left) and SKYDECK (right). Reproduced by permission of PERI.

To give the most economic solution reinforcement should be rationalised fairly heavily. Rationalisation of reinforcement means simplifying the reinforcement layout by having regular bar sizes and spacings. To give the lightest – but perhaps not the most sustainable – layout, many bar sizes and different spacings will be used. Detailing can be done by the designer or the contractor. Prefabricated reinforcement mats, normally detailed by the supplier, can speed up construction on site.

Lead times

Lead times are very short as this is one of the most common forms of construction. If contractor reinforcement detailing or prefabricated reinforcement is used, lengthen lead time to allow for production and checking of detailing information.

Procuring

This is one of the most common forms of concrete construction. Almost all concrete frame contractors can undertake this type of construction.

Cost/whole life cost/value

Flat slabs are particularly appropriate for areas where tops of partitions need to be sealed to the slab soffit for acoustic or fire reasons. It is frequently the reason for flat slab to be considered faster and more economic than other forms of construction, as partition heads do not need to be cut around downstand beams or ribs. Flat slabs can be designed with a good surface finish to the soffit, allowing exposed soffits to be used. This allows exploitation of the building's thermal mass in the design of HVAC (Heating, Ventilation and Air Conditioning) requirements, increasing energy efficiency.

Speed on site

The average speed on site of flat slabs is approximately 500m^2/crane/week.

Mechanical and electrical services

Flat slabs provide the most flexible arrangements for services distribution as services do not have to divert around structural elements – the resulting cost saving on services can be significant.

Holes through the slab close to the column head affect the design shear perimeter of the column head. Holes next to the column should be small and limited to two. These should be on opposite sides rather than on adjacent sides of the column. Large service holes should be located in the centre of the bays away from the column strips and column heads. Location and size of any holes should be agreed early in the design.

Health and safety

Modern formwork systems can incorporate all edge protection and provide a robust working platform.

C.3 (Troughed) Ribbed and waffle slabs

Ribbed and waffle slabs provide a lighter and stiffer slab than an equivalent flat slab, reducing the extent of foundations. They provide a very good solution where slab vibration is an issue, such as laboratories and hospitals.

Ribbed slabs are made up of wide band beams running between columns with equally deep narrow ribs spanning the orthogonal direction. A thin topping slab completes the system.

Waffle slabs tend to be deeper than the equivalent ribbed slab. Waffle slabs have a thin topping slab and narrow ribs spanning in both directions between column heads or band beams. The column heads or band beams are the same depth as the ribs.

Design

Frequently ribs are designed as L-sections (as opposed to T-sections) to allow a hole in the thin topping slab on one side of the rib. This allows design to proceed before the service holes have been finalised. Waffle slabs work best with a square column grid. Ribbed slabs should be orientated so that the ribs span the longer distance, and the band beams the shorter distance. The most economic layout of longer to shorter side is 4:3.

Construction

Both waffle and ribbed slabs are constructed using flat slab formwork but with moulds positioned on the flat forms. Speed of construction depends on repetition, so that the moulds on the forms do not need to be repositioned between pours.

Lead times

Both ribbed and waffle slabs need moulds to be procured before starting on site. The lead-in times, that is, time to order, manufacture and deliver to site, for these moulds depends on whether the mould is standard or needs to be fabricated.

Figure C.5   Exposed waffle slabs provide full benefits of thermal mass.

Procuring

All concrete frame contractors should be able to provide this type of construction.

Cost/whole life cost/value

Ribbed and waffle slabs normally have good surface finish to the soffit, allowing exposed soffits to be used in the final building. This allows the use of the thermal mass of the building in the design of the HVAC requirements, particularly as the soffit surface area of the slab is greater than a flat slab, increasing the building's energy efficiency (Figure C.5).

Speed on site

This is a slower form of construction than flat slabs, but if moulds can be fixed to the flat slab formwork for successive pours the speed can be increased. Where partitions need to be sealed acoustically or for fire up to the soffit, ribbed and waffle slabs take longer on site. Lightweight floor blocks can be used as permanent formwork, which give a flat soffit, although these take away some of the benefits of the lighter weight slab design. If partition locations are known, the moulds may be omitted on these lines, thereby forming strips of flat slab.

Mechanical and electrical services

Holes should be located through the topping slab rather than the ribs where possible. If the holes are greater than the space between ribs, then the holes should be trimmed with similar depth ribs. Post construction holes can be located between ribs.

Health and safety

Modern formwork systems can incorporate all edge protection and provide a robust working platform.

C.4   Beams and slabs (one way or two way spanning)

Beam and slab construction involves the use of one or two-way spanning slabs onto beams spanning in one or two directions. The beams can be wide and flat or narrow and deep, depending on the structure's requirements. Beams tend to span between columns or walls and can be simply supported or continuous.

This form of construction is commonly used for irregular grids and long spans, where flat slabs are unsuitable. It is also used for transferring columns, walls or heavy point loads to columns or walls below. It is not a fast method of construction as formwork tends to be labour intensive.

Design

This is a very common form of construction and as such is well covered in standard codes and guidance. Beams can be designed as either L or T beams using the slab as a flange.

Construction

The formwork tends not to be reused. Beam reinforcement can be prefabricated and craned into place. Slabs tend to be lightly reinforced and can normally be reinforced with standard mesh.

Lead times

Fast lead times as formwork tends to be made on site.

Procuring

All concrete frame contractors, and indeed general builders, are able to do this type of work.

Speed on site

Slow and laborious on site due to time for formwork and fixing reinforcement in the beams.

Mechanical and electrical services

Wide band beams can have less effect on the horizontal distribution of the M&E (Mechanical & Electrical) services than deep beams which tend to be more difficult to negotiate, particularly if spanning in both directions. Any holes put into the web of the beam to ease the passage of the services must be coordinated. Vertical distribution of services can be located anywhere in the slab zone, but holes through beams need to be designed into the structure at an early stage.

Health and safety

Most of the work is undertaken on site; therefore care is needed with all operations. Formwork should include all guard rails.

C.5   Post-tensioned (PT) slabs

PT slabs are typically flat slabs, band beam and slabs or ribbed slabs. PT slabs offer the thinnest slab type, as concrete is worked to its strengths, mostly being kept in compression. Longer spans can be achieved due to prestress, which can be used to counteract deflections. Post-tensioning can use bonded or unbonded systems. Currently the most common type in the UK is bonded. Bonded systems have tendons that run typically in flat ducts, grouted up after the tendons have been taken to full prestress. Bonded systems do not rely on the anchorages after the ducts have been grouted, with the prestress locked into the slab even if a tendon is inadvertently cut. Unbonded systems have tendons that run in a small protective sheath. Unbonded systems are more flexible, with no need for a separate grouting stage.

Normal reinforcement is required wherever prestress is not present. This includes the edges of the slab and in any closure or infill strips. It is also needed at anchorages, where there are large bursting stresses due to high local forces. Normal reinforcement is also needed in unbonded systems for the ultimate load case. In bonded systems this ultimate load case can be resisted partially or fully by the bonded strands. Around column heads shear and bending reinforcement is required for both bonded and unbonded slabs (Figure C.6).

Figure C.6   A bonded PT slab just prior to concreting being placed. Reproduced by permission of The Concrete Centre.

Figure C.7   Stressing pan to provide top access to post-tensioning strands. Reproduced by permission of Kevin Bennett.

Design

For PT flat slabs, design tends to be based on limiting punching shear or deflection. Post-tensioning should not be between two stiff points, for example, cores, as the tension cannot be mobilised in the slab without pulling the stiff points together (or cracking the slab). Cores should be placed in the centre of the building. If this is not possible, closure strips should be used, and concreted after the post-tensioning has been carried out. Guidance is available from The Concrete Centre (TCC, 2008) and in Technical Report TR43 (TCS, 2005).

Construction

Contractors should be aware of the need to protect ducts and tendons from damage prior to concreting. The tensioning jack needs to have a working space of approximately one metre. The tensioning is typically done from the edge of the slab. If the site is constricted it may be necessary to have a normally reinforced strip around the edge of the slab and prestress via a stressing pan which gives access to the end of the strands so as to tension them, from above the slab (Figure C.7).

Procuring

Procurement of PT frames is done via a concrete frame contractor, who may well employ a specialist sub-contractor. All major frame contractors can provide PT frames. Procurement can be with a full design prepared by the designer or with a performance specification suitable for a sub-consultant to the frame contractor to be able to carry out the design. The performance specification should include:

- floor and beam sizes (if critical);
- design loads;
- hole locations;
- restraint locations.

The designer and specialist post-tensioning designer should agree a design responsibility matrix, to ensure that all parts of the design are covered.

Lead times

Lead times depend on the method of procurement. If the design is by the main designer, procurement is only slightly longer than for normal reinforced concrete. If the design of the PT slabs is by a specialist, lead in time should reflect work to be done before start on site.

Cost/whole life cost/value

PT slabs can be cheaper than the equivalent RC frame, particularly for spans exceeding 7.5m/8m.

Speed on site

PT slabs tend to be faster on site than reinforced concrete slabs due to the reduction in steel fixing required and the reduction in the volume of concrete. Formwork can also be struck earlier.

Mechanical and electrical services

Holes for the vertical distribution of services can be provided without a problem between the tendons. If the required hole is too large to fit between them, the tendons can either be displaced around the holes or anchored at the edge of the hole.

Health and safety

PT slabs are not an 'unexploded bomb'. If cut inadvertently the tendons do not whip out of the protective sheath or duct. In particular, the bonded systems, when grouted, are as safe as normal reinforcement.

Alterations can be achieved in bonded systems by back propping the span affected and cutting the ducts as necessary. Often no strengthening will be required, unless the new void is at a critical section. Alterations can be achieved in unbonded systems by back propping all the spans affected by the tendon(s) to be cut. The cut tendons can then be re-stressed against newly formed anchorages.

For a bonded system PT slabs can be demolished by normal methods. For an unbonded system, the slab should be back propped, the anchors broken open and the tendons de-stressed before the slab is demolished.

C.6 Hybrid Concrete Construction

Hybrid Concrete Construction (HCC) makes use of precast and in-situ concrete together, combining the benefits of both to give a robust, durable construction which is fast on site, with an excellent finish. There are many different forms of HCC as different parts of the structure can be precast (Figure C.8). Further information can be found in the publication Hybrid Concrete Construction (TCC, 2005).

Option 1 – Precast twin wall and lattice girder slab with insitu infill and topping.

Option 2 – Precast columns and edge beams with insitu floor slab

Option 3 – Precast columns and floor units with cast insitu beams

Option 4 – Cast insitu columns and beams with precast floor units

Option 5 – Cast insitu columns and floor topping with precast beams and floor units

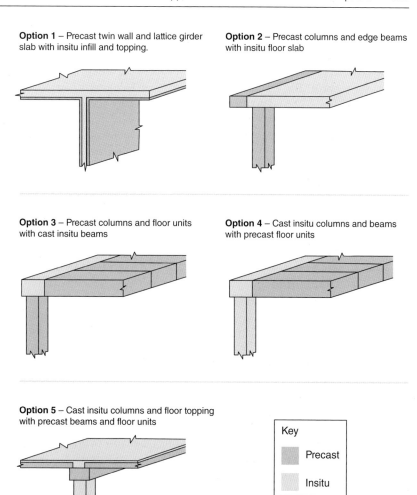

Key

Precast

Insitu

Figure C.8   Various hybrid concrete construction options. Reproduced by permission of The Concrete Centre.

Design

HCC can be designed as a normal reinforced concrete building, with full composite action between in-situ and precast elements. The construction phase needs to be designed, as one of the load cases is normally precast concrete elements supporting the weight of wet in-situ concrete. An additional stage may be considered if de-propping happens before the in-situ concrete develops its design strength. Precast elements should be repetitive, as mould costs are a significant factor. For non-standard areas, in-situ concrete could be used instead, or layout altered to allow a standard form.

Construction

Full coordination of the services through the building needs to take place early in the design process, as they need to be incorporated into precast elements. Also items frequently sorted out on site must be resolved before the project gets to site, allowing faster and safer construction.

Lead times

Depending on the precast elements of the construction up to 20 weeks lead in time can be necessary. However, rapid progress of in-situ elements can be made, with substructure often completed in this period. The design should be fully coordinated prior to the precast elements being manufactured if coordination affects the precast elements.

Procuring

Since a standardised layout allows the full benefits to be realised, use of HCC should be considered from design concept stage. A lead frame contractor (usually a concrete frame contractor) should be appointed early together with specialist supplier(s) of the precast elements. This will provide the best advice to the design team and hence the best finished building.

Cost/whole life cost/value

Initial HCC costs vary, depending on quality of finish required and the extent of repetition of precast units. HCC can provide the best value building, as the procurement process should allow for cooperation between parties to provide best value for client's requirements.

Speed on site

One of the main benefits of HCC is speed. For the Home Office Project in the UK, HCC constructed $4200m^2$ in an 11-day cycle, with three cranes, using in-situ concrete for vertical elements and floor toppings, and precast beams and slabs (Figure C.9).

Mechanical and electrical services

M&E services can be integrated into precast elements, and need to be fully coordinated. Thermal mass can be used to reduce energy consumption of the building in comparison to other similar sized buildings.

Health and safety

Much work is done in the factory, where activities are easier to control. Where precast slab units are used (the majority of cases) the working platform is provided by the slab, giving less danger of a fall from height.

Figure C.9   The Home Office Project used precast elements as shown in option 5 of Figure C8 plus precast columns. Reproduced by permission of The Concrete Centre.

C.7   Precast concrete

Precast concrete can form all types of structures, from cellular type construction such as crosswall where wall and slabs are precast, to 'stick' frame construction with columns, beams and slabs. Precast concrete is particularly suited to uses where either speed on site or a fine fair faced concrete finish is required. A high degree of repetition is advisable, as the cost of the mould required for each element reduces the more the mould is used. Crosswall is suited to repetitive accommodation on orthogonal grids, and some degree of complexity can be achieved (Figure C.10). Rooms of up to approximately 4m × 9m are standard (TCC, 2006a). Precast concrete can also be used as elements within a building. For instance, precast footings or stairs can be used whether the main frame is precast concrete or not.

Design

Grids and layouts should be as repetitive as possible. Precasters can give advice at an early stage to achieve the most economic layouts. Precast concrete is normally manufactured from high strength concrete and the design can take advantage of this. Junctions between the precast elements need to be designed. The specialist subcontractor can either do this, or give guidance to the designer. Code requirements to protect against progressive collapse are fully met by use of tie bars through junctions, bolted details or proprietary jointing systems. Load bearing precast concrete cladding can also be used as

Figure C.10   Crosswall construction – University of East London. Reproduced by permission of The Concrete Centre.

a precast frame ensuring the building becomes weather tight as quickly as possible, allowing finishing works to start early.

Construction

The use of precast can be helpful on a tight site provided access is not a problem. Precast elements can be craned into place from a lorry, eliminating any need for storage areas for reinforcement or shutters. Coordination between the specialist subcontractor and other subcontractors is vital to ensure the best is achieved from precast. The specialist subcontractor should be appointed as soon as possible to enable both coordination and buildability aspects to be fully integrated into the precast design. Some in-situ stitching is required at joints, but normally only involves grouting up connections. The size of the largest piece of precast concrete normally dictates the size of the crane, so similar weight elements should be used if possible. The contractor should beware of the largest lift requiring the largest reach.

Lead times

Lead times are approximately four months for structural precast frames. This includes preparing all drawings for product manufacture and coordinating with other subcontractors. Lead times for simple standard elements, such as stair flights or hollowcore slabs, are significantly less.

Procuring

Lists of specialist precast subcontractors and their specialities can be accessed from trade bodies. Some standard precast frames, such as those for car parks, are frequently procured as a 'turn-key' project where the design, detailing and erection are carried out by a single company who may or may not cast the concrete themselves.

Cost/whole life cost/value

With the use of durable finished concrete, maintenance for precast concrete buildings is kept to a minimum, providing excellent value for the whole life costs. The thermal mass of the building can be used as long as it is exposed (e.g., if suspended ceilings are not provided) so that the long-term costs of heating and cooling the building are reduced.

Speed on site

Precast concrete frames are very quick to erect on site. Speed is one of the main benefits of using precast concrete.

Mechanical and electrical services

Mechanical services can be integrated into precast elements. These systems pass heating or cooling through precast concrete floor slabs, allowing the thermal mass of the concrete to act as a storage heater or cooler. The precast option should be integrated into the design at concept stage to allow the full benefits of servicing the building to be realised. Using the thermal mass of the building reduces both service requirements and size of plant. Electrical services can be integrated into the design of precast elements as conduits can be cast into the elements in the factory.

Health and safety

As the fabrication of the precast elements takes place in a factory setting, health and safety factors on site are much reduced.

References

TCC (2004) *Practical Yield Line: Applied Yield Line Theory*, TCC/03/03, The Concrete Centre (TCC), UK.

TCC (2005) *Hybrid Concrete Construction: Combining precast and in-situ concrete for better value structural frames*, TCC/03/010, The Concrete Centre (TCC), UK.

TCC (2006a) *High Performance Buildings: Using Crosswall Construction*, TCC/03/026, The Concrete Centre (TCC), UK.

TCC (2006b) *How to Design Reinforced Concrete Flat Slabs Using Finite Element Analysis*, TCC/03/027, The Concrete Centre (TCC), UK.

TCC (2007) *Concrete Framed Buildings*, TCC/03/024, The Concrete Centre (TCC), UK.

TCC (2008) *Post-tensioned Concrete Floors*, TCC/03/033, The Concrete Centre (TCC), UK.

TCC (2009) *Economic Concrete Frame Elements to Eurocode 2*, CCIP-025, MPA–The Concrete Centre (TCC), UK.

TCS (2005) *Post-tensioned Concrete Floors: Design Handbook*, Technical Report TR43, The Concrete Society (TCS), UK.

Appendix D: Example on Embodied CO$_2$ for a Building Slab

Carbon accounting is generally used to compare options and determine which design development delivers the solution with least carbon impact. In this example carbon accounting for two slab options is carried out only for Cradle to Gate – that is, raw material to processing, and manufacturing – followed by a Commentary on Gate to Site – that is, transportation and use – and, a Commentary on Site to Grave – that is, operation, demolition and end of life.

D.1 Cradle to gate

Two slab options are compared: a conventional flat slab and a post-tensioned (PT) flat slab. In qualitative terms at the outset, it is known that the former will use more concrete and more steel but for each of these materials the ECO$_2$e/t will be less. Therefore, it is not self evident as to which option will have the lowest overall ECO$_2$e.

This simple example only compares the slabs themselves, and does not include the affect these have on other building elements. It should be noted that the lower weight PT solution will enable weight savings in vertical load bearing structures (walls and columns) and in the foundations. Also, the PT solution is thinner, and hence the building envelope will be marginally smaller leading to savings on cladding.

The design example chosen is for a school building with a floor plan layout as shown in Figure D.1. A typical bay, 8250mm × 7750mm, will be used for comparison.

D.1.1 Step 1 Engineering design solution

A flat slab solution for the example problem is a 325mm thick slab with a weight of 145kg of reinforcement per cubic metre of concrete.

A post tensioned slab solution for the same problem is a 250mm thick slab with 65kg of reinforcement and 20kg of post tensioned strand per cubic metre of concrete.

Sustainable Concrete Solutions, First Edition. Costas Georgopoulos and Andrew Minson.
© 2014 John Wiley & Sons, Ltd. Published 2014 by John Wiley & Sons, Ltd.

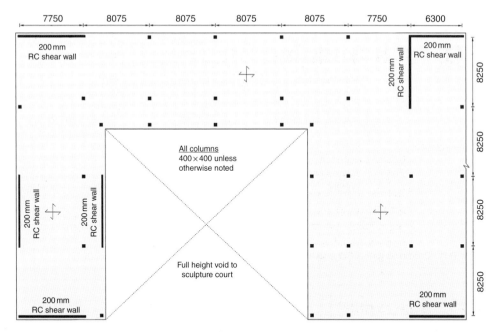

Figure D.1   Structural floor plan for worked example. Reproduced by permission of The Concrete Centre.

Arriving at these designs is not a trivial task as any engineer would appreciate. Nor are the solutions unique, as thickness and reinforcement/stressing may each be changed to give different solutions for the conventional and post tensioned options. For each of the solutions, a range of sub-solutions could be designed and for each of these a carbon footprint calculated.

D.1.2   Step 2 Summary of quantities

Once designed, it is a relatively straightforward task to itemise the materials and respective quantities for each solution as shown in Table D.1.

D.1.3   Step 3 Material ECO_2e values: Cradle to gate

The source(s) of ECO_2e values must be chosen such that they enable valid comparison between the different solutions by treating boundary conditions and assumptions consistently. Also it is useful to have a range of values as this will enable a sensitivity analysis of the results. Example data is presented in Table D.2.

D.1.4   Step 4 Multiplying quantities by ECO_2e rates

This step is analogous to the quantity surveyor taking a bill of quantities and multiplying it by the cost of each quantity (£ rates) to price a project. Rather

Table D.1   **Quantities for each slab solution (data from internal Concrete Centre report).**

		Flat slab solution	Post Tensioned (PT) flat slab solution
Concrete	Slab thickness,	325mm	250mm
	Volume per bay,	20.8m³	16.0m³
	tonnes per bay,	49.9t	38.4t
	Material specification	C32/40	C32/40 with strength gain requirements
Reinforcement	Weight (kg per m³ concrete),	145kg/m³	65kg/m³
	Tonnes per bay	3.02t	1.04t
Post Tensioned strand	Weight (kg per m³ concrete)	0kg	20kg
	Tonnes per bay	0t	0.32t

Table D.2   **Cradle to gate ECO_2e values for slab materials (Kaethner & Burridge, 2012).**

		ECO_2e kg/tonne			
		Low	Typical	High	Notes
Concrete	C32/40 flat slabs	67	110	157	Range due to concrete specification
	Post tensioned slabs	150	166	182	Range due to concrete specification
Reinforcement		430 lower bound EAF*	570 local EAF* value	2750 Upper bound BOS*	Range due to Production method
Post Tensioning Strand		1360 recycled content 60% EU figure	1770 recycled content 43% worldwide figure	2750 upper bound BOS*	Range due to level of recycled content assumed.

*EAF: Electric Arc Furnace; BOS: Basic Oxygen Steelmaking.

than cost, the ECO_2e kg/tonne are multiplied by the relevant quantities as shown in Tables D.3 and D.4.

By amending the concrete specification so as to reduce the ECO_2e, and reworking the calculation using the 'Low' column ECO_2e kg/tonne values in Table D.2, the totals for the flat slab and PT solutions are reduced from 7207kg to 4640kg and from 7527kg to 6636kg respectively. This demonstrates that the material specification is more effective than the design solution in achieving minimum ECO_2e. To further emphasize this, on a typical sized non-domestic building, through careful specification, a structural engineer could save his/her lifetime's personal carbon footprint (Kaethner & Burridge, 2012).

The reader can do further investigation by using the range of low, typical and high embodied carbon rates. Such a sensitivity test is important. It shows that reporting single answer results is far too simplistic.

Table D.3   Total ECO$_2$e calculation for flat slab solution.

	Quantity (t)	ECO$_2$e kg/tonne (Typical)	Total ECO$_2$e for material used per typical bay (kg)
Concrete	49.9t	110kg/tonne	5486kg
Reinforcement	3.02t	570kg/tonne	1721kg
		Total for slabs =	7207kg

Table D.4   Total ECO$_2$e calculation for the post tensioned flat slab solution.

	Quantity	ECO$_2$e kg/tonne (Typical)	Total ECO$_2$e for material
Concrete	38.4t	166kg/tonne	6368kg
Reinforcement	1.04t	570kg/tonne	593kg
Post Tensioning Strand	0.32t	1770kg/tonne	566kg
		Total for slabs =	7527kg

D.2   Commentary on gate to site

The factors to include when extending the scope of a study from 'cradle to gate' to 'cradle to site' are wastage, transport from factory gate to construction site, formwork and site works.

D.2.1   Wastage

Whilst every effort is made to minimise waste, until zero waste is achieved, the reality is that more material is required than is actually specified on the project drawings. There are industry rates available for typical wastages (see Table D.5). The total ECO$_2$e burden caused by wastage can be estimated by summing for all materials the ECO$_2$e wastage calculated for each material using the formula:

ECO$_2$e wastage = Material cradle to gate ECO$_2$e × wastage rate in %

D.2.2   Transport

At a late stage of a project, when suppliers are known, actual travel distance figures can be used. However, when alternative solutions are still being compared there will be a reliance on average travel distances for materials. These can often be obtained from trade associations and national statistics. For materials that are imported and therefore have a primary transport leg by boat, other sources of data are required or estimates made as shown in Table D.6.

The emissions from different transport modes are available from various sources to facilitate carbon foot printing. An example of these is presented in Table D.7.

Table D.5   Example average wastage rates for different material elements (WRAP, 2012).

	Wastage Rate (%)	
Element	Standard	Good
Precast Concrete Piles	0	0
In situ Concrete Pad Foundations	4	2
In situ Concrete Frame	4	2
Wooden Floor	10	5
Steel Frame	0	0
Steel Frame Board Fire Protection	22.5	15
Insulation	15	5

Table D.6   Average transport distances and travel modes for concrete and selected other construction materials (sources as listed in table).

Material	Primary Transport Leg		Secondary Transport Leg		Source
	Distance (km)	Mode	Distance (km)	Mode	
Ready mixed Concrete, Mortar	12	Road			(TCC, 2013)
Precast Concrete	106	Road			(TCC, 2013)
Steel	123	Road	91	Road	(DFT, 2010)
Brick	64*	Road			(DFT, 2010)
Structural Softwood Timber	1200**	Ship	121	Road	(DFT, 2010)
Plaster	64*	Road			(DFT, 2010)

*derived from 'other building materials' DFT category. This category also includes all concrete products, but more specific data for these products is available from The Concrete Centre.
**private communication from Arup.

Table D.7   Average emissions for different transport modes (DEFRA/DECC 2012 © Crown Copyright, reproduced under the terms of the Open Government Licence (http://www.nationalarchives.gov.uk/doc/open-government-licence/).)

	Emissions per tonne transported per kilometre	
Mode	kg CO$_2$/t/km	kg CO$_2$e/t/km (i.e. inclusive of all greenhouse gases)
Road	0.122	0.124
Rail	0.028	0.031
Ship	0.013	0.016

To calculate the total transport emission from materials is simply a case of summing for all the materials the mass used by the distance travelled by the emission rates, that is:

$$\text{Material Transport CO}_2\text{e} = \text{Material Mass} \times (100 + \text{wastage rate})\,\%$$
$$\times (\text{Transport Distance} \times \text{Modal CO}_2\text{e})$$

Table D.8   Site works CO$_2$e emissions.

Size of project	kgCO$_2$e per week
Very large (construction cost more than £10 million, more than 25 people permanently on site)	1879
Large (construction cost £5 to £10 million, between 16 & 25 people permanently on site)	1252
Medium (construction cost £1.5 to £5million, between 9 & 15 people permanently on site)	751
Small (construction cost less than £1.5million, fewer than 8 people permanently on site)	313

D.2.3   *Formwork*

Formwork impacts are dependent on the number of re-uses of the formwork that is achieved. An unpublished study carried out for The Concrete Centre found that formwork impacts were typically 0.1–1% as a percentage of total impacts for a range of concrete superstructure solutions. This assumed re-use factors provided by PERI, a supplier and manufacturer of formwork. It also accounted for a total round trip of 100km from supplier to project site and back to supplier. These results were consistent with those reported for the USA (Johnson, 2006).

D.2.4   *Site works*

The operations on a construction site use energy and have associated emissions. These are typically small compared with material production and operational impacts, but nevertheless should be taken into account. It is the case, as would be expected, that the site works impacts as a percentage of total impacts is influenced by the scale, number of storeys, construction method, design and location. It is difficult to compare published results as they are rarely for comparable cases. Results reported by Johnson (Johnson, 2006) are not untypical: 6.3% for a steel framed office and 5.8% for a concrete framed office. Alternatively carbon calculators provide emissions per week, such as presented in Table D.8. If details of the construction process are known then a more detailed analysis is possible.

D.3   Commentary on site to grave

In-use impacts and operational energy savings will be similar for each slab solution. End of life demolition impacts will be different because of the volume of materials. The lower volume PT solution will have lower impacts because of the reduced volume to be crushed and transported for re-use, and the simpler separation of the lower embedded steel content from the concrete.

The two most important aspects for these stages is lifetime of the project and carbonation.

If a project lasts for twice as long, then simply the ECO_2e is halved. The difficulty with this is predicting the lifetime of a project, bearing in mind that it may be obsolete before it is no longer fit for its intended purpose. It may be argued that in an environmentally constrained future scenario, building obsolescence will be less common as we get used to refurbishing and re-purposing existing buildings.

Carbonation is the chemical process of absorbing CO_2, reversing the chemical process that occurs in the kiln to make clinker. In porous elements such as blockwork this can occur in a matter of months. For structural concrete the desire is to minimise the depth of carbonation, as otherwise the alkaline conditions that help protect reinforcement are lost, and there is a risk of corrosion. Hence these elements only carbonate on their surface until crushed at end of life.

Considering all concrete products and their different uses, it is estimated that on average, approximately 20% of the CO_2 emitted in production is reabsorbed. This re-absorption occurs over the operational and demolition stages and a short period of weeks of stockpiling of crushed concrete following demolition (see also Section 5.3).

References

DEFRA/DECC (2012) *Guidelines to Defra/DECC's GHG Conversion Factors for Company Reporting Annexe 7*, Produced by AEA for the Department of Energy and Climate Change (DECC) and the Department for Environment, Food and Rural Affairs (Defra); Final Version: 1.0 Updated: 28/05/2012

DFT (2010) https://www.gov.uk/government/publications/road-freight-statistics-2010 Table RFS0112, Department for Transport (DFT), UK.

Johnson, T.W. (2006) *Comparison of Environmental Impacts of Steel and Concrete as building Materials using the LCA Method*, Master of Science, Massachusetts Institute of Technology, Retrieved November 22, 2012: //dspace.mit.edu

Kaethner, S. and Burridge, J. (2012) *Embodied CO_2 of structural frames*, The Structural Engineer, vol. 90, no. 5, 33–9, The Institution of Structural Engineers, UK.

TCC (2013) *Concrete Industry Sustainability Performance Report, sixth report: 2012 performance data*, MPA–The Concrete Centre (TCC) on behalf of the Sustainable Concrete Forum, UK.

WRAP (2012) Net Waste Tool Data Set; http://nwtool.wrap.org.uk/

Index